I0754399

From Prof. Frithiof Holmgren's Färgblindhet.
Farveblindhed - Farbenblindheit - Colour-blindness.
Cécité des couleurs - Cecità di colore.

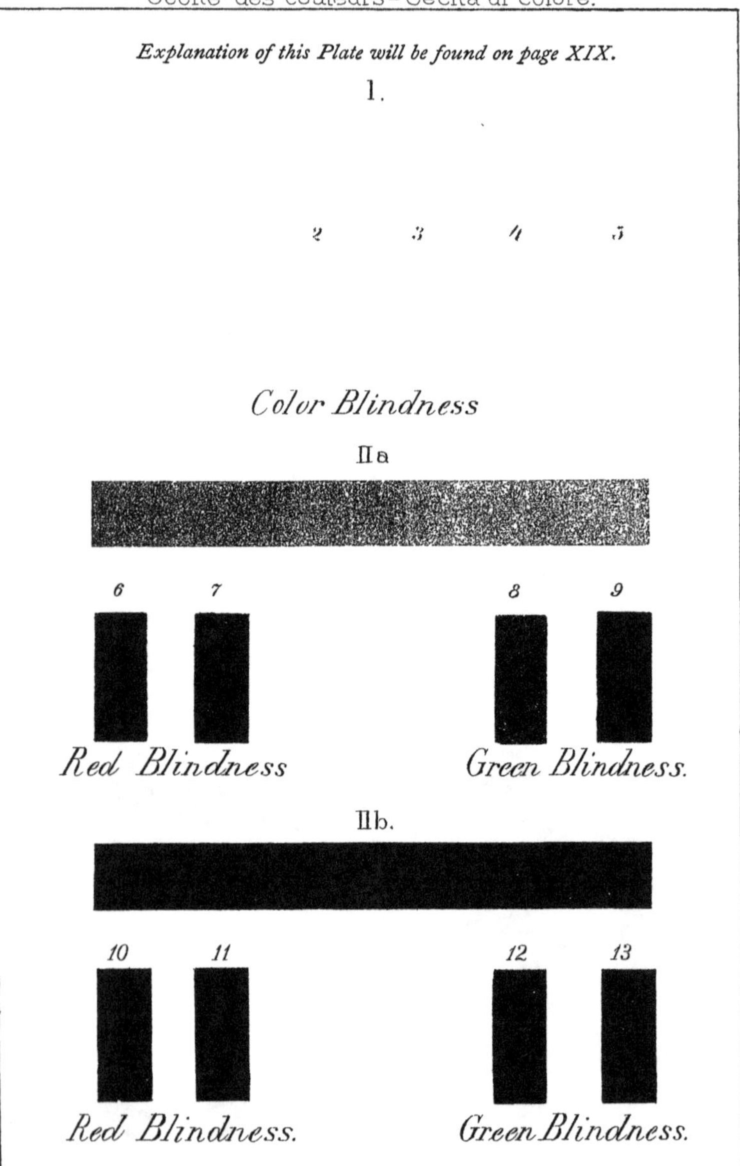

COLOR-BLINDNESS:

ITS DANGERS AND ITS DETECTION.

BY

B. JOY JEFFRIES, A.M., M.D.,

(HARVARD,)

Fellow of the Massachusetts Medical Society; Ophthalmic Surgeon Massachusetts Charitable Eye and Ear Infirmary, Carney Hospital, and New-England Hospital for Women and Children; Member of the International Periodic Congress of Ophthalmology, American Ophthalmological Society, Boston Society of Medical Sciences, Boston Society for Medical Observation, Boston Society of Natural History, &c.

BOSTON:
HOUGHTON, OSGOOD AND COMPANY.
The Riverside Press, Cambridge.
1879.

C. J. Peters & Son, Stereotypers,
73 Federal Street.

TO

FRITHIOF HOLMGREN, M.D.,

PROFESSOR OF PHYSIOLOGY IN THE UNIVERSITY OF UPSALA, SWEDEN,

THIS VOLUME

IS RESPECTFULLY DEDICATED.

"Why should we look one common faith to find,
Where one in every score is color-blind?
If here on earth they know not red from green,
Will they see better into things unseen?"

Dr. O. W. Holmes: *Andover Poem, June, 1878.*

CONTENTS.

PREFACE.

I HAVE dedicated this volume to my friend Professor Holmgren, because I consider that to him above all others do we owe the present and future control of color-blindness on land and sea, by which life and property are safer, and the risks of travelling less.

To his Majesty the King of Sweden are due the thanks of all for his personal interest in the investigation of color-blindness, and his practical good sense in immediately putting into execution the plans and proposals of Professor Holmgren, by which the subject was so prominently brought forward as to command the attention and example of other nations. It is earnestly hoped that this country will follow rapid suit.

Professor Holmgren's book on "Color-Blindness and its Relations to Railroads and the Marine" was published in Swedish, in 1877, at Upsala. Immediately after this a French translation was printed, which soon called very general attention to his labors and their results. An authorized translation into German appeared last year (1878). I had agreed with him to translate the work into English, when an abridged translation appeared from the Reports of the Smithsonian

Institute at Washington. This, of course, prevented any publisher from being willing to risk a complete translation. The very necessary explanatory colored plate was not given in the Smithsonian translation. I understand that it will be in an extra edition. This English translation is so abridged as to greatly interfere with its value and its practical use.

Had, however, I been enabled to reproduce Professor Holmgren's book entire, I am afraid it would not have accomplished its purpose so well in this country as in Europe, from the general lower tone of scientific knowledge on the part of those for whom it was especially written, and also the lack of just the persons — namely, the railroad-surgeons — who could make immediate application of the method for detecting color-blindness, and have convinced the authorities of its necessity. Aside, also, from the difficulties of publication, I found that a simple translation was not likely to be so generally read.

To bring before the community the dangers and the prevalence of color-blindness, I thought it best to prosecute my researches amongst the places of learning and teaching. Hence I chose our immediate universities, colleges, and public schools. Thus, whilst I was pursuing my own individual studies of color-blindness, I was at the same time gathering the necessary statistics in proof of the position I took, and disseminating a knowledge of the whole subject, very especially the important one of its frequency. It is rather curious that this volume is only the third monograph in book-form on this subject. Professor Wilson of Edinburgh published in 1855 a small book, being a collection of his several articles on this subject. Yet the literature of normal and abnormal chromatic power is pretty extensive, as may be seen by the bibliography appended to this volume. I first publicly discussed the subject before the Boston Society of Natural History, March 7, 1877. An article of mine on the "Dangers from Color-Blindness in Railroad Employés and Pilots" was printed in the Ninth Annual Report of the Massachusetts State Board of Health, 1878. April 8, 1878, I gave a lecture on color-blindness before the Society of Arts of the Institute of Technology in Boston. Feb. 23, 1878, I read a paper on the "Incurability of Congenital Color-Blindness" before the Suffolk District Medical Society in Boston, published in "The Boston Medical and Surgical Journal" March 28, 1878. May 25, 1878, I read a paper on the "Relative Frequency of Color-Blindness in Males and Females" at the Suffolk District Medical Society, and also at the July meeting at Newport of the American Ophthalmological Society; published, July 26, in "The Boston Medical and Surgical Journal." The substance of these papers is included in this volume. I have quoted largely from Professor Wilson's book, not only because it is quite out of print, but also because the cases he relates are interesting as being in England, and his deductions are truthful and valuable, although much of the theory presented is now old to science. I have given a good part of Professor Holmgren's book, including what is essential to be known and understood by our railroad authorities and the specialists they must employ in carrying out any system of thorough examinations. The explanations and directions may seem to many unnecessarily minute, and the description too extended; but these are especially intended for examiners, who, I think, when using this test, will thank me for putting them within their easy reach.

The importance of this whole question of color-blindness I need not insist on here. "The Railroad Gazette" of Jan. 24, 1879, after discussing the 740 accidents by which 204 people were killed and 756 injured, says, "What most needs doing now is the improvement of the men who work the roads, — officers and employés, — though there is still plenty of room for progress in the tools with which they work."

I have not in this volume entered into the loss of time and money from color-blindness in the great industries where a perfect chromatic sense is needed; or the mortifications, &c., arising from constant mistakes of dress &c., in every-day life, — as all these bear no relation to the importance of the danger to life and property on land and sea from this curious visual defect. The railroads of England pay two million dollars a year for killed and injured travellers.

I must explain some expressions in my text. I always use the term color-blindness, instead of Daltonism, as more truthfully representing the defect in general, as Dalton was red-blind; and also in order not to continue to attach this defect to his name. This has become pretty universal, except with the French, who, having no one word for color-blindness, still say *Daltonisme* for brevity's sake. My speaking of *a color-blind* I would apologize for by saying, were I to have added "person" each time, my readers would, I think, have preferred the present bad grammar.

I am quite aware, that, instead of presenting the material of this volume in its present shape, I could have given a condensed essay on color-blindness more easily read; but such a book would not meet the wants of the immediate future. The question of color-blindness is soon coming up in a very practical form in this country. Those who have to deal with it will properly ask for the original material which they may themselves study, and which I have here collected. Such material, as my bibliography shows, is widely scattered and in foreign languages; whilst other I here present has never been published. For this reason I risk the natural criticism my work will call forth, rather than fail to give full opportunity for those who from their position must hereafter have my gathered material within their reach.

As this volume is intended to meet the wants of several quite different classes in the community, its contents are somewhat varied. Many of the chapters may be read by themselves, by those who are only interested in the subject from the point of view touched on in that special chapter. General readers will find the historical cases, and the curious mistakes caused by this chromatic defect, of most interest to them perhaps. Physicians will be interested in facts relating to color-blindness from disease, its heredity, and the supposed peculiarities heretofore connected with it, as also its incurability. Scientists and physiologists will naturally turn to the accounts of the precise condition of color-blindness and its relation to normal color-sense, as well as the additional methods of detection. The color-blind cannot but be interested in the palliatives of congenital color-blindness, since we can now do more for them than formerly. The dangers on land and sea concern us all. Railroad authorities will find full explanation of the precise condition of their color-blind employés. The possible change of railroad and marine signals will also concern them and the officers of the navy and mercantile marine. The possibility of detecting and eliminating the color-blind is important to those whose position requires them to avoid employing such. The methods of so doing interest the specialists employed for this purpose. Our national and state legislatures and railroad commissioners will naturally turn to the account of the present provisional European laws in reference to the control of color-blindness on land and sea.

I have hitherto avoided seeking for the color-blind, and discouraged those who I understood would apply to me; because I desired to have my statistics as near as possible precisely represent the truth as to the prevalence of this chromatic defect. My present numbers are so large as to perfectly decide, for myself at least, this point. I therefore am now anxious to hear from the color-blind, by letter or otherwise, as each and every account is of value. The personal observations of any who have this defect would interest me, and be of service to science. All names would of course be strictly confidential. I am at present devoting special attention to the question of heredity, and naturally very anxious to hear from any one on this point. In many color-blind families the facts must be pretty well known as to the different members, and such I desire to have *causa scientiæ*. My professional brethren may be able to assist me in this, and I would hereby ask it of them. I well know that many color-blind persons, whilst shrinking from exhibiting their defect, would not hesitate to give an account of their case when assured their names would not be used.

The dedication of this volume, and the free use I have made of his material, show how much I am indebted to Professor Holmgren of Upsala, Sweden, with whom I have been in constant communication. I have also to greatly thank Professor Donders of Utrecht for advice and suggestions, as well as for the rules of the Holland railroads. I am indebted for information and numerous publications to the following gentlemen, whom I would hereby gratefully remember: Dr. Magnus of Breslau, Drs. Eulenberg and Hirschberg of Berlin, Dr. Stilling of Cassel, Dr. Cohn of Breslau, Dr. Zehender of Rostock, Dr. Schiess of Basle, Dr. Warlomont of Brussels, Professor Delbœuf of Lille, Drs. Favre and Dor of Lyons, Dr. Nicati of Marseilles, Dr. Quaglino of Pavia, Dr. Daae of Kragerö, Norway, and Dr. Hjort of Christiana, Norway, Dr. A. von Reuss of Vienna, Dr. Robertson of Edinburgh, and Mr. S. Wright Dunning of "The Railroad Gazette" of New York.

To the Boston School Board my thanks are specially due for permission to test the scholars of the public schools, in which work I am still engaged.

To avoid cumbering this volume with references, I use an author's name, and the bibliography will enable the reader to turn to the original. There is, I believe, no excuse for a writer not giving his best work to the public; but I must add here, that the time for my eighteen thousand examinations for color-blindness, and the preparation of this volume, has been stolen from the busy hours of a professional life.

B. Joy Jeffries, M.D.

15 Chestnut Street, Beacon Hill, Boston.

INTRODUCTION.

THERE are some points in reference to color-perception which I must first explain to my unprofessional readers, to show what color-blindness is *not*. Our point of best vision on the retina is directly in the centre, and over but a small space here; so that, to see an object distinctly, we must carefully turn the eye, to keep the picture on this portion. In looking at a long word on a page, we unconsciously travel along it to catch all the letters. If we keep our eye fixed on one point, and move a letter away from this point, its form is soon lost, and we fail to recognize it. In other words, if the image of the letter falls on the retina but a little way from the centre, called "the yellow spot" from its color, it is confused. Form-perception diminishes very rapidly from the centre outwards in all directions. Now, this is also the case in reference to color. Let one eye be closed, and the other fixed on a bright-red object, like a wafer, held before it. When moved gradually out from the central field of vision, the wafer will decrease in brightness, and finally appear black. Its *form* we may still discern. This is not color-blindness. A painter has added a bright little scarlet flower down in one corner of his picture, and turns to work in the centre, when suddenly the scarlet flower loses its color, because its image falls far away on the retina from the point of best color-perception. This same will be found in reference to the other primary colors in varying degrees.

Another point: Whenever the retina is tired out with one color, it can only perceive the complementary one. If with one eye we gaze steadily for some seconds at a bright-green disk on a white ground, and then quickly look at another white surface, we shall see a *red* disk. Gazing fixedly at the setting sun when a deep red, and turning quickly to the east, we shall see a rising *green* sun. I hardly need say this also is not color-blindness.

Again: the crystalline lens in the eye becomes, with age, harder, and of a yellowish color, — up to positive blackness. When opaque, it prevents, of course, the passage of light through the pupil: it is called *cataract*. This opaque lens we then remove from the eye, and replace it by a strong convex lens in the spectacles. Whilst the lens has been turning yellow, all the person's light has been yellow; so that, when the lens is removed, the impression will be that of the complementary color, — bluish. Many old persons whom I have operated on for cataract, after it was removed, and they were able to use their sight, complained that every thing was blue; that, for instance, their children's faces appeared blue: and they naturally often expressed considerable disappointment that life was to be to them wholly bluish. This is not true color-blindness, and soon wears off. Santonine, or worm-seed, causes, when taken, all objects to appear a bright yellow, or sometimes its complementary color, violet.

The effect is not permanent, and passes off in a few hours.

Another physiological fact in relation to color-perception is very important, and seems to be generally quite unknown or neglected. Around the point of best vision in the centre of the retina is a zone where we perceive all of the three so-called base colors, — red, green, and violet. Outside of this there is another zone, in which we have a perception of only two; namely, green and violet; and again, beyond this, on the retina, only blue or violet is perceived. We shall hereafter see how these zones resemble color-blindness.

EXPLANATION OF THE COLORED PLATE.

Repeated and inexcusable mistakes have been made in Europe in reference to this colored plate of Prof. Holmgren. It has been spoken of as if intended to be used to test for color-blindness, and has also been so used. But, as he expressly states, it is only intended to *illustrate* the characteristic mistakes of the color-blind, and the colors of the sample worsteds to be employed.

I. The Green Test.

If the person examined takes any of the confusion-colors (1 to 5) to put with the green, he proves himself color-blind; or even if he seems to want to put them together.

II. *a*. The Purple Test. (*This contains Red and Violet.*)

The color-blind puts with it the colors 6 to 7, always a *deeper color.*

If he puts only purple colors, he is *incompletely color-blind.*

If he takes blue or violet, like 6 and 7, or both, either with or without purple, he is *completely red-blind.*

If he takes green or gray, like 8 and 9, or one alone, with or without purple, he is *completely green-blind.*

II. *b*. The Red Test. (*Not necessary to be used.*)

Here the red-blind puts, with the red, dark green and brown (10 and 11), which are much *darker* than the test.

The green-blind puts, with the red, *lighter green and brown* than the test.

The violet-blind matches, with the purple, red, orange, and purple.

COLOR-BLINDNESS:

ITS DANGERS AND ITS DETECTION.

CHAPTER I.

HISTORICAL CASES OF COLOR-BLINDNESS.

THERE seems no good reason to doubt that color-blindness has existed at all times in man. It is therefore certainly very curious that its detection, and consequent mention in literature, is so very recent. A case of Dr. Tuberville's (1684) has been quoted and referred to as one of color-blindness. In a letter to the Royal Society, London, Aug. 4, 1684, he says, "A maid two and twenty years old came to me from Banbury, who could see very well, but no color beside black and white. She had such scintillations by night (with the appearances of bulls, bears, &c.) as terrified her very much. She could see to read sometimes in the greatest darkness for almost a quarter of an hour."

This is too indefinite to be admitted as a case of color-blindness recognized at that date. We probably shall hunt literature in vain for mention of color-blindness till nearly a hundred years later, when we come (in 1777) to Mr. Huddart's account of the shoemaker Harris of Maryport, in Cumberland, Eng. This case is historic, and the description perfect in its way, rendering it quite worthy of being given here in full. Huddart writes to Rev. J. Priestley, —

"I have known Harris ten years, and had frequent opportunities of conversing with him. I had often heard from others that he could discern the form and magnitude of all objects very distinctly, but could not distinguish colors. This report having excited my curiosity, I conversed with him frequently on the subject. The account he gave was this: that he had reason to believe other persons saw something in objects which he could not see; that their language seemed to mark qualities with confidence and precision which he could only guess at with hesitation, and frequently with error. His first suspicion of this arose when he was about four years old. Having by accident found in the street a child's stocking, he carried it to a neighboring house to inquire for the owner. He observed the people called it a *red* stocking, though he did not understand why they gave it that denomination, as he himself thought it completely described by being called a *stocking.* The circumstance, however, remained in his memory, and, together with subsequent observations, led him to the knowledge of his defect. As the idea of color is among the first that enters the mind, it may perhaps seem extraordinary that he did not observe his want of it still earlier. This, however, may in some measure be accounted for from the circumstance of his family being Quakers, among whom a general uniformity of colors is known to prevail. He observed, also, that, when young, other children could discern cherries on a tree by some pretended difference of color, though he could only distinguish them from the leaves by their difference of size and shape. He observed, also, that, by means of this difference of color, they could see the cherries at a greater distance than he could, though he could see other objects at as great distance as they; that is, where the sight was not assisted by the color. Large objects he could see as well as other persons; and even the smaller ones, if they were not enveloped in other things, as in the case of cherries among the leaves. I believe he could never do more than guess the name of any color; yet he could distinguish white from black, or black from any light or bright color. Dove or straw color he called white, and different colors he frequently called by the same name; yet he could discern a difference between them when placed together. In general, colors of an equal degree of brightness, however they might otherwise differ, he frequently confounded together; yet a striped ribbon he could distinguish from a plain one, but he could not tell what the colors were with any tolerable exactness. Dark colors in general he often mistook for black, but never imagined white to be a dark color, nor dark to be a white color. He was an intelligent man, and very desirous of understanding the nature of light and colors, for which end he had attended a course of lectures in natural philosophy. He had two brothers in the same circumstances as to sight, and two other brothers and sisters, who, as well as their parents, had nothing of this defect. One brother is master of a trading-vessel. I met him, and asked him whether he had ever seen a rainbow. He replied he had often, and could distinguish the different colors; meaning only that it was composed of different colors, for he could not tell what they were. A piece of ribbon he without difficulty pronounced striped, and not plain. The several stripes of white he uniformly so called. The four black stripes he was deceived in; for three of them he thought brown, though they were exactly of the same shade with the other, which he properly called black. The light green he called yellow, but he was not very positive. He said, 'I think that is what you call yellow.' The middle stripe, which had a slight tinge of red, he called a sort of blue. But he was most of all deceived by the orange color: of this he spoke very confidently, saying, 'This is the color of grass: this is green.' I also showed him a great variety of ribbons, the color of which he sometimes named rightly, and sometimes as differently as possible from the true colors. These experiments were made in the daytime, and in a good light. I asked him whether he imagined it possible for all the various colors he saw to be mere difference of light and shade; whether he thought they could be various degrees between white and black, and that all colors could be composed of these two mixtures only. With some hesitation he replied, No: he did imagine there was some other difference."

In 1779 Mr. J. Scott reported his own case in a letter to Rev. Mr. Whisson, Trinity College, and communicated by the Rev. Michael Lort. He says that a full red and full green, pale blue and pink, deep red and blue gave him the same sensation; but he readily distinguished yellow and deep blue. The claret color of a garment seemed to him deep black.

We must again seek in vain in literature for cases of color-blindness till we come, in 1794, to the English chemist Dalton's description of his own vision. His report excited so much attention, that his name became attached to this chromatic defect, which, by general consent, is now among nearly all nations called color-blindness, not only from a desire not to connect so distinguished a man's name as Dalton with a physical defect, but as also being nearer the truth, since only the red-blind are Daltonians. Dalton's case is as interesting as historical. He says, —

"It has been observed that our ideas of colors, sounds, tastes, &c., excited by the same object, may be very different in themselves without our being aware of it, and that we may nevertheless converse intelligibly concerning such objects as if we were certain the impressions made by them on our minds were exactly similar. It will, however, scarcely be supposed that any two objects, which are every day before us, should appear hardly distinguishable to one person, and very different to another, without the circumstance immediately suggesting a difference in their faculties of vision; yet such is the fact, not only with regard to myself, but to many others also. Notwithstanding the occasional study of botany, I was never convinced of a peculiarity in my vision till I accidentally observed the color of the flower *Geranium zonale* by candle-light in 1792. The flower was pink, but it appeared to me almost an exact sky-blue by day. In candle-light, however, it was astonishingly changed, not having then any blue in it, but being what I called *red*, — a color which forms a striking contrast to blue. Friends, when asked, all agreed that the color was not materially different from what it was by daylight, except my brother, who saw it in the same light as myself. Two years afterwards I commenced an investigation of the subject, assisted by a friend. My observation began with the solar spectrum, or colored image of the sun, exhibited in a dark room by means of a glass prism. I found that persons in general distinguish six kinds of color in the solar image; namely, red, orange, yellow, green, blue, purple. To me it is quite otherwise: I see only two, or at most three, distinctions. These I should call *yellow* and *blue*, or *yellow*, *blue*, and *purple*. My yellow comprehends the *red*, *orange*, *yellow*, and *green* of others; and my blue and purple coincide with theirs. That part of the image which others call red appears to me little more than a shade, or defect of light; after that, the orange, yellow, and green seem *one* color, which descends pretty uniformly from an intense to a rare yellow, making what I should call different shades of yellow. The difference between the green part and the blue part is very striking to my eye: they seem to be strongly contrasted. That between the blue and purple is much less so. The purple appears to be blue much darkened and condensed."

The next cases reported in order of time are by Dr. Nicholl, 1816 and 1818. One was a boy eleven years old, who was color-blind, like Dalton. The other was a man aged forty-nine, who reported thus: —

"The color I am most at a loss with is green; and, in attempting to distinguish it from red, it is nearly guess-work. Scarlet in most cases I can distinguish, but a dark bottle-green I could not, with any certainty, from brown.

Light yellow I know; dark yellow I might confound with light brown, though in most cases, I think, I should know them from red. The different shades of red and green, I know not to which they belong; but, when they are before me, I see a difference in the shade. Though I see different shades in looking at a rainbow, I should say it was a mixture of yellow and blue, — yellow in the centre, and blue towards the edges."

These cases are about all which may be properly considered historic. I have referred to the original accounts, and quoted from them. It may be noticed that mention of what the several persons called colors — i.e., the names they gave them on presentation — has been generally omitted. The reason of this will be seen later. It need only here be remarked, that asking the examined to name colors is in reality no test of their color-perception; and, where this alone has been done, their color-blindness cannot be accepted as proved.

CHAPTER II.

COLOR-BLIND MISTAKES.

It will be interesting to note what mistakes their chromatic deficiency causes the color-blind to make, and therefore well worth our while to listen to their own report, as well as that of their examiners. Not only shall we find it curious and interesting, but from a long series of cases we may able to deduce, as has been done, some general laws and classification of this peculiar visual condition. Commencing with the cases I have referred to as historical: Dalton said the color of a florid complexion seemed dull, opaque, blackish blue upon a white ground. Diluted black ink on white paper gives a color much resembling a florid complexion. It has no resemblance to the color of blood. Blood appeared not unlike that color called bottle-green. Grass appeared a very little different from red. The face of a laurel-leaf is a good match to a stick of red sealing-wax, and the back of the leaf answers to the lighter red of wafers. Green woollen cloth — such as is used to cover tables — appeared a dull brownish-red color. A mixture of two parts mud and one red would come near it. It resembled a red soil just turned up by the plough. "When this kind of cloth loses its color, as other people say, and turns yellow, then it appears to me a pleasant green. Very light-green paper, silk, &c., is white to me." Blue was the same to him as to other people, both by daylight and candle-light. "Colors appear to me much the same by moonlight as they do by candle-light. By lightning and the electric light they appear as by daylight. A light-drab woollen cloth seems to resemble a light green by day. My idea of brown I obtain from a piece of white paper heated almost to ignition. This color by daylight seems to have a great affinity to green. Browns seem to me very diversified: some I should call red. Dark-brown woollen cloth I should call black."

A most amusing account was given by Babbage of the incidents attending the presentation of Dalton at court: —

"Firstly he was a Quaker, and would not wear the sword, which is an indispensable appendage of ordinary court-dress. Secondly, the robe of a doctor of civil laws was known to be objectionable on account of its color, — scarlet, — one forbidden to Quakers. Luckily it was recollected that Dalton was afflicted with the peculiar color-blindness which bears his name, and that, as the cherries and the leaves of a cherry-tree were to him of the same color, the scarlet gown would present to him no extraordinary appearance. So perfect, indeed, was the color-blindness, that this most modest and simple of men, after having received the doctor's gown at Oxford, actually wore it for several days in happy unconsciousness of the effect he produced on the street." — *Scientific London*, 1874, p. 38.

Professor Whewell reports having asked Dalton what the bright-scarlet gown which he wore resembled, and he pointed to some of the evergreens outside of the window, and said, that to his eye their colors were quite alike. On the other hand, the lining of the gown, which was pink silk, he could not distinguish from sky-blue.

The first case recorded — Harris the shoemaker — noticed, when an infant, what the color-blind nearly always do, namely, the inability to distinguish any red fruits from the surrounding green leaves. Recognition of their chromatic defect dates not infrequently from companions being able to pick strawberries, cherries, &c., more quickly. One of Dr. Colquhoun's patients says, —

"I cannot perceive a bit of red sealing-wax if thrown down upon the grass, nor a piece of scarlet cloth hung upon a hedge, which, I was told, was to be seen a mile off. I once gathered some lichen, as a great curiosity, from the roof of a friend's fishing-house. I thought it was of a bright scarlet, from its seeming to be of the same color as the tiles: in reality it was a bright green. On another occasion I perceived no difference in the complexion of a foreign lady, who had purposely substituted Prussian blue for her rouge."

Dr. Nicholl says of a boy, eleven years old, —

"I placed a scarlet paper on the grass, and afterwards a green baize. He said that the grass and the baize were of the same color as the paper, but that they were a shade lighter. I made him put on a pair of green spectacles, which he called *red* glasses. He said that everybody and every thing in the room had a reddish cast when seen through them. The border of the room had a blue leaf with a green edge: this he called a blue leaf with a red border. A woman passed by with a basket on her arm. He told his mother that the woman had fowls in it, for that he saw the *red* feathers hanging out: these proved to be *green* leaves with which she had covered her butter. He told me, 'What you call purple and pink and blue are so like each other, that I cannot well know one from the other.' He also called the gray eyes of his sister a bluish red. A blood-relative of this lad was in the navy, and purchased a blue uniform coat and waistcoat, with *red* breeches to match the blue. I showed him a doily which was red, having a leaf of the same color traced out on it, and I asked him the color of it. He, having been so often mistaken and laughed at, said, with an air of triumph, 'Why the groundwork is red; but the leaf is of course green.'"

Dr. Nicholl's second case, a gentleman forty-nine years old, said, —

"If railings were painted red, I could not distinguish them from the grass. The grass in full verdure appears to me what other people call red; and the fruit on trees, when red, I cannot distinguish from the leaves, unless when I am near it. A cucumber and a boiled lobster I should call the same color, making allowance for the variety of shade to be found in both; and a leek in luxuriance of growth is to me more like a stick of sealing-wax than any thing I can compare it with.'"

In further illustration of the sort of mistakes the color-blind make, I here quote some of Professor Wilson's cases. A middle-aged gentleman says, —

"As far as I can tell, the following expresses my experience as to colors. Yellow is the brightest color; blue, nearly as bright. These two are the only ones I see distinctly in the rainbow. Red I can distinguish when bright; but delicate shades I confound with stone-color or gray. Green I have no distinct conception of. According to its different shades, it appears black, brown, red, yellow, blue, and gray. I cannot distinguish at any distance the ripe cherries on a tree, or strawberries from their leaves. I have no conception of what is meant by complementary colors, or of the agreement of different colors when blended together; as, for instance, what kind of a carpet accords with red curtains in a room. With regard to my want of perception of green, it appears to me that the blue and the yellow rays neutralize each other, and, when in equal proportions, constitute what is really no color, varying all the way from a very light drab or gray to a dingy black. When the blue rays predominate, it appears a blue drab; and, when the yellow rays are in excess, it appears a yellow drab. When the blue and yellow are properly blended, a lady's green silk dress appears to me very similar, and no more glaring than a drab silk. The dry dirt of the street I could equally suppose to be green. I also confound red and brown frequently. I could not distinguish between treacle and blood spilt in a road by daylight."

Another gentleman gives a very interesting illustration of the extent of his color-blindness in reference to red and green. When acting as assistant to the engineer of the Granton Railway, he frequently returned in the evening from Granton to Edinburgh on one of the engines, without, however, taking any part in managing it. On these occasions he observed, that, although his undivided attention was directed towards the signal lamps, the light of which was visible to him a long way off, he could not, till he was close upon them, distinguish whether they were red or green. He feels certain that he could tell a blue light from a red light at a distance which would make green and red appear the same.

Another gentleman was, like many other color-blind persons, a great lover of fine arts, and a skilful draughtsman. He was led in consequence, early in life, to discover his inability to arrange his own palette, and was accustomed to rely upon a relative to select his colors, whilst he had no difficulty in graduating their shades. In the rainbow he distinguishes blue, yellow, and orange. Green he never sees in it, and he is very uncertain as to red. In colored objects he has no difficulty with blue or yellow; but he stumbles at red and green, and olive and brown. Green moss and red and green velvet make the same impression on his eye, so far as color is concerned. He is foiled also by worsteds of these colors, and on one occasion betrayed his peculiarity of vision by his inability to see the contrast between the scarlet berries and green leaves of the mountain-ash. On another occasion he was surprised to find, on returning home from a journey, that a letter which he had written home during his absence was one-half in black and the other in red ink. A red-brick house, which to others is a conspicuous object in the landscape, even at a great distance, is to him an inconspicuous one, and made out with great difficulty solely by its form.

"Green and red I cannot distinguish from each other. Red cabbage growing, pickled, or in infusion, are all the most beautiful blue I can conceive; and it was by not observing any change by acids in the infusion of red cabbage, when attending Professor Hope's chemistry-class, where I used to stare for the whole hour expecting to see the change, that I first became fully convinced of my great defect. Red, again, in the lips, cheeks, nose (red), gooseberries, inflammations, and the like, looks blue to me! (I never saw a red nose in my life;) and yet, in recently taking up an oil-paint, to illustrate to another my conception of the color of the lips, you will be astonished to hear that I took up a green (terre verte). On another occasion I was very much annoyed at a little boy who could tell a blue line of water-color, drawn across my finger, from blood: I could see no difference. Strawberries, cherries, &c., I can recognize without the slightest difficulty; but I don't trouble myself about their color: I see only a difference as regards what I call *shade*. Pinks, lilacs, purples, and blues are all the same color, only differing in intensity. Browns, russets, maroons, olives, citrines, and a host of others, are just any thing I can guess at; but I never get farther than red, brown, or green. The names of the other colors I don't think I ever uttered. Indeed, I never speak of colors, unless I cannot avoid it; and the only practical mistake I ever made in regard to them was purchasing a purple neckcloth under the impression it was black. That was the only mistake, for a good reason: I never bought a colored piece of dress *alone*, either before or since. A piece of railway red signal-glass, and another of green signal-glass, held up together, close to the eye in daylight, appeared to be shades of the same color."

An engraver reports, —

"Strange as it may appear, my defective vision is, to a certain extent, a useful and valuable quality. Thus: an engraver has two negative colors to deal with; i.e., white and black. Now, when I look at a picture, I see it only in white and black, or light and shade; and any want of harmony in the coloring of a picture is immediately made manifest by a corresponding discord in the arrangement of its light and shade, or, as artists term it, the *effect*. I find at times many of my brother-engravers in doubt how to translate certain colors of pictures, which to me are matters of decided certainty and ease. Thus to me it is valuable. From childhood I have been totally unable to retain certain colors in my mind, nor able to give their names when shown to me a second time. This defect applies more particularly to compound colors, such as green, purple, orange, and brown (this color I can never define); also the difference between pink and pale blue, reds and yellows, blues and greens, reds and greens; but the appreciation of the various shades of colors (or the weight of colors, as I may term it) is exceedingly nice and critical. A few years ago I went to a draper's to buy some green baize, but unfortunately bought a very bright red, which was excessively painful to my eyes by lamplight, but agreeable enough by daylight."

An amateur artist, who also worked with crayons, found his defect an advantage, and reports, —

"I have myself a distinct perception of the whole spectrum, with the exception of the *red* and *green*, which seem to be a very near repetition of the same colors; the difference between them being to my eye much more marked by some accidental variation of tone rather than of *tint*, which to others is frequently imperceptible. The flowers of a fuchsia, the berries of mountain-ash and holly, are scarcely distinguishable to me, excepting by their tone or form."

He also adds, "I recollect the late Lord V. joking his wife for wearing a *scarlet* dress. She assured him it was bright *green;* and, comparing notes with him, I found that our defect of vision was precisely the same, although he had been scarcely aware of it till that time. My brother, who has the same trouble, once picked up a red-hot coal, asking what that funny green thing was."

Another case writes as follows:—

"I do not think I should easily mistake a green for a red, or red for a green; but, if the distant perception of scarlet (or red of that nature) is a necessary qualification for an engine-driver in the conduct of a train, I shall be careful, 'come what come may,' never to offer myself in that capacity to a railway company. At a distance of about sixty yards it would puzzle me to distinguish the color of a soldier's coat, although the general outline of the figure would enable me to pronounce upon its being that of a soldier."

An admiral in the British service writes,—

"A younger brother of mine, long since dead, was fond of drawing; yet once he painted a *red* tree in a landscape without being aware he had done so. I myself, though fond of drawing, never attempted to color, as I should have done the same, unless the cake of color had been properly marked. I find that it is not that I do not see a distinction between two colors when placed near each other, as in patterns or bales of cloth; but I should hardly distinguish a red jacket hung on a tree, unless quite fresh from the loom. A red-tiled barn I should not distinguish in a landscape, but from knowing tiles are red. The shades of green, of brown, and of red, perplex me most. Bright scarlet is unmistakable to me; but I chose a pair of green trousers once, thinking they were brown. As for signal-lanterns, I should know the difference between red and green if they were shown together; but I should be sorry if the safety of a train depended on my lookout, when one light alone was exhibited as danger or no danger."

A young physician answers, "Having often observed a railway signal-light, seen from my window, I am convinced that its colors would be lost upon me; nor dare I trust to their flags. I never venture on the purchase of colored articles without a companion to appeal to."

Professor N. says, "I suppose I can sometimes distinguish red in some objects, but probably this is from knowing that they are usually of this color. At any rate, I am quite sure that I should make a dangerous railway-signal man, as I most certainly would not know a red flag from a green one."

An architect reports having to release a pupil-apprentice in consequence of finding him copy a brown house in bluish-green paint, the sky rose-color, and roses blue.

A tradesman reports his boy offering pink and pale-green paper as good matches, and getting his master into frequent trouble by binding books in wrong colors.

A manufacturer reports that one of his weavers had to have the red and green threads selected by another, as he could not distinguish them.

A carver and gilder, who was color-blind, had a son who painted a head with the face muddy green, which he conceived to be vermilion. A brother of this person, an artist by profession, knew no difference by gaslight between the variously-colored bottles in a druggist's window, and could not distinguish the red from the green signal-lamp at a railway-station.

Six males — uncles, nephews, and cousins — in one family all belong to the Society of Friends;

and their mistakes in selecting articles of dress have been rendered especially conspicuous by the preference which members of that religious body give to the least brilliant and most unconspicuous colors. One of their number provided himself with a bottle-green coat, intending to purchase a brown one; and selected for his wife, who desired a dark gown, a scarlet merino. Another, who is an upholsterer, purchased scarlet for drab, and had to rely upon his wife and daughters to select for him the fabrics needed in the course of his profession. A third, who is a farmer, could not tell red apples from the surrounding green leaves, except by their shape. All of them confounded red with green, olive with brown, and pink with blue; but they are very expert at matching shades of the same color. One of the younger men, whose profession requires him to deal much in colored tissues, has found that the "only way of telling the difference between scarlet and green, or blue and crimson, is to take them into a room lighted with gas or candles," when the distinction which was invisible by daylight becomes apparent. Olives and browns, however, are as undistinguishable by one light as by another. A minister, also in the Society of Friends, selected scarlet cloth as the material for a new coat.

As to females with color-blindness, Wilson says of the Countess of D., —

"Red, green, black, brown, and lilac, she does not venture to name confidently, and greens and drabs are the same color. Mountain-ash or holly berries are undistinguishable from their foliage. In sorting worsteds she can place no confidence in herself in choosing, and all the lightest shades of color are liable to be completely mixed up. 'The yellow tints now (October) seen on the trees appear to me exactly the same as those of their spring shades: indeed I cannot conceive the possibility of any one seeing them to be different.' The term 'yellow' here included all the autumn tints of the leaves; and therefore various shades of orange, red, russet, and brown must have seemed identical with the yellow green and the bright green of the spring leaves."

A lady reports, "I do not know how to express myself well regarding the loss I am at to distinguish colors, as I hardly understand *how it is* myself; but I will try to do so as clearly as I can. There are many colors the shades of which I confound: these are blue, lilac, pink, and purple; and, if the various shades of these colors were put before me and mixed together, I should be quite confused, and *could not* tell to which each belongs, although I see they are different. In the same way I confound green, brown, and some of the shades of orange. In short, were I to tell the name of any color correctly, it would be merely guesswork. I can enjoy the beauties of nature, and the varied hues of the trees, &c.; but that there is *some* defect in my vision I am quite aware. Of this, also, I am certain; I can do nothing (or as yet have not been able) to improve it."

When engaged with colored worsted-work, she always has the skeins marked.

To this long list of foreign and American reports, I could, of course, now add as many more from my own experience with the color-blind. I will forbear giving but a few, merely to show that they all can be brought under the same general laws.

Dr. Blank writes me, "Possibly you may have recollected that I am myself of the red-green group. In 1854–55 Wilson of Edinburgh added me to his list."

Another physician writes me, "I read with interest your color-blind researches: for I am shockingly so, often to my great chagrin and the mortification of my wife and daughter, and, where I feel it most, in surgical practice, — color of throats, gangrene, ulcers, coppery-hued sores, &c.; so that I have to draw out the statements of others for my guidance."

A gentleman tells me, "Yellow and blue are my only distinct colors. Red is the most indistinct. I cannot see certain shades of red. I cannot distinguish scarlet salvias a few rods away."

A member of a well-known American color-blind family sends me word, "Red, brown, and green, of about the same depth or strength of color, appear about alike to me. The red cherry and the leaf of the tree look substantially alike."

A lady, whose father was color-blind, writes me of two of her children, boys (three girls being free of the defect), that "they do not observe when a flaming bush of *Pyrus Japonica* is in flower, unless near enough to discern the form of the flower. After having his attention directed to it, one of them said, 'Oh, yes! I see the flowers now; but they are not so bright as the leaves.' The leaves in their young state are of a very yellow green. Neither of the boys is near-sighted. I first noticed it in my older boy when he was five years old. We were in a field, and the girls were screaming with delight over such columbines all around them. The little boy said, 'Where are they? I don't see any. flowers.' After having one put in his hand, and observing the form, he, too, could find them. There are two colors my boys are quite unable to learn to distinguish. These are a light green and a yellow brown. I do not think they see any difference between them. I enclose bits of the colors I mean. I omitted to mention that my boys always call crimson blue."

The green worsted I found almost the same as the shade used in Holmgren's test, and the yellowish brown just the color the color-blind will select among the first, if not the very first, to match the green.

A colleague at a distance, regarded by his wife as very deficient in color-perception, asked my opinion. I sent him my test-worsteds; and the *matches* he returned me were amusing, fully substantiating the lady's opinion and diagnosis.

A friend told me he painted a pea-green lion for his little boy. Another wore a green and a brown glove. A young architect put a green roof on a church, and was indisposed to admit having made any mistake. Complaints to me from the color-blind, as to the colors of horse-cars by day and their lights by night, have been very frequent. A medical friend tells me that on a yacht he must have a piece of red glass marked *red*, and green marked *green*, to look at, to endeavor to impress on his eye the sensation, and compare it with the red or green light of an approaching vessel. His matches of worsted were amusing, and showed complete red-blindness. I happened to meet him on the street; and, on questioning him, I found he could see no color in a bright-red express-wagon, a brilliant new scarlet "soldier's messenger" cap, nor could he distinguish a lad by his deep-red scarf. His brother was nearly the same. Yellow-stained glass in a door they recognized, but thought pale green was white, or "the color of soda-water."

As has been truly said, "Volumes might be

written on this subject if the different instances of all the peculiarities presented by color-blindness, and all the embarrassment to which they give rise, were cited."

The question of correctly distinguishing colors comes up in a practical form more often than we imagine in every-day life. Such articles as the following, clipped from the newspapers of a day, attract naturally the attention only of those specially interested in or investigating color-perception : —

"NEW BEDFORD, Aug. 30. — Masters of vessels arriving at Vineyard Haven complain, that, since the red light at the East Chop has been removed to the new tower built for it, it is scarcely distinguishable from the West Chop, or any other fixed white light. The captain of schooner 'Hannibal,' of Islesborough, Me., made it on Saturday evening, approaching from the eastward, in thick weather, and called it West-Chop light, and changed his course to run in Vineyard-Haven Harbor, and just escaped running ashore near Oak Bluffs by making the light at that place through the fog. Such accidents as the above can only occur, however, in thick weather, when but one of the two lights on the Chops of the harbor can be seen at the same time."

"An English inventor, J. J. Nickoll, has brought out a system of helm-signals. In describing his invention to the Inventors' Institute, Mr. Nickoll says, 'As my signals move automatically with the rudder, every material shifting of the helm to the port or starboard is at once shown at the head of the vessel by a red or green light, and before she answers her helm, thus giving timely notice to an approaching ship what course she is about to steer. The signals act independently of the regulation mast-head lights.' "

As if the present necessary marine-signals were not difficult enough to read quickly, a writer in "The Scientific American" proposes that there should be exhibited a red light for north, green for south, yellow for east, and white for west. When steering due north a red light is to be shown; when steering north-north-east one light under this; north-east two lights; east-north-east three lights, &c.; and so on for the other points of the compass. Every change of course is to be immediately followed by a change of these lanterns. Such a proposal but expresses the general lack of appreciation of the difficulties with all night-signals.

"The Eastern Railway Company has recently placed upon the whole route of its line patent switches painted red, with an index pointing across the track if all is not right. At night a green lantern signifies the track is clear, and a red one if not. The company claims that by this simple arrangement accidents will not be of so frequent occurrence as under the old system of signals."

A post-office clerk in Prussia was found to be constantly in trouble with the stamps. The accounts would come wrong. Sometimes there was not enough money in return for stamps sold; and on other occasions there was too much. This made dishonesty on his part less likely; but it was incomprehensible how he would make the accounts so entangled. At length it was discovered that he was color-blind, and could not distinguish red from green stamps ("Boston Medical and Surgical Journal," Dec. 27, 1877). No doubt letters in the United States find their way to the Dead-Letter Office as unpaid from the color-blind senders putting on *red* two-cent instead of *green* three-cent stamps, since we all, from habit, regard the color rather than the number on a postage-stamp, especially when in haste.

CHAPTER III.

FORMER CLASSIFICATION OF THE COLOR-BLIND.

By this long list of reports from the examiners or the examined, I have not only enabled my readers to recognize what are the mistakes the color-blind make, but also, perhaps, assisted them in grouping into certain classes those with this chromatic defect. This, as will be seen, is of importance; but it was not done till 1837 by Professor Seebeck. Of course any one observer of this then simply scientific curiosity had hardly opportunity of comparing any great number of cases together, and thereby deducing some laws concerning them, or sorting out the color-blind into classes according to their special form of trouble. Seebeck personally investigated a number for that time very large, — namely, twelve cases; and he was the first to work philosophically, recognizing and insisting on the uselessness of asking the color-blind the color-names of objects. He proved the importance of letting them show their own comparisons by having a number of colored objects mixed up together, and allowing them to select and group together those which seemed to them of the same color. He had some three hundred pieces of variously colored paper, also variously colored pieces of glass. He recommends worsteds, but thinks silks would be too brilliant. He did not use worsteds, but did employ the spectrum and polarized light in addition to the test with the colored papers, &c.

His deductions were, that there was a class of color-blind who seemed quite insensible to the specific impression of all colors, — most so for *red* and naturally, also, its complementary *green*, in that they could distinguish them but little, if any, from gray; then for blue, which they did not well separate from gray. Their sensation of yellow seemed best developed, though this did not appear so different from colorless as to a normal eye. Such persons more or less confounded bright orange and pure yellow; deep orange, bright yellowish or brownish green, and yellowish brown; pure bright green, grayish brown, and flesh-color; rose-red, green (rather bluish than yellowish), and gray; carmine, dark green, and hair-brown; bluish green and impure violet; lilac and bluish gray; sky-blue, grayish blue, and grayish lilac.

Another class he found very similar to the first. They also recognize yellow best, and distinguish red better, blue rather less from colorless, but especially confound red and blue. The colors they confound with each other are clear orange, greenish yellow, brownish yellow, and pure yellow; bright orange, yellowish brown, and grass-green; sealing-wax red, rusty brown, and dark olive green; cinnabar-red and dark brown; dark carmine red and dark bluish green; flesh-red, gray brown, and blue green; pale bluish green and gray (rather brownish); impure rose (rather yellowish) and pure gray; rose-red, lilac, sky-blue, and gray (towards lilac); carmine and violet; dark violet and dark blue.

Seebeck was the first, besides grouping the color-blind into classes, to show also that there were *degrees* of this trouble as varying as the visual power for form, which we now recognize as individual.

Again, from an analysis of our long list of reported difficulties with chromatic vision, we may see how it was, from a study of all the then accessible cases, Szokalski distinguished *five* classes of color-blind, —

1. That of persons in whom the sense of colors is almost completely wanting, and who, in place of the elementary colors, — yellow, red, and blue, — see only different degrees of white and black.

2. That of persons who also distinguish yellows: external objects appear to them colored with shades which generate the different mixtures of yellow, of white, and of black.

3. That of persons who, besides seeing yellow, have a common perception for both blue and red.

4. That of persons destitute solely of the perception of red, which appears to them ash-gray.

5. That of individuals who distinguish all colors, but not in a decided manner: instead of being able to distinguish the mixture of two colors, they never see but one of them.

Professor Purkinje, again, from an analysis of cases observed and then recorded, divides color-blindness into four varieties. The first two relate more to the intensity, the others to the nature, of the imperfection.

Professor Elie Wartman, writing in 1840, says, —

"The various ancient and recent observations which I have to relate appear to me to confirm the division of Seebeck, rather than that of Szokalski and Purkinje. It would be very advantageous to make a strict classification of the color-blind, because for each category means might be offered at once simple and few as palliatives of their imperfections. Unhappily such an undertaking does not seem possible, and we may say that there are as many varieties of color-blindness as of individuals who are affected with it. With regard to the very rational distinction which Seebeck has the merit of having first established between the errors of appreciation of *intensity*, and those of judgment of the *individual kind* of colors, it is to be regretted that we cannot make it in the great majority of the descriptions which writers have transmitted to us. I prefer only to separate the cases of *dichromatic* and *polychromatic* color-blindness; that is to say, where there are more than two colors perceived normally."

I have thus briefly given the earlier attempts to classify the color-blind, that the difficulty of so doing may be recognized. We shall also thus be better able to appreciate the value of the application of the theory for this purpose described in the next chapter.

CHAPTER IV.

PRESENT CLASSIFICATION OF THE COLOR-BLIND IN ACCORDANCE WITH THE YOUNG-HELMHOLTZ THEORY OF COLOR-PERCEPTION.

A PROPER division, and a consequent correct understanding, of color-blindness was not made till this half of our century. Professor Helmholtz brought forward the long-forgotten work of Thomas Young, and applied his theory of color-perception to the results of more modern investigations, with the final development of what is now called the Young-Helmholtz theory of color-sense. Helmholtz says, —

"A reduction of colors to three base colors has only a subjective meaning: it is but reducing or carrying back the sensations of color to three base or final sensations. In this view Thomas Young correctly grasped the problem, and, in fact, his theory gives us a very simple and clear view and explanation of all the phenomena of the physiology of color. Thomas Young holds that, —

"1. There are in the eye three kinds of nerve-fibres. Stimulation of the first produces the sensation of red, the second that of green, and of the third the sensation of violet.

"2. Objective homogeneous light excites these three kinds of fibres in varying degree according to the wave-lengths. The red perceptive fibres will be strongest stimulated by light of the greatest wave-length, the green perceptive by light of medium wave-length, and the violet perceptive by light of the smallest wave-length. Here must not be excluded, but rather accepted in explanation of a series of phenomena, that each spectral color excites all three kinds of fibres, — but one less, the others more strongly. Let us suppose, as in Fig. 1, the spectral colors in a horizontal row from red to violet: then the three curves will represent the intensity of stimulation of the three kinds of fibres, — (1) the red perceptive; (2) the green perceptive; and (3) the violet perceptive elements or fibres.

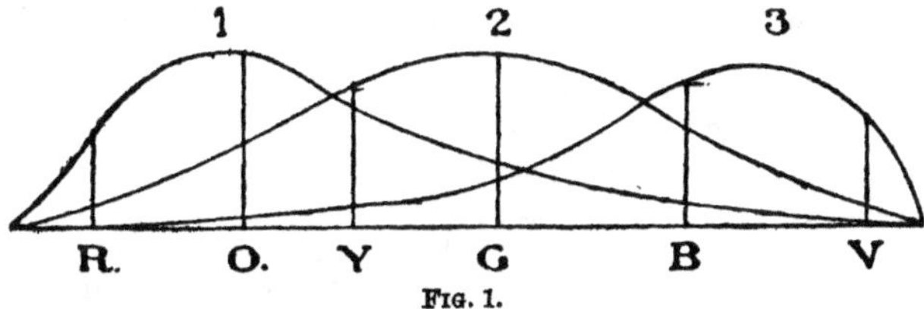

FIG. 1.

"Simple *red* strongly stimulates the red perceptive, less the other two: sensation, *red*.

"Simple *yellow* stimulates moderately the red and green perceptive, feebly the violet: sensation, *yellow*.

"Simple *green* stimulates strongly the green perceptive, much less the other two: sensation, *green*.

"Simple *blue* stimulates moderately the green and violet perceptive fibres, feebly the red: sensation, *blue*.

"Simple *violet* stimulates strongly the violet perceptive, feebly the other fibres: sensation, *violet*.

"Equally strong stimulation of all the fibres gives the sensation of white or whitish colors."

This is not the place to discuss the Young-Helmholtz theory of color-perception. It must be remembered that the facts in relation to color-blindness given in this volume are not collected in support of any theory, nor is any theory argued for. The Young-Helmholtz is used rather as a means of better explaining this defect. It will assist our understanding its relations to color-blindness to read Helmholtz's explanatory introduction of it:—

"Perhaps there will be much objection to this hypothesis, from the number of the necessary nerve-fibres or nerve-terminations being tripled, in comparison with the common theory, where every individual nerve carries all possible color-stimulations. I do not think, however, that in this respect Young's theory is in opposition to anatomical facts, since we know nothing of the number of the transmitting fibres; and then, besides, there are a number of microscopic elements present, whose special function we do not as yet know. Moreover, this is not the most essential in Young's hypothesis. That seems to me to be rather the presenting color-sensations as composed of three wholly independent actions in the nerve-substance. It is not absolutely necessary to suppose separate nerve-fibres for these separate sensations. The same value of Young's hypothesis in this explanation is shown, if we suppose that in each individual fibre three different and independent actions may take place. Since, however, the form of the hypothesis, as originally proposed by Young, is capable of more definite presentation and expression than such a modification of it would allow, we will, in view of its description, retain the original plainer form. Moreover, the physical phenomena of nerve-stimulation — namely, the electro-motor — are not marked in the sensitive or motor nerves by such a variation in action as would necessarily be the case if each nerve-fibre transmitted all color-sensations. By Young's hypothesis we may also apply to the optic nerve the simple conceptions of the mechanism of stimulation and conduction which we have derived from the study of the phenomena in the motor nerves. This we could not do if we must admit that each optic nerve-fibre is to have three qualitatively different conditions of stimulation without mutual interference. Young's hypothesis is only a more special carrying-out of the law of the specific energies of the senses. As the sense of touch, and the sense of sight in the eye, have evidently separate nerve-fibres, so is the same claimed for the sensation of the several base colors. The choice of the three colors is somewhat arbitrary. Any three colors could have been taken whose combination produced white light. So far as I see at present, there is no other means of determining the base colors than the examination of the color-blind."

For further description of the Young-Helmholtz theory of color-perception I would refer the reader to Helmholtz's popular scientific lectures. I have given above the essential points, as this was necessary to enable us to readily follow out the application of the theory thus stated by Helmholtz to the condition of the color-blind. By Young's theory Helmholtz has shown how colors must appear to the color-blind. This has been, however, so well extended and explained in Professor Holmgren's book, that I cannot do better than quote from it here. In deference to the Smithsonian Institute I will give their translation rather than my own. Professor Holmgren goes on to say, —

"These curves (Fig. 1) enable us to explain easily the colors of the spectrum by the theory. We find in what proportion each one of the three fundamental perceptions enters into it by measuring the vertical distance from their place on the horizontal line (abscissa) to the corresponding points of each of the three curves. It is then seen that there is no color of the spectrum into which but one primitive color enters exclusively. The two others also furnish their contingent. No one is therefore perfectly "saturated." They are more or less spread with white, and green is the least sensibly "saturated," or more whitish. The curves also show us that yellow and blue are at the same time whitish colors, and the most intensely luminous in the whole spectrum. When we again add that a color, "saturated" in almost the same degree as the other spectral colors, proceeds from the homogeneous combination of red and violet, — that is to say, purple, and its whitish shade, pink, — we shall have said all theoretically that we have to say in relation to the normal chromatic sense.

"To explain the abnormal sense of colors by the theory of the normal, we can, in advance, conceive various possibilities. Let us suppose that one of the three fundamental perceptions is wanting, or that one of the primitive colors is absent: it is clear that the whole chromatic system will be upset. It is evident, therefore, that this system must be completely different, according to the absence of one or the other of the three primitive colors. It is virtually just in this way that it has been attempted to explain cases of a strongly marked defect in the chromatic sense, or genuine types of blindness to color, found in real life. The term *color-blindness* has been justified by this, as it indicates in each case a genuine blindness to one of the primary colors. In this way, therefore, we distinguish, according to the kind of element wanting, three classes of blindness, —

"1st, Red-blindness.

"2d, Green-blindness.

"3d, Violet-blindness.

"We shall see that the Young-Helmholtz theory, far from being contradicted, as has been recently claimed, by the phenomenon of color-blindness, finds in it, on the contrary, a support; and this theory most certainly furnishes the best guide for attaining the practical end in view for which we intend to use it. Let us, in the first instance, cast a rapid glance over the different kinds of typical and complete blindness to colors as their features are presented by the theory. This sketch will be singularly facilitated by the use of the same kind of curves employed in illustrating the normal sense of colors.

"1. According to the theory, blindness to *red* is due to the absence or paralysis of the organs perceiving red (Fig. 2). Red-blindness has, then, but two fundamental colors, which, adhering strictly to the theory, are *green* and *violet* (blue according to Maxwell).

"The curves distinctly show what aspect the various kinds of lights of the spectrum must have for the chromatic sense, such as the one we have in view. We will give a short list of them, according to Helmholtz, by designating here the different kinds of lights, — by using terms borrowed from the impressions they produced on the normal chromatic sense. The comparison will not be without interest: —

"'Spectral red, which feebly excites the perceptive organs of green, and scarcely at all those of violet, must consequently appear to the red-blind a "*saturated*" *green of a feeble intensity*, more "saturated" than normal green, into which a sensible portion of the other primitive colors enters. Feebly luminous red, which affects the perceptive organs of red in a normal eye sufficiently, does not, on the other hand, sufficiently excite the perceptive organs of green in the red-blind; and it therefore seems to them black. Spectral *yellow* seems to them a *green* "*saturated*" *and intensely luminous;* and, as it constitutes the precisely saturated and very intense shade of that color, it can be understood how the red-blind select the name of that color, and call all those tints that are, properly speaking, green, *yellow*. *Green* shows, as compared with the preceding colors, a more sensible addition of

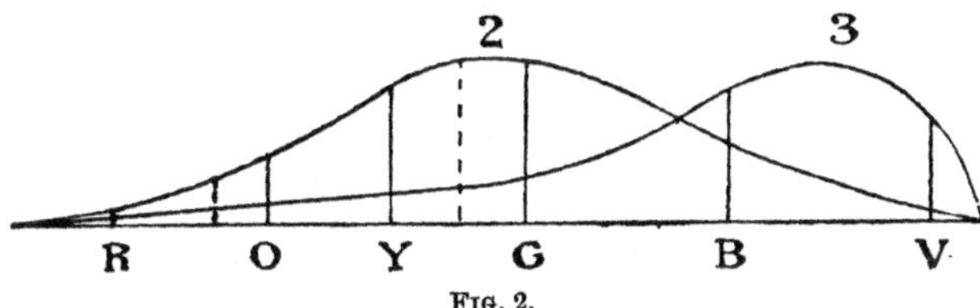

FIG. 2.

the other primitive colors: it then appears, consequently, like a more intense but whitish shade of the same color as yellow and red. The greatest intensity of light in the spectrum, according to Seebeck's observations, does not appear to the red-blind to be in the yellow region, as it does to the normal eye, but rather in that of the blue green. In reality, if the excitation of the perceptive organs of green, as it was necessary to assume, is strongest for green, the maximum of the total excitation of the red-blind must be found slightly toward the blue side, because the excitation of the organ perceiving violet is then increased. The white of the red-blind is naturally a combination of their two primitive colors in a determinate proportion, — a combination which appears blue gray to the normal sight: this is why he regards as gray the spectral transition colors from green to blue. Then the other color of the spectrum, which they call *blue*, preponderates, because indigo-blue, though somewhat whitish according to their chromatic sense, is to them, owing to its intensity, a more evident representative of that color than violet.'

"This description of the manner in which the red-blind forms a conception of the different kinds of light of the spectrum is assuredly a conclusion logically deduced from the theory; but it accords so well, at the same time, with the experience acquired in examining the color-blind, that this might perfectly serve to support and corroborate the theory. We will simply add a point for our especially practical purpose, or rather emphasize one point of this theory. In fact, it is clear that a red and a green light especially excite one and the same element in the red-blind. A ray red and green, or an object red and green, to the normal sense, must seem fundamentally to the red-blind to be the same color; and if, in especial cases, he knows how to discriminate, his judgment is simply guided by the intensity of the light. The intensity of light is much more feeble (as shown by Fig. 2) in red than in green. If, then, a red-blind individual finds that a red and a green tint are exactly alike, it is necessary that the green be to the normal eye much less intense than the red. This is distinctly shown by the vertical dotted lines between R. and O., and also between Y. and G., in Fig. 2; and this is entirely confirmed by experience.

"2. *Green-blindness* derives its origin, according to the theory, from the absence or paralysis of the perceptive elements of green. The green-blind has therefore but two fundamental colors; that is, — still closely adhering to the theory, — red and violet (blue according to Maxwell). The spectrum for green-blindness should be, according to the theory, constructed in the following manner: —

"The spectral *red*, which strongly excites the perceptive organs of red, and but very faintly those of violet, must therefore appear to the green-blind as an extremely 'saturated' red, but of a light somewhat less intense than the normal red, which is comparatively more yellowish, as green forms a part of it. The spectral *orange* is again a very 'saturated' red, but much more luminous. Yellow is undoubtedly a more intensely luminous red than the spectral red, but, on the other hand, more whitish, because a sensible portion of the other primitive color enters into it.

"*Green*, with its shades inclining to yellow and blue, ought, correctly speaking, to be a 'saturated' purple, and with a mean intensity of light: but it is the white (gray) of the green-blind; for it is composed of almost equal parts of the two primitive colors.

"The *blue* is an intense violet, but a little less 'saturated' than indigo, which is more strongly luminous and more 'saturated.' Violet is a little less intense, but more 'saturated' than normal violet. The tints most luminous, and at the same time most 'saturated,' which must constitute the types of the primitive colors of the green-blind, are orange (or its immediate neighbor in the spectrum, red) and indigo-blue. Now, orange is a color which, in ordinary language, especially amongst the uncultivated and unpractised, is indiscriminately called red and yellow: this fact explains why the green-blind denominate their first primary color some-

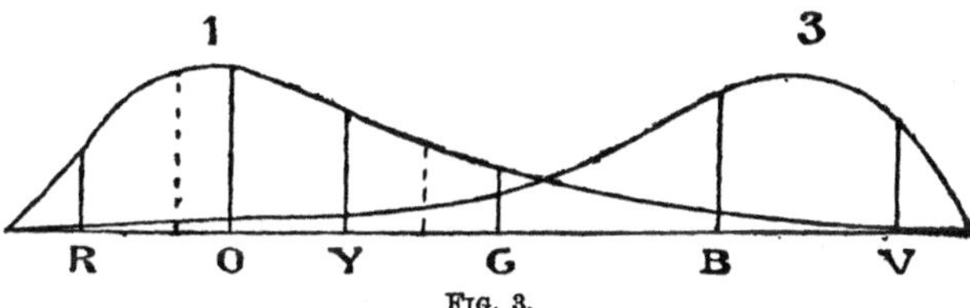

FIG. 3.

times 'red' and sometimes 'yellow.' We will add to this description the same remark made about red-blindness. In green-blindness the same organ is also found affected by spectral red and green light. Red and green are then perceived by the green-blind in the same way, or, in other words, *are to him in fact exactly the same color*. In cases where he succeeds in distinguishing them, it is by the aid of the intensity of the light; but, with regard to this intensity of light, it is the opposite of what occurs in the case of the red-blind. A green tint which to the green-blind must appear exactly like a red one, to a normal sense of color must be sensibly more luminous than red. This is shown by the dotted vertical lines between R. and O., and also between Y. and G. (Fig. 3), and is confirmed in every respect by experience.

"*Violet-blindness* (or blue according to Maxwell) is due,

according to the theory, to the absence or paralysis of the elements perceiving *violet*. The two primitive colors of the violet-blind are then, according to theory, *red* and *green*. The spectrum of the violet-blind must, in consequence, be represented as follows: —

"The *red* is a purer red color (not yellowish) than normal red, but still less 'saturated.' The more it inclines toward orange, the more strongly luminous it is, but is at the same time less 'saturated,' more whitish. The *yellow* is, as it were, a combination of almost equal proportions of the fundamental colors that form white. *Green* is a strongly luminous but whitish green, which, in tending toward the blue, becomes more and more 'saturated;' so that greenish blue must be the type of these hues. The *blue* is a green of moderate luminosity, and strongly 'saturated;' and *violet* is green very feebly luminous, but also 'saturated' in a much

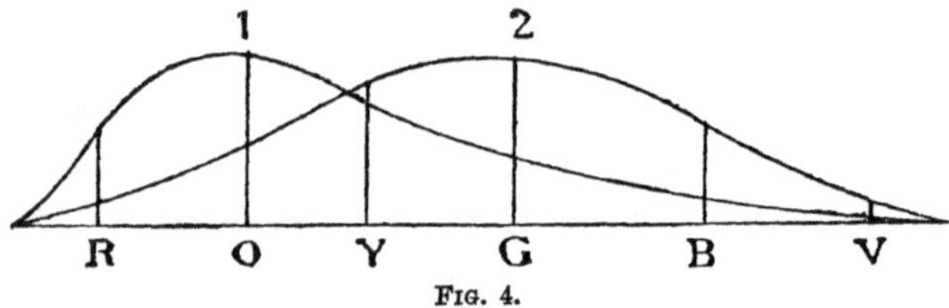

FIG. 4.

higher degree than the normal. A violet strongly luminous is sufficient to induce this green; but a feeble violet, although very sensible to the normal eye, is black to the color-blind in question.

"It is plain that the violet-blind, whose primitive colors are red and green, do not confuse these colors. This kind of blindness, from the experiments made so far, must be very rare. For our part we have not succeeded in discovering more than two cases agreeing quite exactly with the description given by the theory; while the first two kinds are comparatively very common. In order to be abnormal it is not necessary that a sense of color should completely fulfil the conditions indicated in the types we have just described. We might perfectly conceive a resultant, not of an absolute absence or of a complete paralysis of one kind of perceptive elements, but solely of a comparatively very low excitability, or, if preferred, of a much more limited number of one kind of elements, acting on the retina, as compared with the two other kinds. It is very easy to construct curves in conformity with this idea, and not less easy to arrange in this manner a continuous series of transitions and gradual forms between one kind of complete color-blindness on one side and the normal chromatic sense on the other. This kind of defective vision might be called *incomplete color-blindness*, to distinguish it from complete, as we have just characterized the three different kinds. Our experience has taught us that the intermediary forms agreeing with the data given above are met in large numbers in practice, and of very different degrees. These are the forms we designated under the common appellation of *incomplete color-blindness;* but we can, according to the theory, still conceive other forms of a defective sense of color. There is one, amongst others, which has at command only one of the three kinds of elements. Such a sense of sight is not properly a chromatic sense. For it there exists no specific difference in light; that is to say, no color. Every kind of light here acts as if on one element alone. This is why the single perception of differences of intensity of light (quantity), but not of differences of color (quality), is possible. This condition may then be designated under the name of *total color-blindness*. Several cases have been mentioned from time to time; but we have not succeeded in finding a single one, and it may well be questioned whether such a case has actually existed.[1] We may also conceive that

[1] Professor Donders reported an interesting case of congenital total color-blindness at the Heidelberg Ophthalmological Society 1871: An educated young man of twenty-one years of age was totally color-blind. Strong light blinded him: in moderate light he saw very well. He was myopic one-eighth, and read for hours without glasses. Out of doors, all glasses which absorbed light, without difference, — even the brightest colored ones, — were pleasant to him, because they reduced the light. In the dioptric spectrum of a gas-lamp his brightest part was between the spectral lines D and E, close to E: hence in greenish yellow. From here outwards towards the red end the light faded rapidly; towards the violet, at first, slowly, then rapidly. By moderate illumination he lost less of the brightest of the spectrum on this side than towards the red end. With the polariscope, the complementary colors through the quartz plate appeared to him of the same color. In turning the double-refractive prism he had a maximum of brightness at every ninety degrees, or equality of brightness, as if the quartz plate was not there. He had the greatest difference when Donders himself saw purple and green; equality, when he saw yellow and blue. Trials were also made with Chevreul's chromatic circle.

another form of a defective sense of color arises from the three kinds of elements being uniformly of moderate sensibility. We are able to trace the following diagram (Fig. 5), by which the three curves simultaneously approach the abscissa, or horizontal line, and are flattened in such a manner that the vertices disappear the first.

"As is readily observed, green is then precisely the color, which, being ordinarily the most whitish of the primitive colors, is the first to lose its quality of 'saturated' color, and shades into gray. This must then be the exact scheme of pathological color-blindness, according to the theory. In fact, we have found in our examinations a large number of cases perfectly harmonizing with this scheme. We have therefore classed them under the head of *incomplete color-blindness;* and this from essentially practical reasons. To define their nature according to the theory, it is necessary

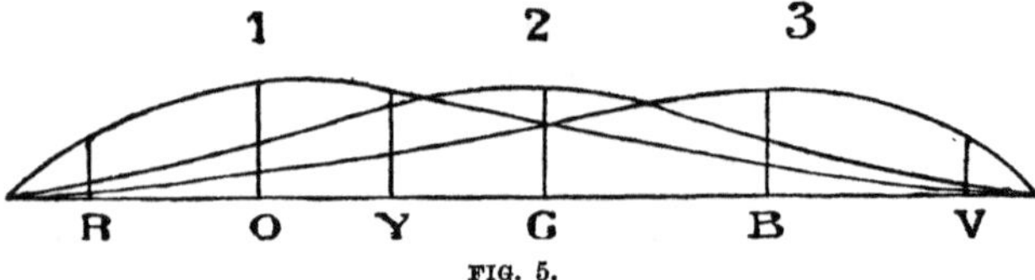

FIG. 5.

to regard them as a particular variety, which we shall call a *feeble sense of colors.* We are not of course able to decide how far defects of this kind should be considered as having a pathological origin, or whether they are ever congenital. For this determination a much wider experience in this particular department than we now possess is requisite, for reasons to be given hereafter. This kind of defect in the sense of color leads — if we fancy it carried to its highest degree, or in such a condition that all the elements lose sensibility — to the complete absence of perception of light; that is to say, to blindness, strictly so called. Every defect in the sense of color must then proceed either from a sensibility anomalously reduced to a complete paralysis of one or several kinds of elements, or from a number relatively diminished in sensibility to the complete absence of one or several amongst them.

"The experience acquired by an examination of colors in

different parts of the visual field elucidates our theory of color-blindness, while at the same time having a practical value. The following is the manner in which this examination is conducted: The eye is fixed upon an immovable point; a colored object — for example, a colored paper one or two centimetres square — is slowly passed from the side of the visual field toward the fixed point. This experiment is performed still better by means of a special instrument, Förster's perimeter. We then find that the colored surface of any color whatsoever appears completely colorless at the extreme periphery of the visual field. Surfaces of different colors exhibit only variations in intensity of light, not in color. The ground on which the surface appears plays here an important part, since, every time our visual sense perceives the light and color of an object, it partly depends upon the comparison with that which surrounds it. Thus a colored surface seems to us, in this part of the visual field, black or gray on a light ground, and gray or white on a dark. If, while following the same direction, the colored object is carried within the region which surrounds the rest of the visual field, like a belt of greater or less width, we begin to see the colored object, but not always in its natural color. Two colors alone — yellow and blue — retain their natural colors. All the others have the appearance of one of these colors consequently, — yellow or blue. It is only after the colored object is carried a little farther toward the fixed object that it is seen in its natural color. Consequently we normally see colors only in the middle of our visual field, within a compass extending in a more or less eccentric manner in every direction from the fixed point. Outside of the central field extends a belt which surrounds it on all sides, and in which our whole system of colors is classed under two heads, — exactly as in the case of the red-blind. We have here, as in the last case, but two colors, — yellow and blue. In other words, we are completely red-blind in this intermediary zone: beyond this there is a peripheral belt, in which we are totally color-blind. These are matters unquestionably of great theoretic value; but it must be acknowledged they are also of great practical importance. Although we have adopted the Young-Helmholtz theory, we must admit that the different kinds of perceptive elements of colors have a different local division upon the retina; and this is why we may speak of the topography of the chromatic sense. The fact is explained in this way: in the retina of the normal eye there are simultaneously three kinds of elements in the central part, corresponding to the central region of the visual field. Toward the periphery, beginning at the central fossa, the elements become more and more rare, but in unequal proportions; so that the perceptive organs of red cease first, and this at a limit corresponding to that of the central region. In a belt which answers to the intermediate zone, or the belt of the red-blind, there remains in consequence but the perceptive elements of *green* and *violet*. At the limit near the periphery of the retina, corresponding to that of the peripheral zone of the visual field, or region of absolute color-blindness, the perceptive elements of green cease also; so that there only remains in this last zone the perceptive elements of violet. We have been especially led to this last conclusion by the examination of two cases of color-blindness, where the visual field was so abnormally small that the peripheral zone seemed to be effaced, and where we, besides, recognized the characteristic features of violet-blindness. This experiment, which perfectly harmonized with the theory, showed us the relation of complete red-blindness to the normal chromatic sense. Red-blindness is distinguished from the normal sight in this, that the normal central field is wanting, but is replaced by a mean corresponding at the same time to the central field and to the intermediary zone of the normal sight. We have also succeeded, owing to the peripheral investigation of the colored visual field, in verifying in a great number of cases the continuous series of forms of transition, which we have classified as one kind under the head of *incomplete color-blindness*, or, in the instance especially occupying us here, *incomplete red-blindness*. In the same way the other kinds of color-blindness may also, as regards the visual field, be classified according to the theory. The visual field of the green-blind is distinguished from that of the normal observer in this, that it has a peripheral field corresponding in extension both to the intermediary and peripheral zones of the normal observer. The visual field of the violet-blind is distinguished on the other hand in this, that it is completely deficient in the normal peripheral zone. These two kinds of *incomplete color-blindness* are characterized by a central field diminished at every degree. With regard to the visual field, we may therefore lay down this rule, that it has as many distinct zones, with reference to the perception of colors, as the chromatic sense has fundamental colors or different kinds of perceptive elements, and that the different degrees of incomplete color-blindness are in the inverse ratio to the dimension of the visual field. If the central field is limited to a circle of ten degrees from the fixed point, all the respective characteristics of color-blindness are usually found in it, sometimes within even a narrower range. A feeble sense of color manifests itself in a much wider central field. All the anomalies that can be discovered in an examination of the visual field might, in consequence of the method employed, be explained by a diminution of excitability as well as of the number of the elements. The intermediary zone of the normal visual field or belt of red-blindness has an especial interest, as it furnishes us with the opportunity of seeing with our own eyes as the red-blind sees, and consequently of exactly comprehending his abnormal perception.

"According to the theory, we see only yellow and blue in this belt, and in consequence we admit that the red-blind not only *call* yellow and blue their principal colors, but moreover *see* them exactly as the normal observer does. This hypothesis cannot assuredly be proved; but this is not necessary, as the explanation Helmholtz has given of the designation of one of the principal colors of the red-blind is perfectly satisfactory. This circumstance, however, has given rise, amongst others, to a doubt about the Young-Helmholtz theory, and to another theory admitting four principal colors to the normal sense of colors, yellow being classed amongst them. But this is useless. It must not be forgotten that colorless light and colored light are subjective perceptions, and that *comparison* here performs an important part. This fact is sufficiently proved by the phenomena of contrasts, accidental colors, &c. White is not a color: it is merely a general, neutral light, and is therefore produced when one kind of element is not more excited than another, or when all the elements are equally excited.

"But, as the theory obliges us to admit that the excitation of the perceptive elements of green and violet may, in certain cases, as in the instance of the red-blind, supply the perception of white, and not bluish green; and that, in certain cases, as in that of the green-blind, the excitation of the perceptive elements of red and violet does not give purple, but white,—it is in no wise contrary to the theory to admit that the excitation of the organ perceiving green gives the perception of yellow in cases where all that remains, moreover, of the system of colors is the complementary color of yellow; that is to say, blue. The excitation of the perceptive organ of green gives the perception of green only on the retina, or on a point of the retina which also contains the organ perceiving red. But this is not the place for further developments of this theory.

"2.—Classification of the Different Kinds of Color-Blindness.

"In the preceding we have indicated, in conformity with the theory, the different forms of a defective sense of colors, to which, we think, should be applied the name of color-blindness, and which, owing to their nature, theoretically must be considered as of different kinds. This division will be sanctioned, if we consider the relations in which it stands to the method pursued for discovering them, and which is based on the Young-Helmholtz theory. It is this we are about to explain.

"We classify the different kinds of color-blindness under especial heads, to be able the better to grasp the whole. We might, indeed, divide this blindness into congenital and acquired; but as such a division has reference alone to the mode of origin, and not to the nature of this blindness, and affects in no wise the manner of its discovery, it has no practical importance in the case now occupying our attention. Besides, our division relates, as does our entire memoir on this subject, essentially to congenital color-blindness. The division is as follows:—

"I. Total color-blindness, in which the faculty of perceiving colors is absolutely wanting, and where the visual sense consequently can only perceive the difference between darkness and light, as well as the different degrees of intensity of light.

"II. Partial color-blindness, in which the faculty of certain perceptions of color, but not of all, is wanting. It is sub-divided into, —

"1. Complete color-blindness, in which one of the three fundamental sensations, one of the three perceptive organs of color in the retina, is wanting, and in which, consequently, the colored visual field has but two ranges. This group includes three kinds; namely, —

"(*a*) Red-blindness.

"(*b*) Green-blindness.

"(*c*) Violet-blindness.

"2. Incomplete color-blindness, where one of the three kinds of elements, or perhaps all, are inferior in excitability or in numbers to those of the normal chromatic sense. Incomplete color-blindness exhibits, like the normal sense, three zones in the visual field, but is distinguished from it by an unusually small central field. This group includes the whole of a series of different forms and degrees, a part of which — the superior degrees, which might be called *incomplete red-blindness* and *incomplete green-blindness* (and *incomplete violet-blindness*) — constitutes the transitions to the corresponding kinds of complete color-blindness; and another part of which — the inferior degrees, which we call a feeble *chromatic sense* — constitutes the transition to the normal sense of colors.

"We will show farther on, that this classification, based entirely upon the Young-Helmholtz theory, is quite practical, and conformable to experience. We know no classification, which, though distinguishing accurately between the different essential forms of a defective sense of colors, draws a surer, more decided, and more practical limit between the defective sense of colors and the normal sense.

CHAPTER V.

PRECISE CONDITION OF THE VISION OF THE COLOR-BLIND.

It will be now asked, What do the color-blind see? Does red look green to them, or green red, or yellow blue, &c.? The fact so long ago noticed that they could not distinguish their faulty color from gray, — a mixture of black and white, — and the more color-blind they were the darker the gray which would match their faulty color, ought, perhaps, to have had more attention paid to it. Through this we can, perhaps, get a better idea of the color-blind's vision. And we may formulate their vision thus: All colors containing their defective one will be grayish, and this in proportion to their individual amount of defect.

But let us have the testimony of the color-blind themselves. Mr. Pole, a red-blind, has tested himself, and shown why his results should be accepted. He thoroughly understands his own condition, although he does not seem to quite appreciate the existence of varying degrees of color-blindness, so perfectly shown, for instance, by Donders in his examination of the railroad employés in Holland: moreover, violet-yellow-blindness has no place for him, which is, perhaps, natural.

In a criticism of Mr. Gladstone's Homeric vision, recently given in "Nature," Mr. Pole briefly sketches his former extended report of his case, and Sir John Herschel's notice of the same. As to how he sees, which interests us, he says, —

"In the first place, we (the color-blind) see white and black, and their intermediate or compound gray (provided they are free from alloy with other colors), precisely as others do.

"Secondly, there are two colors properly so called, — namely, yellow and blue, — which also, if unalloyed, we see, as far as can be ascertained, in the normal manner. But these two are the *only* colors of which we have any sensation; and hence the defect has been given by Sir John Herschel the scientific name of *dichromic vision*.

"But now comes the difficulty of the explanation. It may naturally be asked, Do we *see* objects of other colors, such as roses, grass, violets, oranges, and so on? And, if we do see them, what do they look like? The answer is, that we do see all such things, but that they do not give us the color-sensations correctly belonging to them: their colors appear to us varieties of the other color-sensations which we are able to receive. This will be best explained by examples. Take first the color red. A soldier's coat (British), or a stick of red sealing-wax, conveys to me a very positive sensation of color, by which I am perfectly able to identify, in a great number of instances, bodies of this hue. If, therefore, the investigation of my experience ended here, there would be no reason to consider me blind to red, or as having any grave defect in my vision regarding it. But, when I examine more closely what I really do see, I am obliged to come to the conclusion that the sensation I perceive is not one that I can identify separately, but is simply a modification of one of my other sensations; namely, *yellow*. It is, in fact, a yellow, shaded with black or gray,

— a darkened yellow, or what I may call yellow brown. I find that all the most common hues of red correspond with this description; and, in proportion as they are more scarlet or more tending towards orange, the yellow I see is more vivid. The explanation, I suppose, is, that none of such reds are pure, — they are combinations of red with yellow; so that I see the yellow element of the combination, while the true red element of the combination is invisible to me as a color, and acts only as a darkening shade.

"I obtain a further proof of this by the change of sensation when the hue of red is altered. I find, that, as the color approaches crimson, the yellow element becomes fainter, and the darkening shade more powerful, until very soon the yellow disappears, and nothing but a gray or colorless hue is presented to my eye, although the color is still a positive and powerful red to the normal-eyed; so that there is a hue of red, which, as a color, is absolutely invisible to the color-blind.

"If I go on beyond this point, and take reds that pass from crimson towards the hue called lake, I see my other color come in, — a faint blue, — which increases till violet is reached, when it becomes more decided. Violet is understood, I believe, to be a compound of blue with red; and, accordingly, the red element being invisible to the color-blind, violet hues generally appear to them only as darkened blue. There are, however, examples where, from the red being very strong, the blue appears to lose its effect; and the impression given is colorless, black, or gray. They correspond, in fact, with the neutral red before described, although still called violet or purple by the normal-eyed. This latter effect is much enhanced under the artificial light of gas or candles.

"A similar observation will apply to orange, — a combination of red and yellow, — in which the yellow only is perceived.

"The appearance of green to the color-blind corresponds exactly to that of red. Green, in its true aspect, is invisible to them; and, consequently, when neutral, — i.e., unmixed with any other color, — it presents to their eyes the appearance of gray. When, however, it is mixed with yellow (and most of the greens in nature are yellow greens), they see the yellow only, but diluted or darkened by the invisible green element; and in less frequent cases, where the green is mixed with blue, they see the blue element only in like manner.

"It is therefore easily understood how so simple a defect of vision gives rise to so complex a series of symptoms as those already described. Take first the color red. If it is a scarlet variety, as the majority of reds are, presenting the appearance of yellow to the color-blind, they may naturally confound it with the latter color, as well as with orange, with yellow green, and with brown, — all which cause to them the same sensation. If, on the other hand, the red contains a predominance of blue, it may be confounded, on the same principle, with blue or violet. If it is a neutral red, lying between the two, it will be confounded with black or gray. A pale pink, though very distinctly colored to the normal-eyed, often offers so little color to the color-blind as to be mistaken for white or very light gray. The same explanation will apply to green. Its yellow varieties may be compounded with red, orange, yellow, and brown; its blue varieties with blue and violet; and its neutral hue with black or gray, or, if pale, with white."

These statements of Mr. Pole are so valuable, and so in accordance with the application of the Young-Helmholtz theory of color-perception to color-blindness as we now are enabled to analyze it, that I can not refrain from quoting Sir. John Herschel's remarks in reference to them. We see now how the color-blind perceive the colors they are blind to; and therefore it is important to feel assured that the red-blind — as, for instance, Mr. Pole's — perception of yellow and blue is the same as our own or the normal-eyed. Sir John says, —

"I consider this paper as in many respects an exceedingly valuable contribution to our knowledge of the curious subject of color-blindness, — first, because it is the only clear and consecutive account of that affection which has yet been given by a party affected in possession of a knowledge of what has been said and written on it by others, and of the theories advanced to account for it, and who, from general education and habits of mind, is in a position to discuss his own case scientifically; and, second, for the reasons the author himself alleges why such a person is really more favorably situated for describing the phenomena of color-blindness than any normal-eyed person can possibly be. It is obvious that on the very same principle that the latter considers himself entitled to refer all his perceptions of color to three primary or elementary sensations, — whether these be red, blue, and yellow, as Mayer (followed in this respect by the generality of those who have written on colors) has done, or red, green, and violet, as suggested by Dr. Young, reasoning on Wollaston's account of the appearance of the spectrum to his eyes, — on the very same principle is a person in Mr. Pole's condition, or one of any other description of abnormal color-vision, quite equally entitled to be heard when he declares that he refers his sensations of color to two primary elements, whose combination in various proportions he recognizes, or thinks he recognizes, in all hues presented to him, and which, if he pleases to call yellow and blue, no one can gainsay him; though, whether these terms express to him the same sensation they suggest to us, or whether his sensation of light with absence of color corresponds to our white, is a question which must forever remain open (although I think it probable that such is really the case). All we are entitled to require on receiving such testimony is, that the party giving it should have undergone that sort of *education of the sight and judgment*, especially with reference to the primitive *decomposition* of natural and artificial colors, for want of which the generality of persons whose vision is unimpeachably normal appear to entertain very confused notions, and are quite incapable of discussing the subject of color in a manner satisfactory to the photologist.

"That Mr. Pole's vision is *di*chromic, however, there can be no doubt. If I could ever have entertained any as to the correctness of the views I have embodied of the subject in that epithet, after reading all I have been able to meet with respecting it, this paper would have dispelled it. That he sees blue as we do, there is no ground for doubting; and I think it extremely likely that his sensation of whiteness is the same as ours. Whether his sensation of yellow corresponds to ours of yellow or of green, it is impossible to decide, though the former seems to be most likely."

We thus see that the color-sense of the color-blind may be described as follows: The red-blind sees all objects of this color of a darker hue than they are. The same of the green-blind as to green. Both confound these colors with each other and gray. A mixture of white and black in proper proportions, to represent the luminosity of any shade of red or green, will give the color-blind the same sensation as that shade. The violet-yellow-blind will do the same in reference to all colors containing either of these two. Violet-blindness is so extremely rare, and not causing danger on land or sea, we may omit special discussion of it. Great misunderstanding of the color-blind's sensation has arisen from the natural lack of knowledge and appreciation of *composite* colors. Purple, or a combination of red and violet, or blue, is rarely otherwise spoken of than red in popular language, except when the commercial name "magenta" is used. The blue or violet in it the normal-eyed do not think of, and none would class it with blue. The color-blind, however, do not see the red in it other than gray; but, as their vision is perfect for violet, they see this in the purple, and so class it with blue. Hence the general idea that the color-blind confound red with blue, the sky and a rose. Pure red they never confound with blue.

CHAPTER VI.

COLOR-BLINDNESS FROM DISEASE OR INJURY.

Color-blindness is a congenital defect, and, as will be later shown, incurable. It is not connected with any special color of the eyes, or the humors within the eyeball. The color of the eye depends on the more or less pigment in the iris. The back of this little screen is covered with black pigment, preventing light passing through it, so that its color can have no effect. The ocular humors of a color-blind person have been found exactly the same as the normal-eyed. Whether color-blindness is caused by some defect in the *recipient* organ, the retina, or the *perceptive* organ, the brain, or both, is not yet decided; and I need not discuss the question here.

It is of more importance to know and remember that a similar condition as to blindness to color is caused by certain diseases of the eye or brain. Ophthalmic surgeons have long known that a loss of chromatic sense was associated with a peculiar form of atrophy of the optic nerve, which is hereditary. Certain constitutional diseases, also, cause color-blindness. In some affections of the eye alone, *portions* of the retina become color-blind. As with simple congenital color-blindness, the power of form-perception, in chromatic loss from disease, may be retained.

Tobacco and alcohol, either alone or together, may finally cause color-blindness. The warnings of ophthalmic surgeons have been too little heeded on this point. The loss of color-perception is often overlooked, as the loss of form-perception most troubles the person affected. Excessive smokers and drinkers amongst railroad employés and sailors may become color-blind when their eyesight is still good enough for them to retain their positions, in which perfect color-perception is also needed.

Color-blindness is caused also by accidents, and especially by those accompanied with excessive jar and shock, as on railroads. There are many well-authenticated cases on record where normal color-perception was known to exist before the accident. Professor Wilson reports a physician who was thrown from his horse, and suffered great cerebral disturbance. On recovering sufficiently to notice distinctly objects around him, he found his perception of colors weakened and perverted, and has since continued so. Flowers have lost more than half their beauty for him; and he still recalls the shock which he experienced on first entering his garden, after his recovery, at finding that a favorite damask rose had become in all its parts, — petals, leaves, and stem, — of one uniform dull color, and that variegated flowers, such as carnations, had lost their characteristic tints.

Dr. Favre reports several interesting cases of temporary color-blindness from injury, and says, —

"The majority of cases of traumatic color-blindness are very analagous to congenital natural chromatic deficiency. Railroad employés and sailors are certainly amongst those who are most exposed to wounds and contusions. The large majority of such are habitually or occasionally charged with the observation or transmission of orders given by colored signals. Railroad officials and naval officers ought therefore to have their attention called to the circumstances which may at a given moment and for a certain time deprive an engineer, a stoker, a conductor, a pointsman, a station-master, a guard, a sailor at the helm, a lighthouse-keeper, a signal-man, or a coast-guardsman, of their correct judgment of colors."

In illustration of color-blindness from disease, I will mention Dr. Hay's case : A young woman aged twenty had cerebral trouble, and, with some loss of sight, considerable loss of color-perception. When asked whether she could see the figure on her dress, which was a calico one with red spots, she replied, "Yes, I see the *brown spots*." It was ascertained she could distinguish forms, even of small size, with accuracy; but her perception of colors was exceedingly imperfect. Repeated and careful investigations during this and on several subsequent occasions showed that the only colors she knew with certainty were *yellow* and *blue*. Nearly all other colors she termed brown, or hesitated to name, designating, however, their shades or intensity of color accurately. Thus a deep red she called a dark brown ; a bright green, a light brown ; and a very pale pink, a very light shade of brown. She was not congenitally color-blind, and, after some months of treatment, recovered her form and color perception perfectly. She resembled a red-blind person whilst suffering from her disease.

Tyndall reports a case of Mr. White Cooper's, which, as it contains a word of warning, and is besides very interesting, I will give at length:—

"The sufferer was a sea-captain, and ten or twelve years ago was accustomed, when time lay heavy on his hands, to occupy it by working at embroidery. Being engaged one afternoon upon a piece of work of this description, and anxious to finish a flower (a red one, he believes), he prolonged his labors until twilight fell, and he found it difficult to select the suitable colors. To obtain more light he went into the companion, or entrance to the cabin, and there continued his needle-work. While thus taxing his eyes, his power of distinguishing the colors suddenly vanished. He went upon deck, hoping an increase of light would restore his vision. In vain. From that time to the present he has remained color-blind. Berlin worsted, with which he had been accustomed to work, he at once and correctly pronounced to be blue. He had a keen appreciation for this color, and never made a mistake regarding it. Two bundles of worsted—one a light green, and the other a vivid scarlet—were next placed before him. He pronounced them to be both of the same color. A difference of shade was perceptible; but both to him were drab. A green glass and a red glass were placed side by side between him and the window: he could discern no difference between the colors. A very dark green he pronounced to be black; the purple covering of the chairs was also black; a deep red rose on the wall of the room was a mere blotch of black; fruits, partly of a bright red and partly of a deep green, were pronounced to be of the same uniform color. A cedar pencil and a stick of sealing-wax placed side by side were nearly alike. The former was rather brown; the latter, a drab. Electric light through a green glass, allowed to fall on a screen, gave him no color; but only that portion of the screen was a little less intensely illuminated.

"Capt. C. was assured, that, previous to the circumstances related, he was a good judge of colors; so that, pronouncing on any color, he has an aid from memory not usually possessed by the color-blind. Indeed, he had an opportunity of *reviving* his impression of red. A glass of this color was placed before his eyes while he stood close to the electric lamp. On establishing the light, he at once exclaimed, 'That is red!' He appeared greatly delighted to renew his acquaintance with this color, and he declared he had not seen it for several years. The glass was then held near the light, while he went to a distance: but in this case no color was manifest; neither was any color seen when a gas-lamp was regarded through the same glass. The intense action due to proximity to the electric light appeared necessary to produce the effect. Capt. C.'s interest in this experiment was increased by the fact that the Portland light, which he has occasion to observe, has been recently changed from green to red; but he has not been able to recognize this change. The fare in the fore-cabin of a vessel of his own, which he now commands, happens to be sixpence; and he is often reminded by the passengers that he has not returned their change. The reason is, that he confounds a sixpence with a half-sovereign, both being to him of the same color. A short time ago he gave a sovereign to a waterman, believing it to be a shilling."

Mr. Haynes Walton says, —

"A few years ago I was investigating color-appreciation, and the first instance of the acquired defect that came to my knowledge was in the person of an engine-driver. This man confessed, after an accident through his not distinguishing the red signal, that he had gradually lost his color-power, which had been perfect; and so sensible was he of his loss and its disadvantages, that, before the accident, he had determined to give up the situation. The manager of the company, who told me the circumstance, assured me that this driver had been carefully examined but a few years back, and passed as possessing perfect sight. Does not this show that those who are to be trusted with color-signals should be periodically examined?"

We have thus seen that there is a condition wholly resembling congenital color-blindness, caused by disease or accident, and that it may be recovered from when the results of disease or accident pass away. This must be remembered, as color-blindness, when congenital, is incurable. To the ophthalmic surgeon color-blindness is a recognized symptom of certain affections. This is a question discussed in ophthalmic literature, and out of place here further than I have introduced it. The abuse of alcohol and tobacco is too common not to render possible color-blindness from this cause among railroad employés and sailors,—a point at least to be remembered.

CHAPTER VII.

COLOR-BLINDNESS HEREDITARY.

LIKE all other congenital defects, color-blindness is hereditary, which explains the large ratio of color-blindness individual observers have found when happening to include one or more color-blind families in their statistics. In 1845 Dr. Pliny Earle reported the color-blindness of five generations of his family as follows: —

Of the first he knows nothing as to their color-blindness.

Second: of seven brothers and eight sisters, three brothers had the defect. One was Dr. Earle's grandfather.

Third generation, — children of the grandfather, — three brothers and four sisters: no one imperfect.

Fourth generation, — first family of five brothers and four sisters: two brothers color-blind.

Second family of one child (girl): normal color-perception.

Third family of seven brothers: four had color-blindness.

Fourth, not reported.

Fifth family of three brothers and seven sisters: all perfect vision.

Sixth family of four brothers, five sisters: two of each sex color-blind.

Seventh family of two brothers, three sisters: the two brothers color-blind.

Eighth family: no issue.

Ninth family of two sisters with normal color-perception.

Seventeen of these people of the fourth generation are married, and have fifty-two children. Many of the latter are very young (1845); and, as the defective perception has hitherto been detected in but two of the families, Dr. Earle places these alone on the list for the fifth generation. In one of these families of three brothers and three sisters, one of the brothers has the defect; and in the other a male, an only child, is similarly affected. We have therefore, in these thirty-two males, eighteen color-blind. Of the twenty-nine females, two are color-blind.

The overleaping of one generation by the hereditary peculiarity of vision is satisfactorily shown, since it appears that there are no cases in the third generation. Furthermore, in the cases of the two males of the fifth generation, it will be perceived that neither parent nor grandparent had the defect; so that there was an interval of *two* generations between the manifestations of that defect.

Dr. Earle regrets he is unable to give me a further report of his family to this time (December, 1878).

Such methods of testing as are now only considered to be absolutely certain would, perhaps, have revealed varying degrees of color-blindness in other members of these families.

The first case ever reported, the shoemaker Harris, had three brothers color-blind also, whilst two other brothers and a sister were free from the defect. Dalton had a brother color-blind like himself, another brother and a sister normal-eyed. In one of Dr. Nichols's cases the defect was derived from the maternal grandfather, some of whose brothers were also color-blind. In fact, hardly any of the older cases reported did not show that it was a family peculiarity. Wartman says, —

> "With respect to affinity, there are some color-blind no one of whose kindred exhibits this anomaly of vision. Others have, so to speak, inherited it from their father or their uncle, either paternal or maternal (without, in the latter case, the aunt participating in it). Lastly, it is not rare to find brothers, several of whom are color-blind, without their being all necessarily so. The sisters are almost always privileged."

We must, however, remember that, so long ago as when Wartman wrote, this defect was rather regarded as a scientific curiosity, not particularly affecting practical life. The blood-relatives of a color-blind would therefore rarely be hunted up and tested.

Cunier, moreover, in 1838, reports the case of a lady who was color-blind. Her mother and two sisters were the same. Her brother was free from the defect. The lady had six children, — one son not color-blind, and five daughters affected like herself. The oldest daughter had four children, two of them (girls) color-blind. The second daughter had a boy and a girl, the latter color-blind. The fourth daughter unmarried. The fifth left a boy myopic, but not color-blind. We thus have the remarkable instance of color-blindness appearing only in the *females* of a family for four generations. Dr. Ph. Hochecher says, —

> "Many observers have shown color-blindness to be hereditary. I am not the only color-blind in my family. Three of my mother's brothers are so, one of my cousins, and a nephew. The same is the case with one of the students, whose case I report. He is color-blind, his mother, and his mother's brother, as was also his brother, now dead."

Heredity was frequently very marked, known, and reported on among the many people who replied to Professor Wilson's inquiries. He even says, —

> "No fact is better ascertained than that color-blindness clings to certain families, and is hereditary. With few exceptions, every one of the parties whose cases I have specially recorded in this paper has near relatives as color-blind as himself. It seems, indeed, a safe estimate, that every decided case of color-blindness implies the existence of another case of equal or similar severity in the person of a relative; so that the numbers I have given as representing the proportion of color-blindness in the community may be fairly doubled."

My own experience agrees with Professor Wilson. Few of the adult color-blihd whom I have tested did not know of some blood-relative similarly affected. It has been found prevalent with the Jews, among whom intermarriage and consequent hereditary peculiarity is very frequent.

Professor Horner of Zurich has given the data on which he based the law of transmission of color-blindness, and they are of such value in reference to heredity, that I introduce them here with the remarks accompanying his original article. He says, —

"The hereditariness of color-blindness has been long known. Ribot and Darwin speak of it, as also that it is more frequent in men than women. As I have had opportunity of being familiar with very accurate pedigrees, which illustrate a definite law, I will give the results of these genealogical researches.

"The first family I became acquainted with some years since. In the following Table I., the male descendants are marked with M, and the female with W. The generations go from A to G. The letter of the particular generation stands beside the letter for the sex. To simplify the tables, the unmarried daughters, and the brothers and sisters whose descendants could not be followed, are omitted. I would, however, expressly say that this omission only affects the result in that the law appears more marked, not that an exception to it is thereby concealed. For instance: if, in generation D, several unmarried normal-eyed daughters, in generation G some normal-eyed sons not yet married were included, it would have further illustrated the law, but have rendered the scheme more difficult to express in print.

"From the youngest generation H, the tree is quite certain up to generation C. I have the proofs of this from those who were living in the commencement of the eighteenth century. From here upwards the conclusion as to the common origin is hypothetical. We know nothing of the color-blindness of A. He was the father of two daughters, who have red-blind sons. From the evident law among the descendants, it is fair to conclude that the mothers were not color-blind, but the grandfather was. At any rate, the table, even if we omit the upper row as hypothetical, is of much interest, and plainly shows, —

"1st, That there were no color-blind girls.

"2d, That color-blind fathers had normal-eyed sons.

"3d, That color-blind sons had normal-eyed mothers.

"4th, That the seeming exception in generation F, where a color-blind father had a color-blind son, is explained as still in conformity with the law when we recall that the mother, color-blind, was the daughter of a color-blind father, and we have the descendants of two color-blind.

TABLE 1.

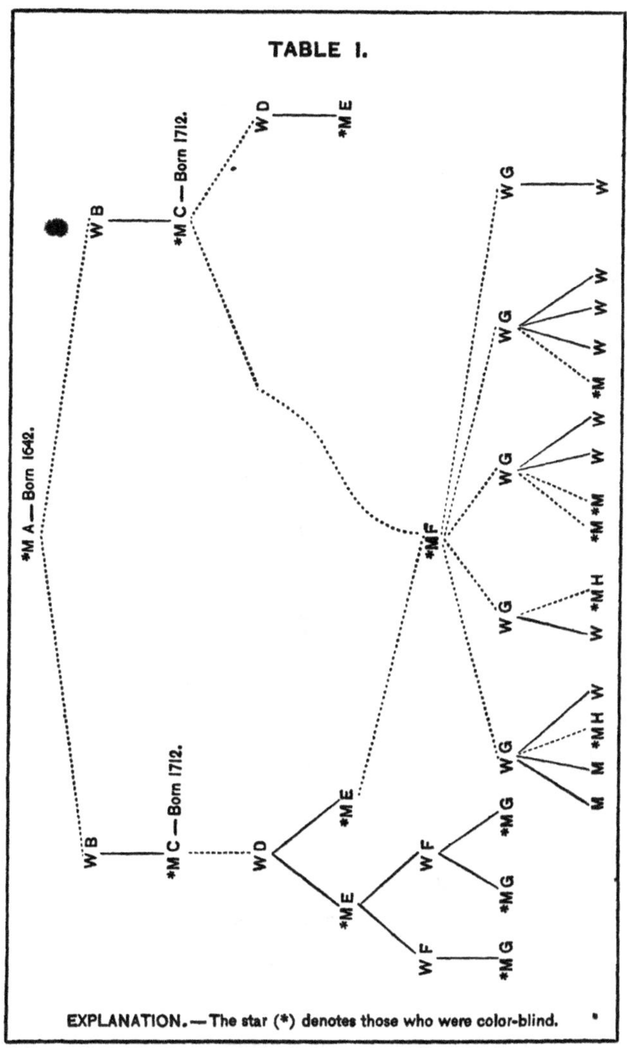

EXPLANATION.—The star (*) denotes those who were color-blind.

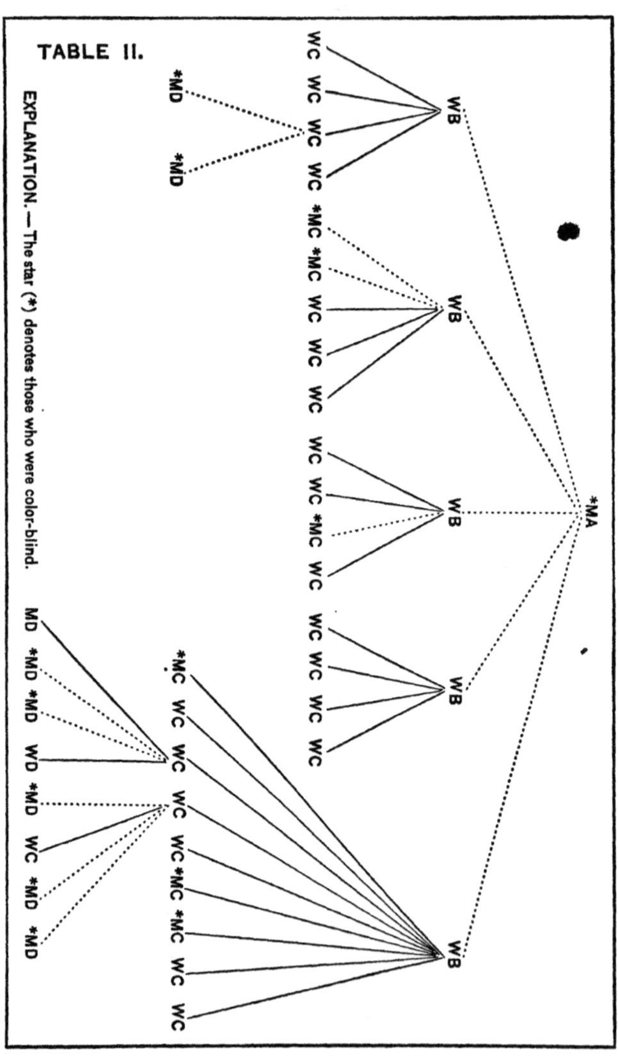

TABLE II.

EXPLANATION.—The star (*) denotes those who were color-blind.

"5th, The general law is, therefore, 'that sons of daughters whose father was color-blind are most likely to be the same, although not without exception (*vide* H); or, color-blindness is transmitted in the revertible type from grandfather to grandchild.'

"I have become acquainted with another family tree which gives, although to a lesser extent, the same type. I place it without comment with the other, calling attention to only one interesting fact; namely, a jump of two generations. The first daughters of generation B bore only girls, whose sons followed their great-grandfather's type. In this smaller pedigree it is seen that in generation C and D the transmission to the grandchildren is not absolute; so that it is the complement of Table I."

Cohn found, among his one hundred color-blind, three times the father red-blind, fifty-six times the parents normal-eyed; in fourteen cases the brothers color-blind; once the father and three sons. In no case were all the children color-blind. A color-blind father had seven children, all normal-eyed; but the mother's brother, a cousin of the mother, and all the sons of this cousin's only sister, color-blind (none of the daughters).

Dr. Magnus says,—

"The hereditariness of color-blindness has been known as long as the defect itself. All who have seen many color-blind will have often noticed that it was in their mother's family that other cases were found. I have frequently been assured that this or that cousin on the *mother's* side was also color-blind; and, now and then, that a more distant relative of the *mother* had also color-blind sons. In view of Horner's law, this is readily explainable; and this peculiar law is all the more interesting since we find that it is the same in reference to the heredity of other physiological abnormities or defects. For instance, we know that in families the tendency to bleeding is similarly handed down, and also, as Dr. Pagenstecher has recently shown, night-blindness. It would seem as if this law of heredity had a more general application. It would be most valuable if family physicians, who know and observe their patients' families for several generations, could interest themselves in carefully elucidating the extent of this important law.

"Naturally this law does not exclude the possibility of other ways in which color-blindness may descend. In some cases I have with certainty found that a color-blind father begat color-blind sons. I remember now two cases in which a color-blind father had two color-blind sons."

In a later publication Dr. Magnus says, —

"The effect of heredity is very marked in my examinations. Of ninety-five color-blind, whose families I could inquire about in reference to this point, I found it in forty-two. Five times the parents were normal-eyed, but the grandfather color-blind, and in three of these cases the father of the mother. Rüte, in 1845, said, 'The defect is hereditary, and, peculiarly enough, rather through the women than the men. For example: the maternal grandfather transmits to the grandchildren.' A very interesting proof of this law I have lately received by letter from Professor Valentine of Berne, Nov. 5, 1878, who writes, 'I naturally can have no opinion as to Horner's law. I only know one case near me which supports it. Professor F., formerly here, was color-blind: his children are not. He had five daughters, who are all married. Their children, so far as I could trace, are mostly color-blind.'"

Again Magnus says, —

"I have also among my color-blind found with certainty six times that the maternal relatives were color-blind, and it was inherited through them. In three of these cases it was the mother's brother, maternal uncle, who was color-blind. Two sisters each had a color-blind son, one of whom I tested. Two cousins, daughters of two sisters, each had a color-blind son. I do not, therefore, think it too hasty to say that the color-blind inherits his defect very frequently from his mother's family. She will be normal-eyed, and transmit color-blindness to her sons, but not to her daughters."

Besides the very many times I was told by those

I tested of some relative being supposed to be color-blind, I had direct testimony from my own observation, or testimony of a character I could depend upon, in the following instances: Sixteen times brothers being color-blind; once, father and son; maternal grandfather and two grandchildren, boys, — three sisters not so; maternal grandmother and grandson; mother and son; male cousins twice; twin brothers red-blind; of two brothers, one red, the other green blind; a lad, his great-uncle and grandfather; three brothers out of five color-blind, but none of their children; two brothers and maternal uncle; three brothers out of four color-blind, the other too young to test.

I have thus called especial attention to color-blindness being hereditary, as it has a direct bearing on the important question of the *frequency* of the defect, upon which of course depends the comparative danger to the community at large.

CHAPTER VIII.

PHYSICAL PECULIARITIES CONNECTED WITH COLOR-BLINDNESS.

I HAVE spoken of the improbability of the color of the iris or hair having any connection with color-blindness other than accidental. My own observations on more than 430 color-blind induce me to discard this at present from further thought. In this Cohn agrees with me. Where light hair and irides are in the majority in the community, they will be so found among the color-blind. Magnus recorded 48 among 93 color-blind with black, brown, or dark hair, and 45 with blonde; 28 had yellowish-brown or yellowish-gray eyes, and 65 blue or bluish-gray. Seebeck, in 1837, found 10 of his 12 cases had blue eyes, but wisely remarks that it is probably simply due to the fact that such are most frequent among all northern nations. There seems to be nothing gathered from testing the refraction or accommodation of color-blind eyes. The results are those to be obtained from the examination of the same classes as the color-blind belong in. The visual power is apparently the same as with the normal-eyed; but

I have seen very extraordinary visual power of form associated with color-blindness. As to the ear and musical power, I can say nothing from my own observation. Magnus could obtain nothing decisive on this point.

In respect to parental relationship, I can only also quote Magnus and Cohn. The former, amongst his 94 color-blind, found but six times the parents related, — always cousins. This point is worth studying; but deductions should be made with great caution. Cohn also found six times the parents related. Five times they were cousins. In one case the father had no color-blind children by a wife not related to him. His second wife was his cousin (their mothers being sisters), by whom he had two color-blind sons.

There is one other physical peculiarity which has been connected with color-blindness; and that is a contraction of the forehead, and consequently of the anterior lobes of the brain. Niemetscheck measured the distance between the pupils of four color-blind, and found it to be 49, 50–54 mm. From this he deduced the idea that the brain mass anteriorily was proportionally smaller; and here was where the phrenologists placed color-perception. The idea was supported by Aubert; but Dr. Cohn measured his one hundred color-blind, finding the distance between the pupils thus: —

54–56 mm. in 20 scholars 9–13 years old.
58–62 mm. in 60 scholars 9–14 years old.
63–66 mm. in 18 scholars 12–22 years old.
67 mm. in a color-blind 67 years old, and 70 mm. in one 40 years old.

His conclusions, therefore, are that, "had Niemetscheck found protrusion of the eyeballs in his cases, he could as well have connected it with color-blindness."

Professor Pflüger, in Berne, measured the distance between the pupils of 1,846 normal-eyed children, and found in those between 7–14 years this to be 54–59 mm.; in those between 15–19, to be 59–62 mm.; also, in older students between 20–22 years, he found it was 61–63 mm. Cohn therefore claims rightly that his color-blind had rather a greater distance between the pupils than the normal-eyed of the same age: hence the theory of Niemetscheck is not true.

Professor Holmgren also reports in 1878 his measurements of the distance between the pupils of 100 color-blind. He employed an instrument he had specially arranged for this purpose. He also finds that there is no measurement of this kind characteristic of the color-blind.

Professor Wilson said in his book, —

"I have to notice a singular expression in the eye of certain of the color-blind, which may assist in their detection. It is difficult to describe it, and it is wanting in well-marked cases. But various of the color-blind, whose cases I have described, have presented a peculiarity of look, which others have recognized on their attention being drawn to it. In some it amounted to a startled expression, as if they were alarmed; in others, to an eager, aimless glance, as if seeking to perceive something, but unable to find it; and, in certain others, to an almost vacant stare, as if their eyes were fixed upon objects beyond the limit of vision. The expression referred to, which is not at all times equally pronounced, never altogether leaves the eyes which it seems to characterize."

In the appendix he also says, —

"I have had the opportunity of observing it somewhat

particularly in four gentlemen not relatives, in two of whom it was readily recognized by others. All the parties referred to have healthy eyes, and excellent vision for every thing but color. One has an absent, anxious glance, with something of the expression which amaurosis gives, only the pupil is small. One has a startled, restless look. The other two have an eager, prying, aimless air. The character common to them all, and to the other cases I have seen, is this aimlessness of look. Macbeth's reference to Banquo's ghost, —

> 'Thou hast no speculation in those eyes
> Which thou dost glare with,' —

very happily expresses the peculiarity which I find so difficult to define. It has not, however, in most cases, any thing repulsive about it. The majority of those I have seen presenting it would be described as having fine eyes. In one, the wistful, somewhat melancholy, but pleasing expression of his eye, had attracted my attention long before I knew that he was color-blind."

I can recall something of what Dr. Wilson describes in reference to two or three of my color-blind acquaintances, but, on the contrary, not at all in reference to others. I recognize his difficulty of describing just what it is. I doubt if I should have noticed it, or at least connected it with color-blindness, except for his remarks in reference to it. Had he spoken of such a look or peculiar expression on the part of the color-blind when being examined, I could corroborate it from my experience with both adults and young persons. I have now and then made my diagnosis correctly, from a peculiar dazed, half-anxious expression of the face and eyes of a looker-on awaiting his turn, as if they were called upon to do something unusual, and sought or expected further explanation than that given the normal-eyed. I do not, of course, mean the natural nervousness of those conscious of some defect; but of those color-blind who had no idea any thing was wrong with their chromatic sense, and who often proved difficult to convince. I believe no other observer than Professor Wilson has remarked on or recorded any thing of the kind.

As to nationality, I have but to say, that, in our mixed population, nearly every European nation is represented. An opinion was expressed long ago, that the defect did not occur in the colored race. My opportunity of testing them has been but very small. Among 102 colored schoolboys I found 2 color-blind; among 94 colored schoolgirls, none.

Whilst this volume is in press I have heard from Dr. Swan M. Burnett of Washington, D.C., who has had an opportunity I could not obtain. He has tested, by Professor Holmgren's method, 1,359 colored schoolboys, and found 22 color-blind (or 1.6 per cent); also 1,691 colored schoolgirls, finding only 2 color-blind (or 0.11 per cent). This smaller percentage among the boys may be due to various causes aside from the difference of race. Moreover, larger numbers may entirely change it.

CHAPTER IX.

FREQUENCY OF COLOR-BLINDNESS IN MALES.

As the magnitude of the danger depends, of course, on the frequency of the defect, it becomes important to know in what proportion of the community color-blindness is likely to occur. Very variable statistics are given by different observers, depending largely upon the methods of testing; the more thorough and scientific these latter are, the greater being the number of color-blind individuals found. Mistakes of excessive ratio reported are now better understood and avoided, since we know color-blindness runs in families, and is hereditary. An observer might thus find 10 out of ·40 individuals examined color-blind. Let us glance at the statistics, such as they are, reported by the earlier observers. Dalton found 8 to 12 per cent; Professor Pierre Prevost, 3 to 5 per cent. Professor Kelland of the Edinburgh University found, among 151 students, 3 "thorough Daltonians," and several less well-marked cases. Wilson again found 2 among 20 students, 1 among 47 other students; on the Edinburgh police, *five* among 158. Dr. Rowe, at the Morningside Asylum, found 5 among 42 male attendants. These I quote from Wilson. Seebeck found 5 color-blind among 100 students. Professor Allen Thomson met with the same result as Dr. Wilson, as also D'Hombre-Firmas in France, and Professor Dove in Berlin. Dr. Wilson also examined a large number of soldiers, who, together with those above spoken of as tested by him, amount altogether to 1,154 persons. Amongst these all, 65 were color-blind, an average of 5.6 per cent, or 1 in 17.7. The red-blind were most numerous throughout all these. This proportion has been now admitted by Professor Helmholtz. Wilson said, in 1854, —

> "The statistics of color-blindness are as yet very imperfect, and do not include females; but there is every reason to believe that the number of males in this country (England) who are subject in some degree to this affection is not less than 1 in 20, and that the number markedly color-blind — i.e., given to mistake red for brown, brown for green, purple for blue, and occasionally red for black — is not less than 1 in 50. We may thus, according to our present knowledge, regard *two* in every hundred of the community as *seriously* defective in their perception of color."

Dr. Goubert estimates 1 in 25 color-blind. Dove, in his memoir of 1872, gives the following figures: Among 860 men, there were 40 color-blind, 4.65 per cent, or 1 in 21.5; among 611 women, 5 color-blind, or 0.82 per cent, or 1 to 122. Among 1,016 scholars at the Lyons Lyceum, he found 16 color-blind for red and green on a visit made in April, 1877.

The last report of Dr. Favre, of the Lyons Mediterranean Railroad, gives the results of examinations of railroad employés since 1855. It shows also how more careful tests discover a greater proportion of color-blind persons. Dr. Favre, up to 1855, had examined about 5,000 candidates for railroad-work, and rejected more than 50 for being *red-blind*. He had not, unfortunately, kept accurate records. From 1855 to 1864 he noted 8 color-blind only, which number does not correspond with the number of men examined. From 1862 to 1872, among 1,196 persons, he refused 14 color-blind who could not tell red. From May, 1873, to July, 1875, his examinations were more particular and exact; and he found, among 1,050 persons seeking railroad employment, 98 who made decided blunders, or hesitated: 10 were refused for being red-blind. His new series since 1875 comprises 600 examinations: the results of these he has not yet sent me (January, 1879). 728 men already in employment were examined in 1872–73. More than one-third of these had been previously tested for color, and the red-blind eliminated. Of these 728, 42 either made mistakes or repeated hesitations. Among 224 conductors examined by Dr. Favre and M. Git, 14 were found decidedly color-blind. In 1874 he found 4 color-blind among 75 office-clerks; the same year, 24 among 65 firemen at the Perrache gas-works. At the Ouillins works, among 148 workmen whom he examined in August, 1877, 82 told the five elementary colors without error or hesitation; 56 either hesitated or made mistakes. May 7, 1877, among 155 students at the veterinary school at Lyons, Dr. Favre found 19 hesitate or make mistakes. Examining, with Capt. Bellecour, 268 sub-officers and men of the Sixteenth line, he found

105 color-blind or color-deficient. Among 138 men of the Twenty-second, Twenty-third, and Ninety-ninth line, M. Paul Guillot found 37 color-blind. Lieut. Gallet of the Twenty-sixth Artillery, in garrison at Mans, examined 116 young soldiers, and found 32 who hesitated or made mistakes on a color-scale of 15 shades. Lieut. Lautheaume found 40 color-blind among 132 men of the train of the Twenty-sixth Artillery. The average among this series of 654 young soldiers was 32.72 per cent. Dr. Mourand, among 200 men of the Lyons station, found 7 color-blind. Dr. Favre says his colleague must have noted only the most marked cases.

Dr. Feris, in his pamphlet, and more recently in a communication to Dr. Favre, reports having examined 775 officers and sailors, amongst whom he found 75 color-blind: 19 wholly confounded *red* and *green*. The average of this series is 10 in 100. Of all the adults Dr. Favre examined, the average was 16.84 to 100. He says, —

> "The results will vary greatly, being dependent on many circumstances and peculiarities I shall hereafter notice; but we may be assured, that in France the color-blind amount to ten in one hundred of the adult males. . . . The study of color-blindness interests at least a tenth of our population (France). This very large proportion gives us the measure of the chances of error the color-blind run in the various industries where good color-perception is necessary or useful. It does not, of course, give us an exact idea of the chances of accident at sea and on railroads, on account of the accessory circumstances which aid the color-blind in his embarrassment; but it shows us plainly how numerous the chances are."

Dr. Favre also reports the results he received from a friend in Algiers, who tested, with great care, 693 persons, and found as follows: Among 203 Kabyles, 5 cases of color-blindness; in 95 Biskris, 4 cases; in 81 negroes, 1 case; in 23 Jews, 1 case; in 15 Spaniards, none; in 62 Italians, 1 case; in 15 Mozabites, none; in 12 Maltese, 1 case; in 8 Tunisians, none; in 19 Europeans, 1 case, — in all, 19 cases among 693 persons examined, or 2.75 per cent.

Dr. A. Lederer has lately found 63 color-blind persons amongst 1,312 men of the Austrian navy, or 4.8 per cent.

Dr. Fontenoy found 31 color-blind out of 1,084 railroad employés of Denmark, or 2.87 per cent.

Professor Donders of Utrecht, Holland, found, among 2,300 railroad employés, 152 color-blind.

Dr. Stilling of Cassel, Germany, found, out of 400 railroad employés, 6 per cent color-blind.

Dr. Krohn, in Finland, found, among 1,200 railroad employés, 60, or 5 per cent color-blind. These and other reports of railroads I shall return to hereafter.

Professor Quaglino of Milan, Italy, writes me (Aug. 11, 1877), —

> "It has been generally believed that color-blindness is more rare in Italy than in Germany, England, or France; but I much doubt this, as there has been little research among us, and I think that a large amount will be found were it carefully looked for."

Dr. Daae of Kragerö, Norway, found, amongst 205 schoolboys, 4.88 per cent color-blind.

Dr. Cohn found, among 2,429 schoolboys of Breslau, 95 or 4 per cent color-blind.

Dr. Magnus found, among 3,273 Breslau schoolboys, 3.5 per cent color-blind.

Professor Holmgren, in Sweden, found, among 32,165 males, 1,019, or 3.25 per cent color-blind.

Dr. Minder of Berne, Switzerland, found, among 1,429 males, 95, or 6.58 per cent color-blind.

To recapitulate the larger numbers and more recent examinations: —

OBSERVERS.	Place.	Number.	No. Color-Blind.	Percentage.	Position in Life.
Dr. Fontenoy .	Copenhagen .	1,084	31	2.87	Railroad employés.
Prof. Donders .	Utrecht . .	2,300	152	6.60	" "
Dr. Krohn . .	Finland . .	1,200	60	5.00	" "
Dr. Minder .	Berne . .	1,429	95	6.58	Schools and various.
Dr. Daae . .	Norway . .	205	–	4.88	Schoolboys.
Dr. Cohn . .	Breslau . .	2,429	95	4.00	"
Dr. Magnus .	" . .	3,273	–	3.50	"
Dr. Stilling .	Cassel . .	400	–	6.00	Railroad employés.
Dr. von Reuss .	Vienna . .	800	–	3.50	Railroad employés.
Prof. Holmgren,	Sweden . .	3,654	166	4.54	Scholars.
"	"	8,682	300	3.45	"
"	"	1,523	47	3.08	Students.
"	"	2,752	105	3.81	Orphan children.
"	"	555	43	4.50	Young people.
"	"	7,953	171	2.15	Railroad employés.
"	"	4,225	94	2.22	Sailors.
"	"	1,851	62	3.34	Soldiers.
"	"	649	31	4.77	Mill-hands.
"	"	321	18	5.60	Prisoners and g'rds.
Dr. Jeffries .	New England,	10,387	431	4.149	Teachers and sch'rs.

The following are the results in tabular form of my own examinations: —

Position of Persons Tested.	March, 1878. April, 1879.	Number.	Ages.	Completely. Red-Blind.	Completely. Green-Blind.	Partially Color-Blind.	Total.	Per Cent.
Instructors and Students.								
Several departments of Harvard University, Cambridge, Mass.; Institute Technology, Boston, Mass.; Amherst College, Mass.; Brown University, Providence, R.I.	March, June, 1878.	1,021	18 years and upw'ds.	22	12	12	46	4.505
Teachers' and Students' State Art-School	–	32	–	–	–	1	1	–
Other adults	–	31	–	8	3	2	13	–
Boys of Public Schools of Boston.								
Latin School	–	415	10 to 17	10	7	5	22	5.301
English High School	–	433	"	4	3	3	10	2.309
Roxbury High School	–	80 } 207	14 to 17	–	–	1	} 4	} 1.932
Dorchester High School	1878. 1879.	38		2	–	–		
Charlestown High School		47		–	1	–		
West Roxbury High School		22		–	–	–		
Brighton High School	–	20		–	–	–		
Phillips Grammar School	–	682	8 to 15 yrs.	24	18	3	45	6.598
Eliot Grammar School	–	774	"	20	2	1	23	2.967
Quincy Grammar School	–	575	"	19	9	–	28	4.866
Brimmer Grammar School	–	606	"	19	2	–	21	3.465
Lawrence Grammar School	–	877	"	21	7	–	28	3.534
Rice Grammar School	–	595	"	12	2	4	18	3.025
Dwight Grammar School	–	633	"	13	5	6	24	3.791
Sherwin Grammar School	–	434	"	16	1	7	24	5.530
Dudley Grammar School	–	472	"	13	1	4	18	3.813
Bigelow Grammar School	–	807	"	19	–	9	28	3.469
Andrew Grammar School	–	366	"	5	1	2	8	2.185
Lincoln Grammar School	–	629	"	26	–	4	30	4.769
Dearborn Grammar School	–	464	"	19	2	1	22	4.740
Comins Grammar School	–	334	"	16	–	2	18	5.389
Total	–	10,387	–	288	75	68	431	4.149

All these examinations were made by Holmgren's method with the colored worsteds, to be described later in this volume. The division into red and green blindness of the first thirty-five hundred, I am not as sure of as that of those afterwards, for reasons I have stated in my last chapter. I have followed Professor Holmgren, and my results correspond very nearly with his and those of observers who have also been governed by his directions.

My work so far has been rather the collection of statistics, and the dissemination of a knowledge of color-blindness, than a study of the defect itself, except in individual cases. I am, therefore, merely presenting its frequency here, which can as well be determined from school-children, since a person born color-blind dies so.

My friend, Dr. Magnus of Breslau, from his own and Professor Cohn's reports of their examinations of the school-children above quoted, concludes that color-blindness is more frequent as we descend the social scale, and also more frequent amongst the Jews. As to this last I was unable to decide whether the schoolboys were Jews or not. In regard to the former, — viz., the greater frequency among the lower classes, — I was surprised to find this did not hold in our community of mixed races, nor did it among the schools where the race was more purely American. Parentage I could not record; but, in a general way, I should say the percentage would be as high or higher among American-born children. My work has satisfied me that we cannot draw safe deductions from a few thousand examinations, but must patiently wait till our lists contain enough to eliminate sources of error from inadequate data and, so to speak, possible local causes.

I have made no column of violet-yellow-blindness, as, besides some very doubtful, I can but report three cases; and these I have allowed to be recorded under "partially color-blind." These three cases I carefully examined again, and found that whilst the red-green perception was not, perhaps, perfect, — so that, on that account, they would propably have been classed among the "partially," — yet as to violet yellow they were wholly blind, as shown by Holmgren's worsted test. In one case there was reduced color-perception for all three of the primary colors, — red, green, and violet. I have no doubt, that, to many of my color-blind, the spectrum would be more or less shortened at the violet end. Many were too young to thus test, and that, moreover, was not the purpose of my work at the time of examination.

I should add here that I made no examination or record of the exact visual power for form of the color-blind I found, as it is wholly uncalled for by this method of testing. They were teachers, students, or scholars at work with their eyes. Neither did I have to regard whether they were normal-eyed, old-sighted, near-sighted or over-sighted (presbyopic, myopic, or hypermetropic), since we need not correct errors of the refraction of the eye when thus searching for color-blindness.

I have not given the percentage of the thirty-one "other adults," as some came to me suspecting or knowing of their defect. There were, however, only three of these. The others were accidental examinations amongst acquaintances or patients and employés. I omit also the special percentage of the art-school.

The instructors and students of the colleges I have added together, to better eliminate sources of errors, as I did not examine *all* the students of any one of these institutions.

In the statistical memoirs of the United States Sanitary Commission, published in 1869, are the only other examinations I know of made in this country. The method of testing — viz., holding up pieces of colored cloth, &c., and asking the names of the color — was, of course, very crude and unreliable. I, however, introduce the report here. The compiler, Dr. B. A. Gould, says, —

> "Serious misunderstandings or calamities have been reported in the army, resulting from mistakes in the color of green and red lights by officers of the signal corps, themselves not fully aware of their failing in this respect; and cases have occurred when ludicrous and even disastrous results have followed the use of a badge of precisely the wrong color."

Instructions were issued to test for color-blindness; and, in the reports received, "the descriptions of the irregularities manifested in distinguishing colors are, in general, neither complete nor adequate, owing propably to insufficiency of the instructions given." Among 8,831 white men, 161 were found color-blind, equal to 0.02. This small ratio is, of course, due to the crude method of examining, which would only detect the most marked cases of color-blindness. Dr. Gould adds, —

> "Notwithstanding the incompleteness of the descriptions returned, and the consequent inadequacy of the classifica-

tion, the well-known fact is distinctly manifest, that the most usual form of color-blindness is that which fails to distinguish between the green and red, and that the confusion of colors sometimes embraces the other half of the spectrum, and sometimes its entire range."

The great variation in the ratio of color-blind persons, reported by different observers, is readily explained by differences in the accuracy of the method of testing.

In testing color-perception by the sun's spectrum thrown on a white surface, the color-blind observer will see the color he is deficient in over a smaller surface. Dr. Edward Ræhlmann, in Halle, reports the test of 70 people with the sun's spectrum. He found only 30 of them saw the red normally: the others varied in their red-perceptive power. He tested only 20 as to the violet end of the spectrum, and found remarkable shortening of the visible portion for this end also. He noticed, besides, that, when the red end of the spectrum was shortened, the violet was also reduced, limiting the spectral row of colors on both ends.

CHAPTER X.

INFREQUENCY OF COLOR-BLINDNESS IN FEMALES.

In an article written in December, 1877, on the dangers of color-blindness, and published in the Ninth Annual Report of the Massachusetts State Board of Health, I stated, —

> "It has been frequently said that color-blindness was less common among females than males. This is *probably* incorrect, and due to the fact that such a defect is of more importance with the female sex, and therefore more carefully concealed. They have not been tested as males have; and most likely future statistics, based on true methods of testing, will reverse the now quite general impression as to their having better color-perception, and hence to be preferred, where admissible, as railroad employés."

My doubt was also based upon the fact that we then had no large number of reliable statistics to prove the contrary, but more especially because methods of testing for color-blindness in females had been employed, calling upon the observed to name colors shown, which females, from habit, could unquestionably do with greater facility than men; and hence fewer appear deficient in color-perception. Professor Wilson, in his "Researches on Color-Blindness," says (p. 75), —

"I have no results to offer respecting the prevalence of color-blindness among females. I have already stated my conviction that it is rarer among them than among males; but only an extended inquiry can show the amount of difference in this respect between the sexes."

In a note in his Appendix (p. 164), he adds,—

"Since the text was written, I have been informed of a few more cases of color-blindness among educated women in England. The general tendency, however, of my later inquiries, as of my earlier ones, is to show that color-blindness is very much rarer among women than men."

Dr. A. Favre, in an article in the "Gazette Hebdomadaire," Oct. 12, 1877, says,—

"We have tested very few adult females, from the difficulty of such examinations, but more especially because the majority of women readily acquire an exact notion of colors, and they do not belong to the professions where color-blindness is dangerous: hence they do not interest us more in an industrial than a medical point of view. Among 236 girls of four schools (three in Lyons, one in Paris), we found 8 children only who made serious mistakes; namely, 3.39 per cent. In the '*salles d'asiles*' and the infant-schools the errors were as frequent among the little girls as boys."

It must be remembered that Dr. Favre reported an enormous number of children of both sexes as color-blind; but he tested them by asking the names of the colors of objects held up before them. He found, as may be readily imagined, many of the youngest children of both sexes unable to answer correctly; whilst, among the older children, the girls had naturally learned the names of colors better than the boys. This, I think, is all that his test proves, as I shall hereafter show.

In 1860 Dr. Henri Dor of Berne tested in Berlin 611 women, using a method similar to that of Professor Holmgren; namely, the sorting of colored worsteds, with the result of finding only 5 — or 0.82 per cent, or 1 in 122 — color-blind. This method does not call upon the examined to name a color; and the eye alone, not memory, guides the hand. Its value is shown by the results it gave. Perhaps these investigations of Dor should have prevented my doubting the less frequent occurrence of color-blindness in women than men. They seemed, however, to stand somewhat alone, and not sufficiently extended.

Professor Holmgren, in his recent work on color-blindness, touches on this point; and, as his experience renders what he says of special value, I quote his remarks: —

"In drawing conclusions from the statistics of the examination of women hitherto made, we must first of all ascertain if the method of testing was such that the previous occupation of the examined had not affected the results obtained. For if the method was based on the principle of asking the names of the colors of objects exhibited, and the chromatic sense of the person examined judged by the reply, then it is very evident that the proportion of color-blind will appear less with women than men. Admitting that color-blindness is less common in women than men, we are by no means justified in attributing this to their greater familiarity or exercise with colors. If exercise can have any such influence, it cannot, as we have seen, cure the individual, but rather affect the offspring, as employment insensibly affects future generations. The laws of heredity are too little known to allow us to indicate, or even conjecture, how this takes place; but we do know with certainty that good qualities as well as defects are transmitted, and amongst the latter we may include color-blindness. We believe, moreover, that the exercise of a sense may favorably affect heredity, although it is difficult for us to prove this."

At the present moment observers in Europe are testing this question of the relative color-blindness of the two sexes. Their results, where Professor Holmgren's method has been employed, are of great value. A number of reports of this character have come to my hand. Dr. E. Hansen of Copenhagen found none color-blind among 50 female railroad emyloyés. Dr. A. Daae of Krageró, Norway, also used Holmgren's method with the worsteds in examining 413 school-children of both sexes, from nine to fifteen years of age. Amongst 208 girls he found none color-blind, and only 5 with imperfect color-perception. He says, —

> "The better color-perception of the girls than the boys was very marked. Is this because the girls have personally more exercise with colors than the boys? If this is the case, then we must assume that even very considerable degrees of color-blindness may be relieved by many years' exercise. This is, however, not probable. It is more probable that the better color-perception which the female sex has acquired and developed by many generations of handling colored objects is essentially sexual, or only inherited by the female descendants."

Since February, 1878, when I published an article on the incurability of congenital color-blindness, my experience with intelligent and educated persons thus afflicted has fully substantiated what I then said; namely, that it has not been and cannot be cured by exercise with colors. The color-blind reported to me their futile attempts to do this, as others, for instance, reported to Professor Wilson years ago, and to Professor Holmgren more recently. Greater familiarity with, and more constant use of, colors on the part of females, seems at first sight to explain their somewhat extraordinary exemption from color-blindness as compared with males. This does not, however, affect the individual. Whether the individual is influenced through generations of female ancestors exercised with colors, I must for the present leave with Mr. Darwin, Mr. Wallace, and Mr. Grant Allen to discuss. The transmission of the defect in the male line alone is very frequent. But there are cases of even the reverse on record. Dr. Pliny Earle reported, out of 61 relatives, — 32 males and 29 females, — 20 cases of color-blindness, *two of these being females.* Again I would recall Cunier's case of a lady who was color-blind. Her mother and two sisters were the same. Her brother was free from the defect. The lady had six children, — one son not color-blind, and five daughters affected like herself. The oldest daughter had four children, — two of them girls, color-blind. The second daughter had a boy and girl, the latter color-blind. The fourth daughter, unmarried. The fifth left a boy myopic, but not color-blind. We thus have the remarkable instance of color-blindness appearing *only* in the *females* of a family for four generations. Heredity has here apparently acted without reference to, or directly against, the accumulated effects of generations of exercise with colors. It is certainly a very curious fact, that, if generations of exercise with colors is gradually eliminating color-blindness from females, this should not have checked its transmission through females exclusively for four generations.

But to return again to the reports I have received from European gentlemen: Dr. Cohn found among 1,061 Breslau schoolgirls *none* color-blind. Dr. Magnus, in Breslau, found but 1 color-blind girl among 2,216.

Professor Holmgren reports from Sweden having found, among 7,119 females of all ages, 19, or 0.26 per cent, color-blind.

Dr. Minder, in Berne, reports, among 846 girls and women, having found 11 color-blind, or the very large per cent of 1.3.

To recapitulate from a number of observers, —

OBSERVER.	Country.	Number.	Number.	Per Cent.	Position of Persons Tested.
Dr. Dor . .	Berlin . .	611	5	.82	Working-women.
Dr. Fontenoy .	Copenhagen .	50	0	–	Railroad employés.
Dr. Magnus .	Breslau . .	2,216	1	.04	Schoolgirls.
Dr. Cohn . .	" . .	1,061	0	–	"
Dr. Minder .	Berne . .	846	11	1.30	"
Prof. Holmgren,	Sweden . .	3,244	9	.27	School-children.
"	" . .	1,374	3	.21	"
"	" . .	97	3	3.09	Confirmed.
"	" . .	1,826	3	.16	Factory-girls.
"	" . .	524	1	.19	Railroad attendants.
"	" . .	51	0	–	Old women.
Dr. Jeffries.	Boston . .	7,942	4	.052	Students and scholars.

My want of success in finding more color-blind females would have at first rendered me doubtful of my testing; but that was not the case when I commenced with females. I have often thought that I had found a case; but was quickly convinced, as were the bystanders, that it would not stand the test, and was but the result of nervousness, carelessness, or stupidity. Females work so rapidly in sorting the worsteds, that the examiner will notice immediately the slightest hesitation or mistake, as do also those who are waiting their turn. The excessive ratio reported by Dr. Minder of Berne, I cannot but think, may be due to a lack of practical familiarity with the use of Professor Holmgren's test with females. He admits that, in cases he thought most perfect, the girl was subsequently proved to have been picking out only the "most brilliant colors." This I have seen often enough among school girls as well as boys. As I have elsewhere said, it is most curious how carelessness and stupidity will at first simulate color-blindness; and if we do not push on with the test long enough, and be on our guard, we may quite readily mark, as at least partially color-blind, females who are really not deficient in chromatic sense. Besides those in my records, I know of two or three color-blind females, and of two families who have color-blind female members. A natural delicacy and sensitiveness render research often difficult or impossible. In time this peculiarity of vision will be found too common to be regarded as a defect, much as near-sightedness now is; and then investigations of heredity will be more easily carried out. At present it is hardly understood and appreciated even amongst physicians, much less amongst the laity, though interested personally.

The following table gives my own results with adults and schoolgirls : —

POSITION OF PERSONS TESTED.	Mar., 1878. Apr., 1879.	Number.	Ages.	Completely.		Partially Color-blind.	Total.	Per Cent.
				Red-Blind.	Green-Blind.			
Female students of Wellesley College, Mass. . . .	-	302	Young women	1	-	-	1	-
Students of State Art-School . . .	-	84	Adults.	-	-	-	-	-
Girls of the Public Schools of Boston.								
Normal	-	123	20	-	-	-	-	-
Latin	-	63	13 to 18	-	-	-	-	-
High	-	796	18 to 19	-	-	-	-	-
Roxbury High . .	-	43	14 to 18	-	-	-	-	-
Dorchester High .	-	39	"	-	-	-	-	-
Charlestown High .	-	89	"	-	-	-	-	-
West Roxbury High,	-	42	"	-	-	1	1	-
Brighton High . .	-	35	"	-	-	-	-	-
Grammar Schools.								
Bowditch Grammar .	-	341	8 to 15	-	-	-	-	-
Bowdoin Grammar .	-	398	"	-	-	-	-	-
Hancock Grammar .	-	486	"	-	-	-	-	-
Wells Grammar .	-	451	"	-	-	-	-	-
Exeter-st. Grammar,	-	90	"	-	-	-	-	-
Sherwin Grammar .	-	500	"	-	-	-	-	-
Andrew Grammar .	-	215	"	-	-	-	-	-
Winthrop Grammar .	-	963	"	-	-	-	-	-
Dearborn Grammar .	-	407	"	-	1	-	1	-
Comins Grammar .	-	348	"	-	-	-	-	-
Dillaway	-	332	"	-	-	-	-	-
Shurtleff	-	653	"	-	-	-	-	-
Gaston	-	411	"	-	-	1	1	-
Norcross	-	731	"	-	-	-	-	-
Total	-	7,942	-	1	1	2	4	.052

CHAPTER XI.

CONCEALMENT OF COLOR-BLINDNESS IN PRACTICAL LIFE.

SUCH statistics as I have given as to the frequency of color-blindness may, perhaps, fairly challenge criticism, and it be asked, If this is the truth, how is it that such a chromatic defect is generally unknown or concealed? Sir J. F. W. Herschel, in 1859, when commenting on Mr. Pole's description of his own color-blindness, remarked, —

"I may be, perhaps, allowed to add a few words as to the statistics of this subject. Dr. Wilson gives it as the result of his inquiries, that one person in every eighteen is color-blind in some marked degree, and that one in fifty-five confounds red with green. Were the average any thing like this, it seems inconceivable that the phenomenon of color-blindness should not be one of vulgar notoriety, or that it should strike almost all uneducated persons, when told of it, as something approaching to absurdity. Nor can I think that in military operations (as, for instance, in the placing of men as sentinels at outposts) the existence, on an average, of one soldier in every fifty-five unable to distinguish a scarlet coat from green grass, would not issue in grave inconvenience, and ere this have forced itself into prominence by producing mischief. Among the circle of my own personal acquaintance, I have only known two, though, of course, I have heard of, and been placed in correspondence with, several; and a neighbor of mine, who takes great delight in horticulture, and has a superb collection of exotic flowers, informs me, that, among the multitude of persons who have seen and admired it, he does not recollect having met with one who appeared incapable of appreciating the variety and richness of the tints, or insensible to the brilliancy of the numerous shades of red and scarlet. It may be, however, that the percentage is on the increase. Certainly we *hear* of more cases than formerly; but this probably arises from the fact of this, like many other subjects, being made more generally matter of conversation."

I introduce these remarks, as they very well illustrate the general position of scientific men — aside, of course, from physiologists — in reference to color-blindness. This has continued pretty much the same till within the last three years; when methods of testing have been used, so simple, so rapid, and so convincing, as to enable us to gather reliable statistics on a very large scale, and detect and expose the color-blind against their own belief as well as that of others.

It must, however, be shown how the color-blind have heretofore, and do now, escape detection in the every-day walks of life. This will, at the same time, give us a clearer idea of the peculiarities of this chromatic defect, and clear up some of its seeming mysteries. In the first place, I must call especial attention to the very great ignorance of the common *names* of colors among the *normal-eyed* below the well-educated class in the community, and the very general misuse of the names of colors known or remembered. This I have seen to such an extent in the thousands of school-children I have tested, as to excite the wonder and even incredulity of the teachers watching my work. Repeatedly an instructor has wanted to mark a boy color-blind because he so utterly failed in designating colors, or even using their names, when my test proved conclusively that he had normal chromatic perception. It convinced those interested of the great necessity of teaching colors and their names in the primary schools, as part of educational work. Now, the color-blind simulate just this sort of ignorance in every-day life, and hence are concealed, or escape detection, through the want of education of the normal-eyed.

There is no greater subject of dispute than the question of color. Hardly any two people will agree as to names of certain given colors. This is often a source of amazement and amusement to the color-blind, who naturally think, that, if there is such doubt as to colors and names, their own doubts and mistakes arise from the same cause. Many persons have been indignant with me for marking them as deficient in color-perception, so assured were they that they lacked only names, and this even when a most amusing and convincing proof of their defect was before the bystanders. Dalton long ago spoke of this. He says, when speaking of three of his pupils, whom he found like himself, "They, like all the rest of us color-blind, were not aware of their actually seeing colors different from other people, but imagined there was great perplexity in the *names* ascribed to particular colors."

Mr. Prior, in "Nature," Dec. 12, 1878, says, as to the general inaccuracy of the names of colors, and the unfixed character of language, "I took to a flower-show at Taunton a dahlia of a rather common variety, and such as most gardeners would call purple, — a dark pink, with a shade of blue over it, — and requested forty-four different people to write me down what they would call its color. In their replies I got fourteen different names for it. I sent a flower of the same kind to a lady, who returned me twelve replies from members of her family and friends, and in the twelve were eight different names." I would here refer to the very interesting chapter on the growth of the color vocabulary in Mr. Grant Allen's book, "The Color-Sense."

I cannot do better than give also the statements of another highly-educated color-blind, from whom I have before quoted (Mr. William Pole), who says, —

"The color-blind must be very liable to associate, almost indissolubly, the true normal name of a color with the sensation it conveys to their minds, *whatever that sensation may be;* and they may, therefore, easily be led to speak of that color as if they saw it like other people, although the sensation they refer to may be really of quite a different nature to that which the name implies. A color-blind person will be especially loth to believe that certain colors, which he hears about and talks about every hour of the day, can be invisible to him. Objects of these hues will probably present to his mind *some* ideas of color (though not the true ones), and he may naturally imagine, therefore, that he does see them, and may give his description accordingly. And this sort of error is very much enhanced by the fact that it is not an easy matter to refer different *tones* of any one color to the same color-sensation; so that a modification of tone, if considerable, may be easily supposed to be a different color. I believe this difficulty is also felt by the normal-eyed; and the popular nomenclature of colors furnishes illustrations of the fact, different tones of the same color having often different names, and being treated as separate colors. Pink and crimson, lilac and violet, are well-acknowledged examples of this; and a dark shade of orange is called brown, which generally passes for a separate color. Hence we may easily see what a great probability there is that the color-blind may acquire the habit of attaching the names of different colors to what are, in reality, only varieties of the same sensation; and as this habit dates from their infancy, and is encouraged by their every-day communication with the world, it is much more difficult to get rid of than might be supposed. The sufferer may find himself continually blundering; but he must go through a very rigid self-examination before he can trace this to the fact that some of the principal ideas he has all his life held upon color are mere delusions. Taking red as an example, it is in the highest degree natural that persons who are continually seeing this color under the appearance of dark yellow should imagine that the latter sensation (which is certainly very distinct from that of full yellow) is what corresponds to the term red; and the notion that they cannot really see red at all is one they have the greatest difficulty in comprehending. Hence the very general assertion by the color-blind that they *do* see red, — an assertion which I think has been far more readily accepted than it ought to be. Red is a more common color than dark yellow; and hence the preference, by the color-blind, of the former name for the common sensation. A great variety of bodies are known to be red by habit and association, and are for this reason often named correctly. My own experience is very decided on this point. It is only after long and careful investigation I have come to the conclusion that my sensations of color are limited to blue and yellow. But, before I found this out, — that is, for nearly thirty years of my life, — I firmly believed that what I now know to be only differences in tone of one or the other of these were different colors; and hence I was in the habit of talking of red, crimson, scarlet, green, brown, purple, pink, orange, &c., — not, of course, with the confidence of the normal-eyed, but still with a full belief that I *saw* them. If, therefore, at that time, any scientific man had examined me, I should have given him a description of my case, which I now, after more careful study, know would have been entirely wrong. I should have told him, among other incorrect statements, that I saw red objects of a full tone, such as vermilion, soldiers' coats, &c., perfectly well; and I could, if necessary, have supported my assertion by naming correctly a great variety of bodies having this color, which, indeed, I am in the habit of doing every day. It would have been inferred, with great appearance of truth, that I was really impressible with the red sensation; but I now see what an erroneous inference this would have been.

"Another source of confusion in interpreting the descriptions of the color-blind is the want of due appreciation of the different sensations that may be produced on their minds by modified *hues* of the same general color. The normal-eyed person considers green, for example, as always green, whether it be yellow green, neutral green, or blue green. Whatever the particular 'shade of green,' as it is called, it still has, in his eye, the distinguishing character of greenness, which cannot be hidden or disguised by any predominance of blue or yellow it may contain. But with the color-blind this identifying characteristic of greenness is wanting; and hence several patients, speaking of green, may, by each having reference in his own mind to some different hue of the color, describe it in the most contradictory terms. One may say, with perfect sincerity, that green appears to him like red; another, that it looks yellow; a third, blue; a fourth, black; a fifth, orange; a sixth, violet, — from which the normal-eyed examiner, impressed with the unity of greenness, may naturally infer that each person is suffering under a different species of the disorder; while, by proper interpretation, these anomalous descriptions would only convey the expression of one consistent truth, and one perfectly uniform defect of vision."

This very clear and admirable description of a color-blind's perception not only shows us how and what they see, but it also explains some of the very many ways in which they escape detection. If so intelligent a person as Mr. Pole could have been so long ignorant of his own perception, we need not wonder that the uneducated color-blind should not be aware of their defect even in adult life, and still less that their defect remains concealed.

Let us turn now to Professor Holmgren's valuable remarks on this point. He says, —

"We must remember that color-blindness is not a *disease*, in the sense of being attended with suffering, obliging the individual to have recourse to a physician. Color-blindness, quite as well as normal sight, is a sense of color, though of another and a more simple nature. He whom we call color-blind is not, correctly speaking, at all blind to colors. He perceives, in the main, the same kind of light as the normal observer, but sees a part of it in another manner. In the system according to which he arranges his colors, he has fewer kinds than the normal observer; and this is why he is obliged to classify under the same denomination a portion of the colors classed by the normal observer under different heads. It results from this that he finds resemblances between colors, or confuses others, that the normal observer finds different; for instance, red and green. These confusions naturally surprise and amuse the normal observer, who readily imagines that it arises from very great ignorance of colors, or from defective training. He ordinarily supposes that there is no limit to the mistakes the color-blind might make in this respect. But such is not the case: he obeys laws quite as exact as does the normal observer. A color-blind person can no more accustom himself to seeing colors as the normal observer does, than the red-blind can see colors in the same way that the green-blind does, or conversely.

"This theory, which is based upon experience, explains to us how the color-blind see colors; but, if we only base our ideas on the names given to colors by the color-blind, we can be easily deceived. To judge correctly of color-blindness, and the various practical questions connected with it, it is of the highest importance to distinctly observe the difference between the manner in which the color-blind person *sees*, and the manner in which he *names*, colors. The sensation is based upon the nature of the sense of color in the organization of the optic nerve from birth. The *name*, on the contrary, is learned. It is conventional: it depends upon exercise and habit. The names of colors are naturally the objective expression of subjective sensations; but, on the other hand, they are regulated by the system of normal sight, and cannot, consequently, agree with that of the color-blind. They can, nevertheless, be learned by the latter, and even applied correctly in many cases. There is connected with this fact a peculiarity of the utmost importance practically to the question in point, and one that has given rise to the most serious embarrassments and misunderstandings. This has been and is still one of the chief causes of our erroneous ideas on the subject of color-blindness existing in the masses, because it is the veil under which this defect usually conceals itself from our observation in every-day life, and under which, even to the last moment, it will succeed in escaping discovery in cases where, as frequently happens, the methods of exploration employed are indecisive, or are based upon erroneous principles.

"If we reflect on the condition of the color-blind, it is difficult to understand how he can avoid being detected in his daily intercourse with men endowed with normal sight. And yet experience has sufficiently controverted this idea. That which we have acquired in examining *en masse* the *personnel* of a railway, for example, where it is required night and day to give attention to colored signals, is singularly worthy of notice. We learn by it that a number of color-blind were discovered, although their defective sense of color had never been suspected by themselves or any one else, and the majority had correctly performed their duties."

Very few of us who have good color-perception are aware how wholly the name of a color becomes the name of an attribute of any special object, and hence how this name may be misplaced. It seems hardly possible that, notwithstanding a good color-perception, the names of color are so much a matter of learning and memory. As Professor Holmgren says, —

"This especially applies to the color-blind, who seek in every way, and without themselves being aware of it, to supplement the chromatic sense nature has refused them. As color is an immutable quality of a number of objects, some of which are of one, some of another color, it is not very difficult to learn by heart the names of their colors. The immediate impression is not necessary for this. We may hear a blind person, even one born so, give the exact names of the colors of ordinary and well-known objects of which he has heard. For a color-blind person this is easier, because he obtains some help from his incomplete chromatic sense."

To practically test this, I thought of examining some young blind people before whom the subject had not been discussed, and who would answer to the best of their knowledge and ability. The following table contains the results obtained in seven such cases. The last, the eighth, a boy of fifteen, was not wholly blind to color; and it will be seen how different his answers were. He was practically as blind as the other seven as to form, &c.

	What Color is—	Boy—14.	Boy—16.	Boy—15.	Boy—10.*
1	Sky?	Blue.	Blue.	Blue when clear.	Red.
2	Grass?	Green.	Green.	Green.	Green.
3	Water?	No color; blue.	No color.	Ocean blue near shore; different colors.	White; no other color.
4	Apple?	Green.	Yellow.	Don't know.	Red.
5	Cherry?	Different colors; red.	Red.	Black and red.	Red.
6	Strawberry?	Red.	Don't know.	Don't know.	Red.
7	Banana?	Don't know; no idea.	Yellow.	Don't know.	Don't know; never had one.
8	Autumn leaves?	Green; kind of brown; dark.	Different colors,—red, blue, green.	Don't know.	Green, white, blue; green at Thanksgiving.
9	Spring leaves?	Green.	Dark.	Green, I believe.	Answer not recorded.
10	Orange?	Think red.	Yellow.	Don't know; sort of yellow.	Very red.
11	This house, Perkins Institution?	Don't know.	Sort of white.	Don't know; think white.	Think it is white, ain't it?
12	Bricks?	Black.	Sort of light; no special.	Don't know.	Black.

* Color of his hair. He laughed, and said *red*.

	What Color is—	Boy — 13.*	Girl — 19.†	Girl — 12.‡	Boy — 15.§ Not wholly blind.
1	Sky?	Don't know.	Blue.	Different colors.	Blue.
2	Grass?	Guess green.	Green.	Green.	Green.
3	Water? . . .	Don't know.	No color; colorless.	No color; ocean is blue.	No color.
4	Apple?	Guess red.	Red and white.	Don't know.	Different colors and shades.
5	Cherry? . . .	Some are green.	Red or black.	Some are red.	Don't know; different shades.
6	Strawberry? . .	Don't know.	Red.	Red.	Red.
7	Banana? . . .	Don't know.	Green; uncertain.	Don't know.	Never noticed.
8	Autumn leaves? . .	Green, I guess.	Different colors; heard they were brown, red, yellow.	Don't know; don't remember.	Green in summer; different tints to brownish.
9	Spring leaves? . .	Don't know.	Green.	Green.	Green.
10	Orange? . . .	Don't know.	Yellow; red.	Some are red, anyway.	Not exactly red; orange color.
11	This house, Perkins Institution? . .	Guess kind of red.	Don't know.	Don't know.	White.
12	Bricks? . . .	Don't remember.	Red.	Think they would be sort of black.	Red.

* He felt his coat, and said it "felt green." Pants "black," quickly answered. † Apron pink, dress green and white, as they were.
‡ Don't remember dress or apron; bed-spread white; boots black. § He can see colors but poorly; says "they are hard to get hold of."

These seven young people were pupils of the Perkins Institution for the Blind at South Boston, who were blind from birth, not only as to form, but also as to color. The importance of this point will perhaps only be appreciated by the specialist, who is aware that those wholly blind as to form may enjoy quite good color-sense. The superintendent had informed me that "there were only eleven who were blind from birth, and about thirteen pupils who were supposed to have lost their sight before the age of four months." I found, however, I had to reject all but the seven from my list. The others were, of course, practically blind; but their knowledge of colors was to a greater or less extent learned through the eye, and not merely a name for a quality. Their answers to my questions were very different, as will be seen by those of one of them, which I append to my list. He had to look for some time at a bright-red book to determine its color, and voluntarily said it was "hard for him to get hold of colors." Before I tried him with the red book, I noticed his answers were peculiar; and he spoke of "shades of color." I was confident that the others were totally blind, both to color and light, from examination of their eyes, and by testing with colored objects, and questioning as to the position of the large windows in the room, &c. These pupils were not aware of what was to be asked of them, and those examined not allowed to communicate with the others waiting. They will naturally be useless for further tests of this character, as the colors of objects will be now pretty thoroughly talked about in the institution, and much learned from intercommunication as to the "color-name" of objects, if I may use this term. I doubt if any but a specialist, and one wholly on his guard, could have obtained just this interesting series of answers. Difference in intelligence and memory was marked, and largely decided the answers given, as also the way they were given. The examination was extremely interesting; and the pupils seemed to be rather pleased at being put to the test of their knowledge and memory. The two girls answered quickly as to water, having lately heard a lecture about it. As to the sky and water, teaching had, of course, a direct bearing; the very way some replies were given proving they were learned by the ear, and not by the eye. Could the look of the face or gesture or tone be added to these answers here simply written down in short, much more force would be given my argument. Through the ear alone these answers were learned, and retained by memory. The attachment of the name of a color to an object is an attribute not learned by the eye alone. A wholly uneducated person who handles bricks, if he hears them called black, will so call them when questioned as to their color.

Dr. Stilling says, as a word of warning to those who are testing for color-blindness, —

"It is a well-known fact that color-blind persons, by exercising their faculty of judgment, can aid their want of sensibility, and are able to conceal their defect to a certain extent. They have learned the names of colors quite as well as normal-sighted people; and by the help of every outward sign they have acquired a certain knowledge of those pigments to the characteristic tints of which they are blind. Very often that knowledge is developed in a surprising degree. Therefore, in testing one who is color-blind, we must take away the possibility of employing any of those outward characteristics which he is wont to make use of according to long experience. This is so much the more important, as most persons of this description have not the least suspicion of their imperfect power of sight. Only very intelligent people understand their defect."

Professor Holmgren very shrewdly observes, —

"If we watch the development, or rather the education of the child's color-perception, it will be seen that they first learn the names of colors, and afterwards their correct use, in defining characteristic peculiarities of known objects. It is much later that they notice the quality of the light in correctly designating colored objects they have not previously seen. The child with defective color-perception differs from the normal-eyed only in not being able to reach this degree. He learns, like the others, that the sky is blue, the grass green, bricks are red. He learns that the corn is green in spring and yellow in autumn; that the poppies have a green bud, but red flowers, &c.: these and many other things are retained in his memory. If he thinks over the meaning of these names, he soon meets with difficulties which may lead to very various results. Upon the color-blind eye the brick, the tile, the barley in spring and in the fall, and the poppy-flower produce the same color-sensation, and he can with difficulty comprehend why different names are given to these colors. Most persons do not reflect so far, and, regarding the problem as one they cannot solve, lose therefore all interest in the study of colors; concerning themselves with them only when forced to. This readily explains why the color-blind grow up without others detecting their defective chromatic sense. This is generally the case with the lower classes, and especially in the country. The majority get into no difficulty from their intercourse with colors; and, if they make gross mistakes, this is attributed to lack of practice, or carelessness. Hence nothing more is thought of it.

"Other persons, however, reflect further. In seeking why there are two separate names for similar colors, as the grass and bricks, they look for some more delicate mark of difference, and finally find it; but this is only the varying degree of the intensity of the light. One color is, perhaps, paler than the other. From the time this is noticed, they become very timid in discriminating colors. They accustom themselves to find a difference of color in the difference of the intensity of light, the luminosity, and lead others as well as themselves into the error of supposing that they see the external world like other people, and that their uncertainty is wholly due to want of practice. We find, in fact, in the color-blind a very practised and sharp eye for variations of intensity of light. They often have acute vision, and can see well at a distance. The first color-blind known to science, Harris, observed this of himself; and it has been supported by nearly all observers since. There are, moreover, very few color-blind so interested as Dalton to study their own case, and detect their fault."

As we have seen, Mr. Pole is the only one since Dalton's time who has studied and reported his own chromatic defect.

I have now shown how the color-blind deceive themselves and others, and, growing up in ignorance of their defect, escape detection. To this must be added the very important fact, that, till very recently, methods of testing for color-blindness have been used which were wholly inadequate to expose particularly the lighter forms of the trouble. It must be remembered that red or green or violet blindness may exist in any degree from the most complete to almost normal vision. Formerly, if a color-blind gave the right color-names to objects, he was regarded as normal-eyed; and this has been continued notwithstanding the repeated warnings of Seebeck, Helmholtz, Holmgren, and others. Thus many have escaped detection; whilst, on the other hand, the normal-eyed's ignorance of names has been set down to color-blindness, giving us, as in France, most extraordinary percentage.

But we now know that about one male in five and twenty is color-blind. It is impossible for all to have grown up ignorant of their defect. How, therefore, has this class, who are aware of their color-blindness, escaped detection in every-day life?

The color-blind, who are quick-witted enough to discover early that something is wrong with their vision by the smiles of their listeners when they mention this or that object by color, are equally quick-witted in avoiding so doing. They have found that there are names of certain attributes they cannot comprehend, and hence must let alone. They learn, also, what we forget, that so many objects of every-day life always have the same color, as red tiles or bricks, and the color-names of these they use with freedom; whilst they often, even unconsciously, are cautious not to name the color of a new object till they have heard it applied, after which it is a mere matter of memory stimulated by a consciousness of defect. I have often recalled to the color-blind their own acts and words, and surprised them by an exposure of the mental jugglery they employed to escape detection, of which they were almost unaware, so much had it become a matter of habit. Another important point is, that, as violet-blindness is very rare, the vast majority of defective are red or green blind. These persons see violet and yellow as the normal-eyed, and they naturally apply these color-names correctly. When, therefore, they fail in red or green, a casual observer attributes it to simple carelessness, — hence a very ready avoidance of detection. It does not seem possible that any one who sees so much correctly, and whose ideas of color so correspond with our own, cannot be equally correct throughout, if they will but take the pains to notice and learn. Color-blindness is also a constant source of petty mortification, which teaches its possessor to be on constant guard over himself in avoiding exposure and its accompanying irritation. The intelligent color-blind finds many ways of drawing a decision of color from those he is in contact with, and always lets shopkeepers pick out the colors he calls for, just as the color-blind shopkeeper lets his customer do the same if he can; and when he fails in this, and makes mistakes enough to lose his place, he can take refuge in the mourning stores, where his defect is an advantage.

This brings us again to their extraordinary appreciation of light and shade. They can sort and place in correct order a series of shades of red or green much better and more quickly than the normal-eyed, because to them the color is but so much light and dark. Now, an educated color-blind is asked by a lady friend to buy a skein of red worsted to match the pattern. He asks the attendant in the store for red worsteds, and selects the one which corresponds in *luminosity* with his pattern. Such good "shopping" forbids the idea of any chromatic defect. But the worsted attendant is away, and another, who is color-blind, quietly hands over the greens to the purchaser: the latter will then complacently select the one which matches in luminosity his *red* pattern. If he is green-blind, he will select a lighter green — if red-blind, a darker — than his pattern. In either case his defect is exposed; and, in fact, it thus often happens.

This sensitiveness to light and shade has enabled color-blind painters to follow their profession with success, and even avoid discovery, until accident or design has interchanged, for instance, their reds and greens. A color-blind engraver has an advantage over his fellow-workmen. It seems hardly possible that a color-blind person should have the ideas and thoughts, and power of expressing these, which are derived wholly from the perception of, and acquaintance with, colors. Hence I quote the following as a peculiar instance of concealment of color-blindness, where it would seem that it must show itself. Of a member of a well-known color-blind family, the reporter says, —

"Another of the gentlemen whose case of defective perception of colors is herein noticed, is generally acknowledged as one of the first and greatest of American poets now living. He also is unable to distinguish one tune from another; yet his poetry is not deficient in the requisites of perfect cadence, harmony, and rhythm. In regard to color, his defect is such as is described in the 'worst degree' of the arrangement of Dr. Hays. He says, that, previous to the time at which he ascertained this peculiarity of vision, he always wondered that people should talk of 'glorious sunsets' and 'beautiful sunsets,' inasmuch as he could detect neither 'glory' nor 'beauty' in them. The kaleidoscope of nature and the harmonicon of art are the Utopias of his mind. The magic hues developed by the prism, the iridescence of shells and minerals, the inimitable colors of the beasts and birds of tropical climates, the verdure of the fields of spring, the splendor of the autumnal foliage of the forests, the myriad hues of flowers, and the realm of beauty which springs, as sprang Minerva from the brain of Jupiter, from the genius of the artist, — all these, it would appear, are, comparatively, 'as a sealed book' to him. *Yet from his writings no evidence of this can be detected.* The *poet* throws his gossamer veil of ideality before the vision of the *man*, converting a sombre world into a paradise like that of the Persian. Seated on the borders of Helicon, he looks abroad upon a universe transformed by imagination and glowing with all the colors of a phantasmagoria. The iris of heaven lifts its expansive arch in hues as varied and as vivid as when first placed there 'to establish a covenant' between God and man; the sun descends, now invested with the mellow tints of the skies of Italy, and now surrounded by clouds emblazoned like those which attend its setting in America alone; fields are clad with a carpet of emerald, and flowers blossom with all the diversity of coloring that ever decked them in the gardens of the East; birds spread to the wind pinions as gorgeous as those that wave over the Amazon or the Ganges; and the mineral world glitters with the concentrated beauty of amethyst, topaz, beryl, and all the precious stones adorning the foundations of the wall of the New Jerusalem which was revealed unto the apostle at Patmos."

As the color of most of our common berries and fruits, when ripe, is the complementary of that of the green foliage, the inability to see and collect them is a very frequent source of the exposure of the color-blind both to themselves and their surroundings in early life. It is therefore a wonder how a person can grow up, and not be found out, much less not find themselves out.

Professor Wilson, in his book, says of a chemist aged twenty-eight, green-blind, —

"He worked five months in my laboratory; and some time elapsed before I discovered his color-blindness, which he was not ready to acknowledge, and could to a great extent conceal by his sagacity in observing those properties of bodies which are not affected by color. He unconsciously betrayed an effort to supplement his defective vision of colors by all secondary aids. If colored papers were shown him, he fixed upon any difference in shape, smoothness, or configuration which they presented, and, when they were shown him again, recognized them by differences which would have escaped most other eyes. He would frequently, accordingly, have appeared to a stranger to recognize colors, when in reality he was only recalling form, or condition of surface, of the colored body."

I was lately called upon to test some employés in a large printing-house, and found two, among the seventeen presented to me, color-blind. The astonishment of their fellow-workmen was very great; and they would not believe one of the men could be defective, since his employment was cutting up colored cardboard and paper. They carried him to his post, and asked him to pick out the colors, which he did, as they were always kept in *certain positions* on the shelves. The members of the firm, however, were convinced by the examination, and quickly realized the risk of loss of material and time from the man's defect, hitherto unsuspected.

An interesting instance of what constant practice will do in helping a color-blind to avoid mistake and detection is given by Dr. Minder, who says, —

"On this point (of possible alleviation or cure) a description of three cases of color-blindness in a Jewish family of Berne will be of value. They are brothers, the youngest already over fifty years of age. They are all feebly red-blind, and happen to be in business which requires daily intercourse with colors. They all make the same mistakes when tested with the worked-worsted tables. I could unfortunately only persuade one to be more thoroughly tested. To my surprise I only detected him by Holmgren's test after repeated trials, and that by his matching bright-blue and rose color. He is a very intelligent gentleman, whose business has required him for more than thirty years to be daily busied with colors, with which, according to his own and his wife's report, he formerly made constant mistakes. These have, in the course of years, occurred less and less frequently. He was even very highly valued for his fine appreciation of colors, and taste in their selection, by a Paris ribbon-factory with which he was connected. He attends alone to all the buying for his large business, and is only liable to mistake with dark green and black, rose and light blue. According to his statement, he could not, in early years, be certain of violet and green. I was perfectly astonished at his power of distinguishing the various colors, and the number of names he had at disposal for the finest shades. I was equally surprised at his so accurate comparison of the several colors with each other. To this he attributed his so greatly cultivated color-perception. He laughed, therefore, at Holmgren's method of comparison, by which he was, he thought, not to be caught; and, in fact, this could only be done with difficulty. The results of other methods were negative, except with the polariscope, where he always stopped at rose and bright blue, which, he declared, were alike, and sometimes called them both rose, and sometimes bright blue."

This case led Dr. Minder — as it would also likely lead others — to suppose that there was a basis for Dr. Favre's belief in the curability of color-blindness by exercise and practice with colors; but no one can have tested and talked with many color-blind without being convinced that we can hardly set any limit to their capacity for learning other attributes of colored objects, and recognizing and remembering their color-names through this alone. Thus, as we now well know, they may even deceive themselves, as well as others, into the belief that they have gained by *practice* a color-perception they were not born with. This we shall see in Professor Delbœuf's supposed correction of color-blindness by looking through certain transparent media.

A brother-practitioner, who is color-blind, and whom I was testing by Holmgren's method, after sitting some time with the one hundred and fifty little skeins of worsted before him, finally said, "I have tried so hard to supplement my defect by every possible means, and catch other attributes than color to recall the names of them, that, if you will give me two or three days to study over these worsteds, and tell me what their colors are, I will afterwards pick them all out correctly; but I shall *see* them no differently."

My friend, Dr. Henry Power, writes me from London, June 1, 1878,—

"Color-blindness is a subject of great public concern. As showing also its private relation, I may mention an interesting case that came under my care lately, in which the man was a draper, who had long, by great ingenuity, conducted a business on his own account; always getting an assistant to bring down the particular *bundle* of color demanded by the customer, and then selecting the particular tint by its shade. He was now going into a much larger business, and wanted to know if his disease could be cured, or whether his future partners should be told of his defect. A "no" and a "yes" settled these points, and I have heard no more of him; but it was curious, that, in the course of twenty-five years, he had never been found out."

I was recently told of the following: Some five and twenty years ago, before color-blindness was so well known or talked of, a student of the Royal Academy in London — who was selected, not only by the authorities, but also by his fellow-students, as having about the best perception for form, and power of light and shade — turned to the use of colors. In this it was naturally supposed he would exhibit extraordinary talent, and become a great painter. He was allowed to take a portrait by Titian from the National Gallery, and have it in a small room to himself. There he copied it to his best ability, as he stated to the principal and his brother-students. No one had seen him at work. His result was the most perfect copy as far as light and shade went, but in *pea-green*. He finally became an engraver.

CHAPTER XII.

INCURABILITY OF CONGENITAL COLOR-BLINDNESS.

The question of the curability of congenital color-blindness is one of considerable importance; for certainly the color-blind railroad employé or pilot should not be dismissed from service if he can be cured of his defect.

It has been till lately universally admitted by ophthalmic surgeons and physiologists that congenital color-blindness was incurable by any known means. In August, 1874, Dr. A. Favre of Lyons, France, reported to the French Congress for the Advancement of Science, at Lille, some observations, which seemed to him to prove that congenital color-blindness was curable both in children and adults by exercising the chromatic sense. Dr. Favre has for the last twenty years or more, as consulting surgeon of the Paris, Lyons, and Mediterranean Railroad Company, pressed the necessity of examining all railroad employés for color-blindness, led so to do principally by the results of Wilson and Potton. He has succeeded in inducing other roads to adopt similar precautions, and deserves great credit for his exertions. It is therefore due him to look carefully at his statements, as, if correct, they are of the utmost importance.

He reports the results in eleven different schools of the examination of 1,002 boys between the ages of four and fifteen. These their teachers tested by asking them to name the color of objects exhibited of five principal colors. The teachers reported to Dr. Favre that they found at least 218 defective in chromatic sense, and that almost all were perfectly cured by being repeatedly shown objects, and told the names of their colors *till they were learned.* Amongst 138 girls, from seven to fourteen years of age, Dr. Favre himself found only 2 whom he regarded as color-blind. These girls, he remarks, were under excellent teachers, and a large number had passed through the *salles d'asile*, where colors were taught. Dr. Favre then says, —

"The examination of these several reports shows that many children of both sexes come into the *salles d'asile* and schools without a notion of the elementary colors. The number of children lacking in this sensation in the majority of boys' schools I have visited is from twenty to thirty per cent. This ratio diminishes in proportion as the attention of the scholars is directed by their teachers to colored objects. Certain exercises, the painting of plans, geographical cards, lessons in natural history, &c., have an evident influence on the scholars' progress in this sense. Amongst the girls, sewing-work, embroidery, the care of the clothing, the handling of flowers, much reduces at eight years of age the number of those who have difficulty in distinguishing one or more of the elementary colors. At this age the number of boys who make marked mistakes in naming colors is still quite large; and we have found, that, if the majority easily acquire a knowledge of colors, many of these need watchful and continued care, requiring to be examined periodically, so to speak, till we are assured of their cure. What is the best method to use in the schools? Experience may teach us further; but, from our observations during the last five years, we feel authorized to draw the following conclusions: Male and female teachers should be required — (1) To question separately the scholars of their class as to the five elementary colors, and also as to white and black. (2) To carefully record, at the time of examination, the scholar's replies against his name. (3) The scholars who have made mistakes should be individually called twice a week, and the colors named before them; they should be questioned and taught till it is shown that they have acquired an exact notion of the elementary colors. (4) There should be periodic examinations. (5) Whenever occasion presents, the precise names of colored objects exhibited should be spoken before the whole class. (6) An advanced course on colors should be given scholars destined for special professions, by the aid of Chevreul's color-chart and the most commonly manufactured articles.

"The treatment of color-blindness in the adult also has given us very conclusive results, which we have embraced in an unpublished article presented to the Academy of Science."

Dr. Favre says again elsewhere, —

"I call for the introduction of exercises with colors in all the schools, in the army, in the marine, and on the railroads. I am persuaded, that, by the precautions I have indicated, a great number of accidents may be avoided; and I hope to be so fortunate as to cause congenital Daltonism to be stricken from the nosological list."

Dr. Favre has here undoubtedly simply mistaken the lack of knowledge of the *name* of a color for a lack of *perception* of the color. In this mistake he has been confirmed by the rather extraordinary reports from his several friends who were teachers. These latter, I must at once insist, were wholly incompetent to decide whether their scholars were color-blind. We must of course first positively prove the existence of the defect before we can talk about having cured it. It is next to impossible for even an expert to decide whether a child is color-blind by simply asking him to name the color of pieces of paper or other objects. It is, on the other hand, very possible to teach him a name which he shall attach to the object, as it would also be to teach a congenital blind person. These children, supposed color-blind, are reported as cured by more or less exercise with colors, according to their individual quickness and memory in catching and retaining their names. Those that were dull, inattentive, and forgetful, required repeated exercises before they retained the names of colors which were seemingly readily forgotten. This is perfectly shown by the teachers' reports.

The reported percentage of defective color-perception found would of itself throw much doubt on the method of testing. For instance, as many as thirty out of fifty, and fifteen out of thirty-five, children are reported having "no notion of color." But ten per cent is a very large ratio, even when we include all cases of only slight color-blindness. Now, these children were from four to fifteen years of age. How many schoolboys at this time of life know the names of five colors, or, having heard them, will apply them correctly when questioned, without being specially taught?

We have found it very different with girls, as did Dr. Favre. They use the names of colors much more frequently, and have more to do with colored objects in dress, trimmings, &c.

Those of us who possess normal color-perception know how difficult it is to tell the difference between light greens and blues. This formed a large class among these supposed defective children, and they were reported cured in four or five exercises. A further convincing proof of the inadequacy of the test employed, and of the disqualification of the teachers as examiners, is shown by their reporting children as confounding those colors which the color-blind never do; for example, red and violet. I would not, of course, deny that amongst these thousand children there were any color-blind. Proof to the contrary exists in the statement of one teacher, who says, "I sometimes despaired of curing one child, six and a half years old, who, after sixty-five exercises, could not tell me a single color without hesitation. Eleven exercises more, however, cured this unexampled Daltonian, who began by first distinguishing green, and finished by not always calling red yellow when shown him." This child, no doubt, was color-blind, and took this length of time to learn the name of a color to be repeated whenever *the same object was shown him.* If alive, I am certain this boy is as color-blind now as then; and any test not calling for the use of names would undoubtedly prove it. Professor Helmholtz, in his "Physiological Optics" (p. 299, 1867), said, —

"As to the examination of the color-blind, simply asking them to name this or that color, will naturally elicit but very little, since they are then forced to apply the system of names adapted to normal perception to their own perception, for which it is not adapted. It is not only not adapted, because it contains too many names, but, in the series of spectral colors, *we* designate differences of tone as such, which to the color-blind are only variations of saturation or luminosity. It is more than doubtful whether what they call yellow and blue correspond to our yellow and blue."

At first sight it seems only natural that we should be able to improve our color-perception by use, as we may sharpen our other senses by exercise; but in the color-blind there is a congenital defect or deficiency. With the ear we may learn to distinguish sounds whose vibrations come within the range of our scale; but no amount of instruction can make us hear a note above or below the vibratory scale of our ear. A little practice will enable the normal eye to discriminate between the lighter shades of green and blue, which at first it had confounded; but no amount of exercise with colors can cause the color-blind eye to perceive those colors as we do, to whose ethereal wave lengths or numbers it is not adapted. However much practice may cultivate the power of an organ, it can never give that organ a different or additional power. I admit that constant exercise may enable a person only partially color-blind to improve his capacity for discriminating colors; but even then I do not believe he has altered his color-perception, but only supplemented it by additional means, as we so often see other senses, when deficient, supplemented. Whether we shall ever be able to cure color-blindness is another question I am not in position to decide. I desire here only to state my belief, shared in at present by all physiologists and ophthalmic surgeons, that it has not been and cannot be cured by exercise with colors. From Dr. Favre's valuable researches, and his well-known and recognized connection with the present great advance in the testing for color-blindness amongst railroad employés and elsewhere, his belief in the curability of this defect might have undue weight. It must be remembered that he stands almost alone in this. I have therefore endeavored to show how and why he was mistaken, as others also might well be. To this opinion I must still hold, notwithstanding Dr. Favre's more recent article before the Lyons Medical Society, and the supposed cases of congenital color-blindness he there describes.

I should, perhaps, not dwell on this point further, were it not that Dr. Favre's mistake might lead to dangerous consequences by quieting the fears of those whose attention had been roused to the necessity of testing for color-blindness. I therefore quote from one or two authorities in support of my opinion, to show that not only is it incurable, so far as we yet know, but that it does not change with time. A congenital color-blind person dies so. Professor Wilson says, —

"*Congenital* color-blindness is certainly incurable, and, when induced by injury or disease, it may become as irremediable as if it had been an inherited peculiarity; but certain forms of this affection from disease or injury are transitory, and admit of cure. So far as I can ascertain, from the examination of the cases of congenital color-blindness within my reach, the amount of modification in the perception of colors, induced by age, is inappreciable, even though no allowance be made for that alteration in all the powers of vision which time produces on every eye. Thus Dalton was certainly as color-blind at the Oxford meeting of the British Association in 1832, when he compared the color of his D.C.L. gown to that of the leaves of trees, as in 1792, when he first discovered his color-blindness; nor did any change, so far as his associates were aware, occur in his perceptions of color up to his death in 1844. Mr. Milne, of Edinburgh, is still (October, 1854) as color-blind as he was when Mr. Combe described his case thirty years ago, and as he had been for years before his case was described.

Professor N. was examined as to his perception of color, some thirty years since, by Sir David Brewster, who has recorded his case. He writes me recently, 'I am under the impression that some change in appreciating colors took place in my eye between childhood and youth. As a child, red gooseberries seemed to me altogether blue, so far as I remember. Latterly I have observed what I fancy red in this variety of fruit.' And again: 'I suppose sometimes that I can distinguish red in some objects; but probably this is from knowing that they are usually of this color.' But he adds, 'At any rate, I am quite sure I should make a dangerous railway-signal man, as I most certainly would not know a red flag from a green one.' This gentleman further states, in answer to some queries, that *pink* still appears to him by daylight *blue*, and by gaslight *green*, and that he continues to confound carmine red by daylight with blue. There plainly has been nothing deserving the name of improvement in his case. Lastly, the Countess of D. has not (in 1853) appreciably altered in her color-blindness since her peculiarities were described by Wollaston many years ago.

"Dr. K., a medical man, says, 'When a boy at school, my attention was directed to my want of knowledge of color by finding I could not see what my father called the *bright-red* berries of the holly. When other children easily found out the trees which were loaded with ripe cherries, I never could, till I came so near the tree as to detect the form of the fruit. The discovery of this defect in vision distressed my father exceedingly; and he endeavored to cultivate in me a knowledge of color by giving me lessons in painting, making colored charts for me of the prismatic and other colors, wishing to believe that the defect resulted from want of education in color, not from a visual defect. I destroyed many a painting of flowers, &c., by putting on wrong colors, — as blues for purples, green for some kinds of red, and yellow for others. I still remember the surprise he exhibited when he found I could not detect a red cloak spread over a hedge across a narrow field. Hedge and cloak appeared to me the same exact hue, and they do so to this day.'

"Dr. T., aged twenty-seven, early became aware of his inability to distinguish colors, and has cultivated painting in the hope of curing or diminishing his defect, but without any success. He has himself favored me with an account of his case; but, as he very strongly realizes the want of a common language between himself and those who have not his defect in distinguishing colors, he regards this account as hopelessly imperfect.

"It is quite certain that dyers, painters, weavers, clothiers, and the members of other callings much conversant with color, are not unfrequently color-blind. I myself have very recently been offered any 'reasonable fee' if I would cure a worthy working tailor of almost total inability to distinguish colors.

"These cases may suffice to illustrate the permanency of this affection of vision; but they are not singular. Among my color-blind acquaintances there are probably none who would not sacrifice a great deal to see perfectly, and nearly all have endeavored to cure themselves of their visual idiosyncrasy; but not one reports a cure, and the best educated and most observant among them are the most decided in declaring that they have given up all hopes of amendment.

"It is difficult to convince many that this conclusion is a just one. Those whose own sense of color is delicate, and who are led by taste or profession to live much among colored objects, are slow to believe that any eye can be so peculiar in its endowments as to make the blunders which the color-blind do, even in reference to what they call a 'staring' red or green. Such colorists insist that carelessness, indifference, or improper education lies at the bottom of the mistakes which the 'supposed' color-blind make, and profess themselves willing to undertake their cure, of which, however, they record no case.

"When we find an engraver, who for the greater part of his life has been gazing all day at paintings, purchasing a red window-curtain for a green one; a tailor, whose eye has been for hours daily fixed on cloths of very varied colors, matching green tape with scarlet linen, at the risk of losing his situation; an experienced field-geologist compelled, when surveying a red-sandstone district, to take a companion with him to point out where grass ends and sandstone begins; and a teacher of chemistry evading as much as possible the questions of his pupils concerning the colors of bodies, — we cannot doubt, that, after education has done all that it can towards developing the sense of color in the color-blind, they remain as helplessly prone to make their characteristic blunders as before. A crowning example of this has recently presented itself to me. In the establishment of a painter and glass-stainer, who is an obstinate disbeliever in the existence of color-blindness, my attention was recently directed by his fellow-workmen to a youth who had been set to repaint the devices on the shafts of a sheaf of arrows. These devices, consisting of alternate circles of red and green, had not been effaced, but only dulled; yet the painter executed his task by painting all the *red* rings *green*, and all the *green* rings *red*. The case was remarkable for the direct reversal of the colors in question, and this by one who held them before him to compare, both on his palette and on the arrows. Yet the party who committed the mistake was an excellent draughtsman, much esteemed by his master, and surrounded at his daily work with splendid specimens of stained glass. This mistake which he made soon ceased to be a solitary one: for his fellow-workmen, having, since its occurrence, put him to the test, found him uncertain in his judgment of many colors; and, on examining him, I found him commit the characteristic errors of the color-blind. Here, then, was the possessor of an educated color-blind eye making such mistakes as no normal-eyed person, however uneducated his power of vision might be, could or would make. Education, then, can do nothing towards curing congenital color-blindness; nor, in truth, can any thing else."

Dr. Goubert, in 1867, says, as to treatment of color-blindness, —

"I have here no more consoling words or fruitful resources to present. Whatever the symptoms characterizing this peculiar imperfection, it belongs to that large number which the divine art of Æsculapius is powerless to cure, perhaps even to mitigate. All ophthalmic surgeons are unanimous on this point."

Professor Holmgren has very thoroughly discussed Dr. Favre's publications; and he is in position, both theoretically and practically, to test attempts to cure color-blindness by exercise with colors, &c. After citing from his pamphlets, he says, —

"We, on our part, have not yet seen the result of a systematic exercise in learning colors pursued months or years; but the observations we have made on the exercise of the color-blind and their general effects may not be without interest, and throw some light on the importance of such exercise. We have said that the color-blind railroad employés learn to distinguish the flag-signals in common use, and rarely make a mistake when examined, especially on this point. Does this result depend on the training, and in what way? The color-blind who are not railroad employés can answer this. If we show them the ordinary flags (green and red), one after the other, they will nearly always name one or the other wrongly, and often both, and even sometimes frankly admit they do not know the true names of the colors. But if we show them the two flags at the same time, and ask which is green and which red, they at once see a difference; and, having fixed the name in their memory, they no longer make mistakes, but will tell the true name of the colors, even when shown one flag after the other. From this we see how the color-blind railroad employé has learned to distinguish the flags.

"But, after all, what have they learned? and what, strictly speaking, have they gained by such recognitions? If we ask a color-blind person who is intelligent and honest, and who has no interest in concealing his fault, he will openly admit that he has no idea of the color itself, but that he notices a sensible difference in that the green flag is darker to his eye than the red. At the next trial he will make the same mistake if the first flag is shown him alone, and will be as surely correct if the two are shown together. A railroad employé who daily sees the two flags will not in general make this mistake when the test is repeated: we readily understand why. The color-blind has learned to apply the names, guiding himself by the difference in the intensity of the light; but he still continues destitute of any idea of color. He is always color-blind, and has simply learned an artifice."

"Dr. Favre's plan of gradual exercising depends, of course, on the same idea ; only that he uses several shades of the same color. Hence the intensity of the light is not necessarily the distinguishing mark. The fact that in his proposed exercises the objects are looked at close to, assists in no small degree their being distinguished; for, close to, there are other attributes besides color and intensity of light observable, whilst the flags are always at a much greater distance. The coloring material of the different wools may present peculiarities, which we do not generally notice, because the color itself is enough for us, but which are of great assistance to the color-blind. What these differences are is not readily determined. The wools, for instance, may be smooth, rough, soft, or shining, — all qualities appealing to the eye.

"The history of science tells us of cases of persons completely blind who could easily and correctly distinguish wool of different colors by means of other senses, — smell, taste, or touch. The power of touch in this case deserves especial attention, as it is of importance in distinguishing the peculiarities of the wools above mentioned. The close connection between touch and sight in determining whether an object is smooth, rough, &c., is well known. The assistance which these two senses render each other in a general appreciation of every material surface is not less well known. These are the very qualities, beyond any doubt, that the color-blind call to their aid to supply the place of their defective color-sense. Therefore many color-blind place the samples of wool in different lights, bring them quite close to the eye and in different angles to the visual axis. But many color-blind, who knew the difference between red and green, or purple and green, frankly acknowledged that they only recognized them because one wool was coarser, harsher, or rougher than the other. Consequently it was not the color, — that is, the quality of the reflected light, — but the coloring matter and its peculiar effects upon the wool, which were to them the distinguishing features. The color-blind may, however, be assisted by still other more accidental peculiarities; for instance, they may notice whether one bunch of worsted is larger or thicker than the other. The results of such exercise will be as useless as a lesson simply learned by heart. The scholar may repeat a whole page of his book word for word, and yet have no idea of the meaning of the contents."

As to the necessity and value of teaching the names of colors in the schools, I entirely agree with Dr. Favre. No better proof of it can be given than the reports of his teacher-friends, who found twenty to thirty per cent of their pupils who did not know the names of colors, or could not apply them. Such recreations as color-teaching would be interesting and valuable, since most probably all marked cases of color-blindness would be detected, and a scholar thus be warned in time not to attempt work in after-life for which his defect unfits him, of which he cannot be cured by any now known means.

Something in the way of teaching the names of colors has been already commenced in our Boston schools. I have shown those interested how necessary some instruction is in colors, as also how useless it would be to attempt to correct color-blindness by teaching *names*, which would only be associated with objects, and not placed as the expression of an attribute recognized by the eye. But the teachers must first be taught what color-blindness is, and how frequent it is, in order not to set down as stupid, or punish, an unfortunate boy, who seemingly *will* not learn colors he cannot see.

As to the possible mitigation or cure of color-blindness, my own experience with educated color-blind adults has been very interesting. All had attempted, in one way or another, to overcome their defect by practice, but in vain. Those who best understood their trouble most realized this, and eagerly asked for relief, which can be but partially obtained.

I think the necessity of discussing, as far as I have, what at first sight seemed perhaps only a medical opinion, has now been made apparent. The very mistake Dr. Favre has been led into has also deceived railroad officials, who here and there have tested an employé, suspected of color-blindness, with the flags or lanterns used on their individual roads. It requires considerable argument and positive proof to convince a railroad superintendent that one of his men, whom he has had cause to suspect, and has seemingly thoroughly tested, is, after all, color-blind. It is very difficult for him not to believe his employé has learned, or can be made to learn, to see colors as they appear to a normal eye. He, however, will be convinced against his reason, when the color-blind man is in his presence subjected to a proper scientific test, applied by a competent specialist.

CHAPTER XIII.

PALLIATION OF CONGENITAL COLOR-BLINDNESS.

As congenital color-blindness cannot be cured by any at present known means, the question of its possible palliation becomes somewhat important. Many methods have naturally been suggested and tried, and of these I will now speak. Wilson says, —

> "A means of guarding against mistakes, relative to colors, which is unquestionably of some service to the color-blind, is the reference of doubtful hues to a chromatic scale, accurately tinted and named. But this means of correcting error soon finds its limit, as the mismatchings of red with green, olive with brown, and purple with blue, characteristically made by the color-blind (although both colors are presented to the eye together), are sufficient to show. Moreover, we must remember, that, to the color-blind, his defective color perfectly corresponds with gray, or white and black, as readily shown by experiment with Chevreul's '*gammes chromatiques*,' or with the worsted test. Hence, by comparison alone, he might decide that his scarlet or green cloth is a neutral tint or gray."

Szokalski and Seebeck, as Wilson also remarks, recommended, as a means of ameliorating the condition of the color-blind, their steady gazing, first on a colored surface, and then on a white or black one; but, for reasons already given, this proposal seems of no value, nor is any proof offered that it has been of service.

There nevertheless exists, says Wartman, a very easy means of rectifying, to a certain extent, the error of the appellation of color. This means consists in examining colored objects through a transparent medium — as a glass or a liquid — of a certain known tint. Suppose this tint red: the impression of a green body and of a red body, the same at first to the naked eye, will become manifestly distinguished by the use of the transparent screen. This method appears to have been practised for the first time by Professor Seebeck (the father) towards the year 1817. Their employment, however, only remedies mistakes in the specific nature of colors, and leaves in general those which apply to one and the same tint. Wilson says that Dr. Steebach carried out this proposal the length of recommending the use of colored spectacles. Trinchinetti advises that the glasses should be of the color which is the complement of that liable to be seen falsely. To this Wartman justly objects, because "the color-blind do not judge correctly of complementary colors;" but his own proposal to employ transparent media of other colors is liable to as great objections. Wilson adds, —

"I am far from wishing to affirm that a color-blind person may not be aided in correcting his chromatic errors by such a use of colored glasses as Seebeck and Wartman recommend; but, after many trials with my color-blind acquaintances, I have found none who could turn the suggestion to practical account. My trials have been chiefly made upon those who confused red with green, to whom

Wartman, in illustrating the use of colored transparent media, specially refers; but I have met with no success."

In 1855 Mr. J. Clerk Maxwell suggested and tried the employment of red *and* green glass simultaneously, which frees it from Wilson's objections. He says, as to the effect of colored glasses on the color-blind, —

"Although they cannot distinguish reds and greens from varieties of gray, the transparency of red and green glasses for those kinds of light is very different. Hence, after finding a case in which red and green appear identical, on looking through a red glass they see the red clearly and the green obscurely, while through a green glass the red appears dark, and the green light. By furnishing Mr. X. with a red and a green glass, which he could distinguish only by their shape, I enabled him to make judgments in previously doubtful cases of color with perfect certainty. I have since had a pair of spectacles constructed, with one glass red and the other green. These Mr. X. intends to use for a length of time, and he hopes to acquire the habit of discriminating red from green tints by their different effects on his two eyes. Though he can never acquire our sensation of red, he may then discern for himself what things are red; and the mental process may become so familiar to him as to act unconsciously like a new sense."

It is very generally remarked of and by the color-blind, that they can distinguish reds and greens better by artificial light than in daylight. Many a one has avoided detection by carrying objects, especially goods, to the gas to enable them to determine. The simple reason of this is that they can see, as the normal-eyed, blue, and its complement yellow. The artificial light adds the yellow, and increases the yellow in the object itself, thereby assisting their vision. In lesser degrees of color-blindness this result is very marked.

Wilson found that the whiter and more intensely luminous artificial lights, such as the lime-ball and the electric charcoal-light, induce the same confusion in the perception of colors as sunlight does. He says, —

"The contrast in appearance under the opposite illuminations is so great, that, among the cases of color-blindness which I have recorded, there are as many as six persons who have discovered that they could mitigate their peculiarity of vision by the employment of artificial light. Thus Mr. N., Professor Y., and Dr. E. have resorted to candle-light as a means of increasing their enjoyment of flowers, which, if crimson, appeared, when seen by it, much richer in color than by daylight. Dr. E. and I had admired flowers together for years without my discovering his color-blindness. Mr. N. states that 'it is quite an *enjoyment*' to him to look at crimson flowers by candle-light. Professor Y. has always delighted in going into a conservatory by candle-light, because then all the purple and red flowers stood out in such brilliant *contrast* to the green leaves. A gentleman who deals in colored goods has long been in the habit of appealing to a gas-flame in a dark room to decide between scarlet and green, and crimson and blue."

Hence Wilson proposed for the color-blind such colored glasses as rendered sunlight nearest to artificial light. These are pale yellow or orange, stained with oxide of silver. Such glasses were supplied to the above-mentioned gentlemen. There were four shades or depths of the yellow color. One reported, "The glasses deepen, or rather brighten, the reds, but do not affect the greens so much. I can distinguish the reds by the aid of the glasses much better than I can the greens. On a bright day they gave a decided and very marked difference between red and green. Scarlets it made very bright and light; while crimsons were made decidedly red and fiery." Another found he could, through the yellow glass, see the same difference between green and scarlet, and crimson and blue, as by artificial light. The color-blind, therefore, can assist themselves and avoid mistakes by selecting and looking through such yellow glass as renders daylight nearest to artificial light.

An interesting notice of a red-blind having discovered his ability to see better by lamp-light is given by Dr. Minder. The person was a member of the Bernese family, whose color-blindness, from documentary evidence, has been known to exist two hundred years. In a letter dated Paris, 1799, to his color-blind brother, he says, —

> "You will find enclosed a pretty Swiss cockade. I have separated it, but you can readily put it together. In the centre is the yellow, then red, then green. Formerly, if I had been torn on the rack to get this arrangement from me, it would have been useless. About a year ago, however, I made the brilliant discovery, that by lamp-light I could distinguish the colors. Rose-red, which by daylight is blue to me, then appears a bright carmine; green, which by day is red, appears blue: so that, give me twenty-four hours, I should seldom be deceived. Write me if you have ever made this discovery."

In March, 1878, Professors J. Delbœuf and W. Spring of Lille published a very interesting and important article on the amelioration of color-blindness by looking through certain colored solutions. Professor Delbœuf is color-blind; and hence his observations, guided by Professor Spring who is normal-eyed, are of such value, that I will give here quotations from the original article. Delbœuf's theory as to color-perception, deduced from his results, is not of course in place here. I would only mention that he endeavors to disprove the Young-Helmholtz theory.

After various trials with one and another colored fluid, he hit upon "fuchsine" five parts in weight to fifty thousand *d'eau alcoolisée*. This he placed in a wedge-shaped glass receptacle, with sides meeting at one end, and separated at the other a centimetre. Thus he could look through any thickness up to a centimetre. He employed other strengths, but the above gave the best results. Of these results he says,—

"The effect obtained was marvellous: not only did the colors which I usually confound — blue, carmine, and violet on the one hand, and scarlet, red, and brown on the other — appear very different, but the scarlet red especially assumed a brightness wholly unknown to me heretofore. It had appeared to me dull, but suddenly it became flaming and brilliant. This was to me an extraordinary and unlooked-for result. The same effect was produced on two of my pupils who were color-blind, and on those whom Professor Spring and I have examined."

Professor Delbœuf found, in brief, that the fuchsine corrected the usual mistakes as to red fruits and flowers, the foliage, &c. With Professor Spring he also tested himself with large numbers of pieces of colored silk.

"Two of the ribbons were of special service, — a marked brown, which I had confounded with a bright scarlet red; the other, a violet, which produced on me precisely the same effect as a pure blue. The fuchsine showed me the difference between the colors and their shades with more or less distinctness, and we found the same with the two color-blind we tested.

"I had here, then, a positive fact, and reason to suppose that the fuchsine rendered my vision like the normal-eyed. But this was a presumption I had to verify by producing color-blindness in the normal-eyed by some solution before their eyes. The hazard which brought us the fuchsine did the same for *chloride of nickel* one part, and twenty-five of water. Through a centimetre of this solution Professor Spring found the violet ribbon looked blue, red identical with brown, and nature assumed a certain uniform tint without brilliancy. Glass stained with copper has also largely this effect of rendering the normal-eyed color-blind. Holmgren called attention to this, and says, 'We may get a good idea of the difficulty the color-blind have in sorting colored objects if one tries to do the same through greenish-blue spectacles. We shall see and sort the colors pretty much as a red-blind does, and have the same difficulty as he, or all who attempt to do that which they have not the power to.' I have said that the fuchsine gave me a very marked difference between blue and violet, brown and scarlet, and that the violet and scarlet became always more brilliant, whilst brown and blue retained their ordinary aspect. Chloride of nickel does not affect the normal-eyed, except as to red or violet; green, blue, yellow, remain, so to speak, unaltered. The reverse holds true with us; namely, considerable thickness of the green solution but slightly interferes with the harmony of colors as I see them: and, through weak solutions of fuchsine, the normal-eyed do not see objects very differently from generally. Stronger solutions only render the violet brighter, and especially the scarlet, which becomes whiter.

"We need now only see if the fuchsine re-establishes the vision of a normal-eyed rendered color-blind by chloride of nickel. This is the case. When a normal-eyed looks at our silks through a solution of chloride of nickel sufficiently strong to render the red and brown ribbons, the violet and blue, appear either brown or blue, and then adds a proper thickness of fuchsine, the colors regain their distinctive characters. So, also, a color-blind corrected by fuchsine becomes again color-blind by chloride of nickel."

Professor Delbœuf remarks, in closing his paper, —

"These researches have an epilogue. Having determined the cause [as explained by his theory] of color-blindness, we should not have thought of broaching the question of its treatment, had not a singular circumstance caused us to believe in the possibility of its cure. I have a painting of flowers, — a bouquet of poppies. What alone always pleased me in it was the correctness of design, the freshness of the flowers, and their true and natûral appearance. Returning in October, after an absence of six or seven weeks, I found a new charm in this painting. I first thought this was, as is so often the case with works of art, but a momentary caprice. Yet finding it each day more and more attractive, I thought whether, by looking through the fuchsine, and thus giving myself the sensation of red, I could not now see distinctions which in reality were hitherto powerless to act on my visual faculty. This conjecture is the more plausible as, at the commencement of our experiments, I had looked at this picture with our apparatus. This was my thought when, in the beginning of November, I made some tests of the railroad-signals, to see if our liquids were sufficient to render distinguishable the red and green lights. The results were not conclusive. I had a vague sensation that my naked eye could recognize distinctions formerly impossible for me. But towards the middle of last December, whilst walking in the city, I noticed, or thought I did, red lights a few hundred steps off. I approached them, and found they were dim lanterns to mark an excavation in the street. It was the first time that any such light seemed to have a distinctive color. Formerly I saw no difference between the yellow and red lights, except that the former were brighter, and the fuchsine had but made them look alike. Much interested, I went over to the American tramway, where the cars are lighted by red lanterns. I used to notice but little distinction between them and the gas-jets; but to my surprise I recognized them quite well, even at a distance. I thought I had perhaps corrected my color-blindness. Some days after, when the weather was dull, I took out the box of ribbons in my laboratory. Formerly, on such a day, I should have unquestionably found them identical in pairs; but it was no longer so. The brown ribbon remained the same; but the scarlet struck me vividly by its brightness. In no possible position could I confound them, and the difference remains still quite marked. I asked Professor Spring to attempt to deceive me by showing them to me singly; but he could not. This I could not say of the blue and violet. I thought I noticed a certain variance, but did not feel assured of not being deceived. I have therefore to improve in this direction; but, no doubt, my inexperience with the blue and violet is due to my sensation of red not being yet very strong. In fact, the fuchsine gives the red of my ribbon a color much stronger than I have as yet recognized. It is probably a matter of time and exercise. Some time after, I thought to ascertain if the solar spectrum looked different from what it formerly did. Going to my laboratory, and taking up the ribbons, I found the red brighter than the brown; yet it seemed as if the contrast had somewhat decreased lately. I looked, therefore, very carefully at the spectrum. I thought, at first, the gradations more marked in the yellow, and hence, on the whole, that there was no change. Accidentally, however, turning my eyes to the ribbons, I still saw one was more brilliant, and, on going to it, found it was the brown! It was only after a time, and repeatedly gazing through the fuchsine, that the red again assumed in part its relative brilliancy."

The following very misleading notice, based upon the above, I quote from "The Scientific American," Dec. 28, 1878 (p. 408): —

"REMEDY FOR COLOR-BLINDNESS. — 'La France Médicale' states that M. Delbœuf has found, that, if a person afflicted with Daltonism looks through a layer of fuchsine in solution, his infirmity disappears. A practical application of this discovery has been made by M. Javal, by interposing between two glasses a thin layer of gelatine previously tinted with fuchsine. By regarding objects through such a medium, all the difficulties of color-blindness are said to be corrected."

More important still is a report from a committee of the Belgian Royal Academy to the minister of public works in answer to certain questions. Professor Delbœuf was secretary of this committee; and, owing to his supposed discovery of the effect of a fuchsine solution, they report, —

"In all cases there can be attached to the engine an apparatus which prevents even the most color-blind from possibly confounding red or green with any color, and which would add to the contrast of the signals. The apparatus would consist of a red and a green glass having the properties spoken of. When the engineer had the slightest doubt, he need but look through these glasses. Looking through the red, the signal of that color would become brighter, and contrast more with the general visual field. On the other hand, it would be weakened by looking through the green. The reverse holds true of the green signal. This apparatus, infallible for the day-signals, would be efficacious to a certain degree for the night-signals also, but perhaps less practical here."

On this point Dr. Magnus says,—

"Whether the method, lately proposed by Professor Delbœuf, of palliating or improving color-blindness by fuchsine-colored glasses, will prove of service, time must decide. Professor Delbœuf, himself color-blind, believes the method of practical value, as tested in his own case. But, as we have already pointed out, deception here is very possible; and one may readily mistake for a cure of color-blindness the practice which a color-blind has gained by any increased sensitiveness to shades of light in distinguishing colors. Moreover, there has as yet been no practical experience with Delbœuf's method."

In order to fairly test Professor Delbœuf's supposed remedy or cure of color-blindness, I have had the apparatus made as he directs in his original article. With the fuchsine solution I have pretty carefully tested six color-blind, both red and green blind, and of various degrees. Two of these were physicians, who had not only paid a good deal of attention to the subject, but also to their own cases. The result was quite unsatisfactory. A red-blind, after carefully working with the fuchsine solution, reported that he could obtain but little more benefit than he did by gaslight, or a pale, lemon-colored glass, which simulated gaslight. He, as they all, reported that the green worsteds in Holmgren's test, or other objects of this color, were darkened, and thereby the *relation of light and shade altered.* This assisted him in selecting them. The same darkening takes place, of course, with the normal eye. We can see what a change in light and shade is produced by even a small amount of fuchsine, and thus understand how much the color-blind may hereby gain; that is, how much is added to their already highly developed sense of light and shade perception. A color-blind person who had not studied his defect, or the subject generally, might very readily mistake the help of the fuchsine solution for a change of his color-sense, and suppose, also, that the comparative new world to him was something permanent, — this also more especially as the fuchsine solution intensifies the reds, and allows a red-blind to get a much better idea of the sensation red to the normal eye. This is probably, therefore, the explanation of Professor Delbœuf's enthusiasm over his discovery. But those who have studied the vision of the color-blind — particularly the educated — can readily understand the fictitious assistance of a change of light and shade, which, as I have said, one of my color-blind soon found out.

Professor Holmgren, some years before Delbœuf's investigations, discussed the effect of colored glass and colored solutions in rendering the vision of the normal-eyed like that of the color-blind.

In a review of articles on color-blindness, published in the "Revue des Sciences Médicales," October, 1878, Dr. Javal says of Delbœuf's method, —

> "I obtained sheets of gelatine stained with fuchsine, which produced the same effect as Professor Delbœuf's solution, and which were much more manageable. But, notwithstanding this better arrangement, I much doubt if this means of correction of color-blindness has a great future; for the majority of those affected are too habituated to live with their infirmity to be willing to suffer the slightest inconvenience in correcting it. This correction will therefore be only applicable to those persons, relatively few, whose occupation is such that their infirmity is a positive hinderance. And from these should be excluded railroad employés, pilots, &c., who are color-blind, as such must be absolutely removed from posts where their deficient chromatic sense may cause accidents."

In reference to Delbœuf and Spring's statements as to chloride of nickel in solution, — one part in weight to twenty-five of water, — I must say I have carefully followed *their* experiment, as also with a stronger solution arranged as they describe; but I obtained no such effect as they report, — of thereby rendering the normal eye color-blind. All normal-eyed with whom I have tried it tell me the same. It did not interfere with my sorting the worsteds with Holmgren's test perfectly. Looking through such a solution dulls the red a little, but nothing more so far as I can yet see; with which, as I said, others agree. Moreover, the effect of the fuchsine solution was not negatived by it to the color-blind. I confess myself at a loss to understand Delbœuf's statements.

CHAPTER XIV.

DANGERS ARISING FROM COLOR-BLINDNESS.

THE mortification, inconvenience, and loss of position or employment, from the lack of power to choose proper or appropriate colors in dress and costume, to distinguish and match colored goods, to mix or use colored pigments, I have already sufficiently described. The *dangers* to which the community are subjected from color-blind railroad employés and pilots will be explained in this chapter, and how and why these should be avoided by the action of the community in protecting itself. For instance, an engineer has run on one road for some five or ten years without accident of importance. The superintendent requires him to pass examination by an expert, who finds he is markedly red-blind, and shows it most convincingly to the officials of the road. It becomes known; and they then do not, of course, dare to keep him in his place. He is dismissed, to protect the community from danger.

We need no better proof of the recognition of the danger than the measures so rapidly taken for the last two years on so many of the European roads, and which are being initiated by the others.

Our very practical American people have recognized the danger from numerous colored lights or signal-flags in having gradually discarded them. Many roads already use only *red* by night or day. *Green* and *red* are, however, most generally used to signify *safety* and *danger*. From experiment and experience I agree that they are right. We cannot give up *color* for *form* by night. It is, however, possible by day. Is the danger any less great here in the United States? I believe the danger from *ignorance* of its existence is not small. The chief of the Brotherhood of Locomotive Engineers told me he had not heard of color-blindness, although he had run an engine twenty years; and asked me, with some feeling, whether I "thought a man was fit to run an engine who could not tell green from red."

The Massachusetts Board of Railroad Commissioners reported to me (Feb. 17, 1877), that "the subject of color-blindness is one which has never come to the attention of the board;" and they "have not known of the subject being investigated in this country."

There is danger from color-blindness, also, from the general and the scientific press never having taken it up in discussion in this country. I am at present unacquainted with any thing on this special topic, except one or two brief articles in "The Chicago Railway Review," "The Scientific American," and an occasional paragraph in some medical journal. So far as I know, the whole question of color-blindness and its natural danger was first publicly discussed by myself March 7, 1877, before the Boston Society of Natural History, and previously at a scientific club, where the necessity of a color-test examination was urged. I speak of this only as showing, that, notwithstanding the number of very competent ophthalmic surgeons in the larger cities of the Union, the subject has failed as yet to arise for discussion through their efforts. We naturally should have looked to them for warning from the danger, especially as their daily practice renders them so familiar with color-blindness from injury or disease. The subject, I confess, forced itself on my attention.

Thanks to the efforts of such men as Drs. Wilson, Favre, Donders, and Holmgren, railway and marine collisions or accidents will now be investigated in relation to color-blindness; and when one is proved amongst us, as they have been elsewhere, to have occurred on this account, then the community will be suddenly awakened to a realization of the danger they have always incurred, and corporations forced to make some effort to avoid similar accidents in future. Then will be brought forward the facts presented in this volume. And it will be shown, that, through the efforts of some railway surgeons and scientific men, the world has been taught that color-blindness exists to a greater or less degree certainly in one in twenty-five of the whole male population; that this must hold good, therefore, among railroad employés and mariners, where it is a source of very great danger. Hence a court or jury will not be slow to accept and apply the verdict of the general community, that the accident was *preventable*, and the corporation liable.

The teaching the community cannot be done by the single or united efforts of scientific men. By examinations in the schools, a knowledge of color-blindness and its dangers can be disseminated, as well as the individual warned of his defect. If the medical, popular, and daily press would take the subject up, as they did in Sweden, the railroads would soon feel forced to act immediately in the matter. It also would not be long before an international commission would be appointed, and laws for the control of color-blindness in the marine *personnel* agreed upon. Professor Wilson closes his book with the following: —

"The professions for which color-blindness most seriously disqualifies are those of the sailor and railway servant, who have daily to peril human life and property on the indication which a colored flag or lamp seems to give. Fortunately a ship is seldom under the guidance of a single person; and in her majesty's vessels the color-signal men are selected from a large number, and are ascertained to have a quick eye for color. In merchant-ships the choice must necessarily be made from a much smaller number; and the appalling yearly list of lost vessels which appears in our wreck returns awakens the suspicion that more than one of these fatal disasters may have resulted from the mistaken color of a lighthouse, beacon, or harbor-lamp, which on a strange coast, and with perhaps the accompaniments of a snow-storm or a thick fog, has been wrongly deciphered by a color-blind pilot.

"On railways the danger attending mistakes of signals is much greater than at sea; especially in this country (England), where trains travel at a very high rate of speed, and succeed each other at very short intervals. . . . I am happy to say that the publication of my papers has induced the Great Northern Railway Company to require that in future all their porters shall be tested as to their freedom from color-blindness before they are admitted."

The attention of railroad managers, and also that of the community at large, has in Europe been repeatedly called to the great danger likely to arise from color-blindness. I would, for instance, refer to Noel, in the "Courier des Sciences;" and I would particularly call attention to the efforts of Dr. A. Favre of Lyons, France. I cannot do better than quote from the *résumé* of his memoirs. He says, —

"I have proved, by facts personally observed from 1855 to 1873–77, the necessity of testing for color-blindness all candidates for railroad service, and the exclusion of those who are *red-blind;* also the necessity of specially examining employés who have been injured about the head, those recovered from severe illness, smokers, and drinkers. I call also for the periodic examination of all in active railroad service. The majority of these precautions, adopted on the Lyons road since 1857, have been gradually enforced on other lines, and quite recently, also, on the Belgian roads. . . . Feb. 8, 1875, I called the attention of the 'Conseil de Santé des Armées' to the use of the colored signals employed in war, and the necessity of testing those giving or receiving orders by colored signals. . . . In February, 1875, I called the attention of the Medical Society of Lyons to color-blindness caused by injuries. . . . On Nov. 4, 1875, I addressed the Medical Society of Marseilles in reference to color-blindness in navigation. My conclusions were adopted, and communicated to the marine authorities of the port and the minister of marine. At the same time the Academy of Sciences and Letters of Lyons voted to call to my publication the attention of the ministers of public instruction, public works, war, and marine."

Wilson says, —

"The majority of even color-blind persons are able to distinguish bright red from bright green when they are *near* the eye and well illuminated: but this power of distinguishing between these colors diminishes with great rapidity when they are removed to a distance from the eye;

so that a separation of a few feet or a few yards, according to the severity of the case, abolishes all sense of distinction between red and green. As the colored day-signals on railways — especially the flags, which alone are available in some of the most pressing emergencies — soon tarnish and darken, the effect of time is to change light reds and greens into much darker shades, and thereby continually to diminish the distance (small at the best) at which the two danger-signals can be distinguished from each other by a color-blind observer."

The danger, therefore, depends on the number of color-blind employed on the railroads. They have been found as frequent there as elsewhere.

My friend, Dr. Edmund Hansen, a distinguished ophthalmic surgeon of Copenhagen, Denmark, writes me, June 24, 1877, —

"The railways of Denmark are in the possession of two parties: one is a private company, which owns the railways of the larger island called Seeland, and of the adjacent smaller islands, Laaland and Falster; whereas the railways on the island Funen and on the peninsula Jutland belong to the government. The investigation for color-blindness has just been completed by the private companies: on the government railways it will be done in the course of the summer. (I will give you the results of the private company, and shall send you the other when the results have been made known.) The examination on the Seeland, Laaland, and Falster roads has been made according to the method of Professor Holmgren. 1,084 persons were examined, of whom 50 were women. Of this number, 31 men (or 2.87 per cent) were color-blind, — all congenital cases. None of the women were color-blind. Of the 31, 10 were perfectly color-blind, 21 imperfectly. Of the perfectly color-blind, 6 had red-blindness, 4 green-blindness. Their occupations were: 2 station-masters perfectly green-blind; 1 engineer perfectly red-blind; 1 train-conductor, 1 fireman, perfectly green-blind; 4 porters, 3 blacksmiths, 7 railway guards, of whom 2 were perfectly red-blind; 2 assistants, 1 pupil, perfectly red-blind; 1 *concierge*, 2 foremen, of whom 1 was perfectly green-blind; 4 workmen on station, 1 perfectly red-blind; 2 extra conductors, 1 perfectly red-blind."

These examinations, I understand, were made by Dr. Fontenay.

Professor A. Quaglino, of Milan, Italy, writes me, Aug. 11, 1877, "I do not know whether there are any statistics of color-blindness published in Italy, though I am sure that all the railroad employés are subjected to a rigorous examination in reference to their color-perception."

Dr. J. Stilling, of Cassel, also writes me, Dec. 6, 1877, "I have but once had opportunity of examining railroad employés, about four hundred in number. Of these, six per cent were color-blind."

Dr. Magnus reports the result of one of his colleagues on a Breslau road as four per cent of color-blindness among the employés.

Professor F. C. Donders of Utrecht, Holland, with the assistance of twelve physicians and ophthalmic surgeons, whom he had specially instructed in a method of his own, examined 2,203 employés on the Holland roads. He found 152 of these more or less color-blind. These he subsequently — with his assistant, Dr. Bouvin — still more carefully tested, thereby confirming his previous results.

Dr. A. von Reuss writes me March, 1879, having found 3.50 per cent color-blind among 800 of the employés of one of the Vienna roads.

I have perhaps quoted enough to show by statistics, and by the precautions railroad corporations in Europe are taking, the extent to which color-blindness prevails amongst employés, and its consequent danger. But I should quite fail in giving the subject due prominence as to the prevalence of color-blindness, the value of scientific investigation in detecting it, its danger for the community, and the success of true methods of testing in convincing railroad people of all this, &c., were I not to quote from Professor Holmgren's work. He says, —

"In a case called the Lagerlunda, arising from a railroad accident at Lagerlunda, in Ostrogothia, Nov. 15, 1875, and which excited great public attention, there was evidence leading me to suppose that color-blindness was one of the principal causes of the disaster. This led me to think that control should be exercised among railroad employés as to color-perception.

"In June, 1876, I had an opportunity for testing this matter. By the courtesy of Major-Gen. von Knorring and Major Rudbeck, I was permitted to examine 2,200 men of the infantry and dragoons of the guard in camp in Upland. From this examination we learned, in reference to the existence of color-blindness among the population of the province, that, out of the 2,200 men, 11 were red-blind, 17 could not perceive green, and 1 violet (?); 31 besides were *incompletely* color-blind in accordance with my classification. There were, then, 60 defective, or 2.7 per cent. The cases of 'feeble sensation of colors' are not here included.

"July 14 of the same year I had opportunity, at the Scandinavian Medical Congress assembled at Gothenburg, to describe my method, report the results of its employment, and also to express my views as to the necessity of taking measures on a large scale in reference to the detection of color-blindness, especially among railroad employés. In consequence the congress voted unanimously on the necessity of instituting examinations to detect color-blindness, first, among railroad employés; second, among pilots, lighthouse-keepers, and sailors in general; and, third, in the schools. During the congress I had time to show the physicians the practical application of the method, by examining in their presence, by permission of Col. Carlsohn, 100 men of the artillery regiment in Gotha, amongst whom we found 4 color-defective, — 1 for red, 1 for green, and 2 incompletely blind to color. At the same time I found one green-blind among the physicians, members of the congress, and one red-blind among the assistants.

"I was then prepared to apply directly to the railroad administration. Thanks to the press, which followed attentively the discussions in the congress of Gothenburg, the question came to the knowledge of the public. It naturally attracted the attention of the railroad officials, who for the most part looked upon it with a certain distrust, as rather the result of learned imagination or over-solicitude than as a practical matter for the railroad service. We have heard a railroad official use almost literally these words: 'If color-blindness really exists, it cannot be amongst the employés, or it would have been noticed. This must at least be the case with the engineers and conductors, all of whom obtain their places after passing through inferior grades, and consequently after having sufficiently proved their faculty of distinguishing colors.' It was, therefore, very important to obtain some certain data on this point. This soon arose. Mr. Jacobsson, *chef d'exploitation* of the Upsala-Gefle line, asked me to accompany him on a tour of inspection, and examine all the employés under his orders. The tour was undertaken in the fall. We left Upsala Sept. 7, and, to carry out our examinations, halted at all the stations, at all the guard-houses, and at every gate; in short, we stopped at every point where an employé was to be found. The examination was finished at Gefle Sept. 8. All the force — 266 men and women — were tested. Amongst them we found 13 defective; viz., 4.8 per cent. Six were completely *green-blind*, and 7 incompletely color-blind. Their positions were, 1 chief of station, 1 engineer, 2 conductors, 1 chief of equipments, 2 men of the equipment department (one a supernumerary), 2 overseers, 2 road-guards, 1 clerk, and 1 stoker. Immediately after the examination, the *chef d'exploitation* dismissed all those who were blind for *green*.

"This first expedition was interesting in many respects. It showed that the method of examination was adapted to, and could be used on, the railroads. It showed, moreover, that there were really color-blind, in nearly every degree, employed on the Swedish roads, of which no one had had the slightest suspicion."

Professor Holmgren reports later in September, 1878, having to date tested 7,953 railroad employés, and found 171 color-blind, or 2.15 per cent; viz., 45 red-blind, 48 green-blind, and 70 incompletely blind.

"In Finland Dr. L. Krohn, who was by correspondence instructed in the method and principles applied in Sweden, has already examined the *personnel* attached to the railroads of his country. A locomotive and car were placed at his disposition to enable him to test the employés on the whole length of the line. It was completed in twelve days. He found, among 1,200 persons tested, 60 color-blind; namely, 5 per cent. They were as follows: 4 red-blind, 25 green-blind, and 31 incompletely blind."

Professor Holmgren brought this matter before the various railroad directions in Sweden. Moreover, experiments were made in the Physiological Institute at Upsala; so that, by Nov. 9, 1876, throughout Sweden, it was ordered that all the railroad employés should be tested for color-blindness by the methods there used. What Professor Holmgren has accomplished leaves no excuse for our American railroads in hesitating or refusing to thoroughly and properly test all their employés for defects of color-perception, and dismissing those who are color-blind, and providing also for the future by testing all applicants for employment.

If long before this my readers have been astonished at the facts here collected, they, no doubt, have also been equally disposed to question them, or at least their practical bearing. They will naturally say, "We do not hear of railroad accidents from color-blindness, and rarely of marine collisions attributable to this cause." Of this I shall again speak; but I must first here explain how it is that the color-blind employés get on so well, conceal their defect, and perhaps avoid accident. I shall confine my remarks to the railroad *personnel* and mariners. How the color-blind escape detection in every-day life, I have already fully described. Professor Holmgren explains this so readily from his experience, that I do best to first quote from him. He says, —

"We should imagine a color-blind railroad employé would be immediately detected, or would have at least discovered his own defect. This very natural idea has greatly tended to retard the reform we have called for. It is, however, incorrect, and does not stand the test. On the contrary, examinations showed that a large number of color-blind were employed in nearly all the positions on a railroad, without they or others being aware of their faulty color-perception. And further: a number of these, far from being convinced of their defect, even after the examination, insisted on repeating the test (even six or seven times), giving all sorts of excuses in explanation of their constant mistakes. They all agreed in saying that they had excellent sight, never had experienced the slightest difficulty in distinguishing the signals, and though a long time in service, and in most important posts, as locomotive-engineers for instance, never had made the slightest mistake.

"Certainly we may well be astonished at this condition of things, and very naturally ask how it is possible for any one to perform the duty of engine-driver, for instance, any length of time without exposing a deficiency of vision so important for the performance of this duty. There are, so far as we know, only two explanations: one is in the peculiar visual sense of the color-blind, and the exercise of this sense in distinguishing the signals; while the other depends on the conditions under which an engine-driver ordinarily does duty.

"As to the first explanation, we must remember that every color coming from an illuminated colored surface may be more or less bright or dark, and every lantern-light, even colored, may be stronger or weaker. Hence, in a colored object or colored light, the eye does not alone take note of the color or quality of the light, but also of its *quantity* or *intensity.* When two objects or two lights appear of the same color to the eyes of a color-blind person, they may differ as respects *intensity.* This being the sole difference between these lights, it is particularly noted; and thus, often as a result of special exercise, such color-blind person may strengthen his perception so as to in a certain degree make up for his color-deficiency. He resembles somewhat the persons who, deprived of one sense, replace it to a degree by the greater exercise of one or more of their other senses. We have already noticed this point, so very important in practice, but could not refrain from again reverting to it here. Any one who has experience from conversation with intelligent color-blind, or experimenting with Maxwell's rotating disk, will have noticed their peculiar sensitiveness to *varying intensity of light* whilst comparing two colors, and hence can have no doubt as to how a color-blind person can so often distinguish between railroad-signals, and give the colors their true names.

"Did we not know this, we should be greatly astonished to find with what facility a color-blind railroad employé can distinguish between the red and green flag, and generally call the red, green, and yellow lanterns by their right color: but it is the intensity of the light, and not the color, which governs his decision ; *and this is the whole secret.* The flags and lanterns have, in fact, usually a constant difference as to intensity. The green flag is to the color-blind, as also to the normal eye, undoubtedly of the deepest or darkest color, and the red the most brilliant. As to the lanterns, the red-blind always recognize the red light by its being darker than the green, and the yellow by its being clearer or more brilliant than the other two. The green-blind finds also, in his turn, the red more brilliant than the green, and distinguishes it by this.

"The other explanation lies in the conditions under which an engineer has to observe the signals. First of all, we must remember the great regularity with which all the details of railroad service take place. An engineer starting from a station at one end of the line knows very well in advance what stations to stop at, and which to pass. Under ordinary circumstances he knows which light ought to be exhibited on the signal-posts above the several stations. The hand-lanterns are not as important, since their color is not so essential, being supplemented by movements. Hence it is only under exceptional conditions that accidents can happen at *stations* from mistakes as to the color of fixed lights. There may, of course, be a number of other cases exceptional to the ordinary regularity: but we must here notice one circumstance, which probably has been and still is of very great importance; namely, that the engineer is not the only one who has to watch for the signals. There is always with him the stoker, and near him a conductor, an oiler, &c., to aid him at critical moments. It must be extremely rare that all the *personnel* of a train are affected with color-blindness.

"Considering only practically the fact mentioned, and the explanation we have given, one might perhaps imagine that color-blindness had some scientific, but hardly any practical, interest, and hence that all the talk that has been made about its existence among railroad employés in our country was unnecessary; because, as may be said, the color-blind have often been employed a long time in railroad service without its being noticed, and without accident or the slightest inconvenience arising; and finally, that, since they can really distinguish the signals (although this is otherwise than by color), their kind of blindness need not call for any preventive measures. It is thus that a great many persons still reason.

"We do not stop here to give the testimony of experience on this point in our country. One fact is certain; namely, that color-blindness in other countries has caused numerous and very fatal accidents. Even if this had not been definitely proved, it is none the less evident that we have no right to await another such experience before passing to words and acts, and in every way showing, that, notwithstanding the numerous circumstances which assist the color-blind in responding to the signals, danger is not wholly avoided, and the uncertainty remains. This is readily shown. Neither the fact that the color-blind have been employed many years on the railroads without causing accident, or even without their defect being discovered, nor the circumstances we have cited in explanation of this fact, furnishes the least assurance of security.

"A typical color-blind person cannot distinguish between red and green. This is an incontestable fact, readily explained by theory, and sufficiently proved by experience. All his judgment as to the difference of colors rests, in consequence, on conjecture. If, perhaps, exercise enables him, up to a certain point, to distinguish between the red and green railroad lights, this is dependent on the intensity of the light telling him the color. But there is, of course, great uncertainty in this means of reading the signals; and the man who may be right in a certain number of special cases will surely go wrong in some other. It is a principle not dependent on theory, but confirmed by our experience in examining more than two hundred color-blind; and we may extend it beyond the limits we have here kept, — in other words, to the majority of cases also of *incomplete* or *partial* color-blindness.

"That the situation of the color-blind in respect to signals may be thoroughly understood, we must here add a few important words on the point. What is the intensity of light? Strictly speaking, it is nothing but the force of the impression of the light which our eye receives. This, however, is dependent on two factors, — one, the quantity of light radiating from the object observed or reflected by it; the other, the strength or amount to which the eye re-acts to this, or, in other words, the sensibility of the subjected visual sense. We may readily understand that both of these factors are extremely variable under the circumstances of the engineer's service. The amount of light which comes to his eye depends naturally on the amount reflected from the colored object, or which, for example, radiates from a railroad-lantern. It is very evident that this quantity may vary from many causes, such as the nature of the illuminating material and the wick, the coloring matter of the glass, its thickness, the peculiar property of the glass, &c. If a little moisture or smoke, vapor, ice, snow, &c., adheres to the glass, the lantern is less luminous. A lantern illuminates differently in clear from what it does in foggy weather. All this may give rise to mistakes. But, on the other hand, the sensibility of the eye differs greatly under different circumstances. The nervous apparatus of the eye may, like all other parts of the system, vary in its sensitiveness. The same light is brighter to a healthy eye in repose than to an eye fatigued and weakened. Every modification of the intensity of the light is, however, for the color-blind *a change in color.* From this we may judge how little dependence can be placed upon a recognition of the signals which the color-blind gain from exercise.

"Hence, if we admit among a large number of color-blind an extraordinary faculty gained by the exercise of the eye with different degrees of intensity of light, we must equally deny that this is sufficient for the security of the roads, as we cannot be assured of all the lantern-flames being of the same strength; all the glass of the same kind, of the same thickness, purity of color, allowing the radiation of the same quantity of light; and, finally, of the eyes of the employés being always at rest to the same degree, this being practically impossible. No person in his senses would deliberately trust his life in the hands of an engineer who could only distinguish the signals by the difference in the intensity of the light. Ask any superior official of a road if he would be willing to take charge of and run a locomotive, assuming the responsibility, when uncolored signals alone were permitted, and a feeble light meant '*danger*,' a medium one '*attention or caution*,' and a strong one '*road clear*.' If he says no, tell him that these are just the conditions under which every color-blind engineer has performed his duties. The absurdity is evident at once.

"The aid an engineer can expect from those within his reach is as little to be depended on as the intensity of the light, especially as he himself is directed to observe the signals, and is responsible for what happens. Without noticing all the possible cases when he may at the moment of danger find himself without help, it will suffice to mention but a single one; namely, when his neighbors are also color-blind like himself.

"To sum up: we may grant that a number of circumstances concur in rendering railroad accidents from color-blindness of the *personnel* relatively rare, even when no measures have been taken to avoid them, and experience has fortunately confirmed this opinion; but, on the other hand, it is self-evident that such accidents may happen sometimes. Here also experience testifies; and there are probably many more accidents due to this cause than those proved to have so occurred. Under these circumstances it is the absolute duty of railroad managements and maritime authorities to look to it that no measure which can aid in avoiding the possibility of these accidents shall be neglected, and to do all in their power to guard the lines of communication in the land and on the sea against all the dangers which menace them."

Direct testimony on these points is of so much value, that I quote from Dr. Magnus, who says, —

"I knew an engineer who was red-blind. Red and green were absolutely undistinguishable to him; yet he could tell the red from the green signal, from having cultivated his perception of the difference in the intensity of the light. However valuable this capacity may be for the individual color-blind, there is danger in it. It may happen — and, no doubt, often does — that the color-blind, by the cultivation of their power of appreciating varying intensities of light, conceal their defect, and induce their surroundings to suppose that they are normal-eyed. But this cultivated power of distinguishing the lights by difference of intensity must always be a very unsafe artifice, which succeeds a hundred times to fail the hundred and first. It is, therefore, a very critical thing for a color-blind railroad employé — for instance, an engineer — to be able to conceal his defect for any length of time. So long as he does, so long are the trains in danger under his control; for how readily may his artifice fail him by which *alone* he distinguishes the red and green signal-lanterns from each other! Only the most careful examination of all railroad employés can protect the public, which, thanks to our railroad authorities, is now conducted on all the German lines."

Dr. Minder, in Berne, reports among his cases that of "a very intelligent young man who was red-blind, but was not aware of it. He held the position first of fireman, and then of engineer, on one of the Swiss roads. He was hardly at work before his defect troubled him. Thinking it was due to the spirit he drank, he stopped this for a while; but, the trouble continuing, he became convinced that 'something was wrong with him about the colors,' and left the distinguishing the signals to his normal-eyed assistant. When another man took this assistant's place, — who also seems to have been color-blind, — the work began to be 'uncomfortable.' As our red-blind engineer now had no control by his side, and very frequently was mistaken in his decision, there occurred a series of mistakes, fortunately only whilst manœuvring in the stations, which brought him occasional fines and other disagreeable consequences.

"The red signal-lantern gave him the most trouble, because, as he said, he could only distinguish it when so near with his engine as not to be able to stop, and hence run by it. He did better with the green signal; and, when asked why, replied, 'Because it was brighter.' To the question how, then, could he tell the green signal from white, he, in a roundabout way, compared green to weak white; and stated, that, with a lantern of white glass, he could, by screwing up and down the wick, and thereby changing the amount of the light, himself imitate the usual railroad-signals. Very bright light was white; very weak light, red; medium intensity, green, — quite corresponding to Holmgren's statements based on theory. The seeming impossibility of his power of distinguishing being dependent on the amount or intensity of the light, induced me to search farther, and ascertain what a complete color-blind understood by pure white. I found for this, also, much greater color-sense than the normal-eyed possess. A whole series of color-blind were expressly asked to select only the purest white. Of worsteds and papers they picked out, besides the white, several shades of bright green, gray, pure gray and dirty gray, light rose, and very light violet.

"The possibility that a color-blind may, through his life, under favorable circumstances, remain undiscovered, and as engineer or switchman perform his duty, cannot be denied. That the filling such posts by the color-blind, however, is a constant source of danger, can be readily understood. For instance: a white lantern exposed to the weather by snow or rain, by the absorption of light from the dimmed glass, may appear green to a color-blind who depends upon the intensity of the light alone. So also a green light may give the impression of a red one. By the accidental use of thicker or darker green glass, or thinner and brighter red glass, the difference in the intensity of the light may also be destroyed; and hence arise all the conditions for the occurrence of dangerous mistakes."

There is a point in reference to steam worth mentioning here, — viz., its varying color; and hence its possibility of causing mistakes. Professor Forbes, in 1839, noticed the sun, through a column of steam from the safety-valve of an engine on the Greenwich Railway, of a deep orange-red color. This he again noticed on the Newcastle and Carlisle road, and it induced him to experiment with white lantern-light seen through escaping steam. It appeared red under certain pressure of the steam, and also green or violet under other pressure. Mr. R. Phillips, in 1852, followed this up, and found that the transmitted light was red; and the reflected, blue. As to this, Professor Wilson well remarks, "Now it must often fall to the lot of engine-drivers to watch lamps through such an atmosphere, which will convert the (white) safety-signal into a danger-signal, completely alter the color of the (green) caution-signal, and so darken the aspect of the (red) danger-signal as to render it invisible."

To the even very slightly color-blind this will be intensified, and to the completely color-blind his only means of distinguishing the signals will be gone; viz., the difference in the intensity of the light.

One of the dangers from color-blindness on our railroads arises from the supposed cure or palliation of it by exercise of the *personnel* with the colored signals, &c. Upon this latter point I dwelt when discussing the incurability of congenital color-blindness. It becomes therefore necessary to here criticise Dr. Favre's ideas and proposals in reference to such exercise. The whole matter, however, is put so practically by Professor Holmgren, and is of such importance, especially in this country, that I shall quote from him. In his criticism of Dr. Favre's ideas, after speaking of the various ways the color-blind supplement their defect, he says, —

"The color-blind railway employé has always a certain assistance at his disposal in distinguishing the flags by day: for he sees not only the flags, but also the person who holds them; a green grass-plot, a tree, a house,—in short, objects whose color-name he already knows. The importance of this is the greater from what we know of the value of comparison in the use of our other senses, and hence, also, of our color-perception.

"From this it might be judged that it was a matter of indifference whether the color-blind could be cured by exercise with colors or not, so long as they can by other means distinguish the signals. We admit they are thus by day less liable to mistake them; but we cannot grant more. The color-blind can, however, never be *sure*, since they can never calculate beforehand all the circumstances leading to mistakes. Sunlight on a green flag, with the surroundings in the shade, makes it appear red to them; or, what is worse, the red flag on a bright day, when in the shade and the surroundings bright, will appear green.

"The condition is much worse with night service. No comparison is then possible. Only the light itself is now visible; and what adds to the difficulty of distinguishing the color of a lantern as compared with distinguishing a colored surface, is our accustomed way of using our senses. In fact, we do not take cognizance of the action of our sense. We do not ever think of the light radiating from or reflected by the object: we rather refer all these to the object itself, and regard them as inseparable attributes of it. We recognize the light of the lantern, without thinking of the material on which it depends. We do not see the lantern or the flame burning in it, but only the light which has neither the form of the lantern or the flame, but is isolated and immaterial in the air. Now the color-blind must distinguish whether this is strong (colorless), medium (green), or weak (red). This is asking more of the human eye than it can do with certainty."

"The color-blind are therefore more often mistaken in distinguishing colored lights than colored surfaces. If we show them one of the lanterns, they cannot distinguish it, unless previously practised. Showing them the red and green together, or in rapid succession, they generally distinguish these from each other; and, if we tell them the names, they remember and call them correctly. The red-blind find that the red of the signal-lantern, such as used on the

Swedish roads, is darker (that is, weaker in light) than the green. The latter, however, seemed to them darker than the common yellow light. The green-blind, on the other hand, find that the green light is weaker (that is, darker) than the red. With the next opportunity these color-blind find the same. Railroad employés are therefore rather more sure; yet much is dependent on the special lanterns used. One familiar with the nature of color-blindness will do better to use lanterns with different glass from that commonly employed, when desirous of exhibiting the precise character of this defect. Let him take one with a thin pale-red glass, and another with thick dark-green glass. The color-blind will then readily take the green light for red, and red for green or colorless. If the glass of the green light is smoked, he will take it for red. Cover the colorless light with steam or dew, and it appears to him green. Or let one do as I, — namely, have lanterns, the glasses of which are prepared for this purpose, and differ from each other, some having colorless or so-called smoked glass of varying absorptive power, — and they will quickly be convinced that the color-blind is guided in his decision *solely by the intensity of the light.*

"Another circumstance assists the color-blind in telling the lantern's light at a distance, which is also dependent on the intensity of the light, though this connection is not at once seen. It is the varying way in which the light radiates outwards. This radiation is most intense with the ordinary lantern, since this is the brightest (strongest in light); whilst, when the lantern-light is weak (red or green), the radiation is very little or nothing. A color-blind railroad employé told me he thus distinguished the signals. It need be hardly said how unsafe this is."

"We see, therefore, that practice is of no avail for the color-blind. Otherwise an employé, who has had daily exercise with the colored lanterns for a series of years, would have been cured of his defect. A pretty wide experience has, however, shown us that *not one of the many color-blind we have examined stood the test.* We must confess that a large number, from constant practice, had attained extraordinary facility, and frequently told the colors correctly."

"As a proof that comparison plays such a strong part, it

is often necessary to make special choice of the particular lanterns for the test. If we use the ordinary lanterns, the color-blind will only make mistakes at the commencement. If they see all the three lantern-lights together, they are deceived much more seldom. A colorless glass, with moisture on the surface, will at first be readily taken for green; a smoked green glass, for red."

There is another peculiar danger on railroads. A mixture of the two complementary colors, red and green, necessarily employed, produce white light. This, of course, does not affect the color-blind in the same way as the normal-eyed; yet it adds to their confusion. The law of the mixture was naturally well-known; but Mr. W. H. Tyndal, in 1853, first, I think, called attention to its very practical bearing. He says, —

"Now, we have this curious fact, that on the railways the union of the two colors — the primary *red* to indicate danger, and the secondary *green* to denote caution — together makes white, the signal for entire safety. This, perhaps, does not practically appear in experiment, when the mind is on the alert to distinguish between the two colors. If the rays from a green lamp, such as are used on railways, are thrown upon a white board, and those from a red lamp are directed to the same spot, — the distance of the two lamps from the board being equal, — the red rays, though rendered paler, predominate. There is, in fact, too much red. But the red lamp may be removed so much farther from the board than the green one as to allow the green rays to predominate; and there must be a point of distance where neither color would predominate, and at which the mixture of the rays on the board would be white. I recently made an experiment on one of the metropolitan railways with a green and a red signal-lamp. A man was stationed at the end of a tunnel, about four hundred yards long, and directed to wave the two lights together. The pointsman at the other end, not knowing any thing of the nature of the experiment, was asked what light was waved. He was satisfied it was white, and could not be persuaded that two lights — a red and a green — were really used, although the matter was afterwards explained to him. Now, it may sometimes happen that, in rapid travelling, the rays from a red lamp and a green one shall flash together across the sight of an engine-driver; or the unsteady motion of an engine may render the driver unable to see distinctly and separately two signals of different colors, the rays from which may fall upon his eye in parallel lines. In either case it is not improbable that the light might be regarded by him as white. A light may be discerned without the color of it being distinctly seen. In such case it would most likely be regarded as white, — that being the most common. It is not improbable that some of the accidents which have occurred in railway travelling have arisen from the colors of the lights shown being indistinctly seen; perhaps from a confusion of rays from two or more lamps. In some cases most contradictory evidence has been given as to the color of the signal shown. The subject is perhaps worthy of the attention of railway engineers."

The following is an interesting proof of how a shrewd observer may, from lack of knowledge of the peculiar condition above explained of the color-blind's perception, fail to explain cases presented to him: —

Mr. Thomas Nelson, an optician in Chicago, Ill., in an article in "The Chicago Railway Review" of March 30, 1878, says, —

"I have kept records of various accidents that have occurred, both upon land and water during the past few years; and I have gathered such information about some of them as I could get outside of official sources. Often I was unable to get any of any value; but I am convinced beyond a doubt that a large proportion of them could have been traced to color-blindness for a correct solution as to the primary causes of the accident. The query has been made, that if these defects in their various forms are as numerous and of such a dangerous character as has been shown, how can we account for such a comparatively small number of accidents occurring which might be charged to them? I have attributed it to the high average intelligence and acquired cautiousness of engineers and pilots as a class. They have become so accustomed to be on the lookout for danger, that their suspicions are easily aroused, which creates a sort of instinct that governs their actions, and they do not recognize but that their perceptions are correct. My convictions in this respect have been greatly strengthened within the past few months, there having been related to me some experience with an engineer, who was continually making narrow escapes; and, after watching his actions under different circumstances for a time, color-blindness was suspected, proved, and afterward acknowledged by him. The correctness with which he formed conclusions under the existing circumstances would indicate that he had some means by which he was enabled to form a plan of action; but he declared that he had nothing upon which to base his actions but the cautiousness acquired in that branch of service."

The means he had to assist him were of course the to him varying intensity of the light, when red, green, or white. This is an interesting proof of how totally unaware a color-blind may be of the *way* he supplements his chromatic defect, as also how he may escape detection.

CHAPTER XV.

DANGERS FROM COLOR-BLINDNESS ON THE OCEAN.

IF we turn now from the land to the sea, we shall find the dangers from color-blindness as great, or even greater. The largest majority of those color-blind are so for red and green. These, however, are the colors necessarily chosen by all nations to be by law carried on the two sides of all vessels from sunset to sunrise, — the green light on the starboard side, and the red light on the port side. These are so arranged that they can only both be seen when the vessel is directly ahead, and far enough off to allow us to see both sides. These lights show us, therefore, the position and the direction of motion of a vessel. Mistaking their color will of course be most disastrous.

Dr. Romberg has classified the reports of some maritime accidents from 1859 to 1866. They number 2,408.

Want of skill, or carelessness, of the ship *personnel*, or the accidents which it was impossible to prevent or avoid	1,562
Error of the pilot or captain	215
Want of observation or proper interpretation of the rules of the way	537
Undetermined causes	94

Under the last three heads, in the large number of 846, there are probably some attributable to color-blindness. They all are not accidents from carelessness or want of skill; for those are included in another series.

M. Léonce Raynaud and M. Degram have demonstrated the effect of fog on the color of lights. Fog or mist makes white lights reddish. In thick weather green lights appear white. A sailing-master meets a green light rendered pale by a thick night: in whatever amount he is color-blind, in that degree will the light appear white to him, causing most dangerous hesitation; or, even if convinced he has not a green light ahead of him, he manœuvres as if it were a *red* one. Color-blindness may therefore well be considered as one of the causes of collision at sea. This imperfection may, however, occasion the loss of a vessel in another way: I mean in the recognition of lights on the coast, &c. Dr. Feris reports three cases of such mistake from the "Annales du Sauvetage Maritime," vol. iii., 1873. He says,—

"If color-blindness is considered a grave danger on railroads, how much more on the sea! Colors are very important to the mariner: the flags, the side-lights, and even the lighthouses and buoys and beacons, present various colors. It is impossible for a helmsman or a signalman to interpret or transmit signals if they have no appreciation of color. Errors with flag-signals are not so likely on board of vessels, as they are employed in daylight, and more often controlled by officers in charge. But the men at telegraph-stations are often alone, not under observation, and hence more likely to make mistakes. National flags may be mistaken, but more especially the white, red, and green Bengal lights used as night-signals. . . . If good color-perception is necessary for a helmsman, how much more for the commander of a vessel!

The increase of collisions at sea is an indisputable fact. How many remain unexplained, or referred to another cause, which are no doubt due to the color-blindness of a single man!"

The testing for color-blindness has already commenced in the navies of Prussia, Russia, Norway, Sweden, Denmark, and Austria. My friend, Dr. Ed. Hansen of Copenhagen, writes me, June, 1877, —

"I have had the opportunity of examining a large number of the individuals who enter the royal navy: I hope some day to be able to give you some statistical information on this point, if you still take an interest in it."

Professor Holmgren reports as to the examination of 4,225 Swedish sailors, finding 94 (or 2.22 per cent) color-blind.

Dr. Lederer was appointed by the medical department of the Austrian navy to test sailors at the naval station at Pola. He examined of the sailors at the station and on the artillery schoolship "Adria" 1,312, finding 63 (or 4.8 per cent) color-blind. There has been some misunderstanding as to his report due to his employment of Stilling's cards and pieces of colored glass and paper, instead of Holmgren's infinitely more sure and ready method with the worsteds.

Dr. Feris of the French navy found, among 501 officers and men, 47 "who presented in varying degrees an alteration of the chromatic sense." Their ages were between seventeen and fifty years.

Dr. Favre, in France, records the examination of 1,050 men for the navy or lighthouse department, and finding 61 (or 5.8 per cent) more or less color-blind. In discussing the question, he also makes some remarks in reference to the loss of the French steamer "Ville du Havre" by collision with an English sailing-vessel. This fearful accident most painfully interested us Bostonians, since so many were lost from our midst in that ill-fated vessel. I have frequently expressed in private my own suspicions that the accident may have been caused by color-blindness; but I will here simply quote Dr. Favre:—

"After the loss of the 'Ville du Havre,' the newspapers which described the collision stated most positively that the green light was not recognized in time. If the steamer's officers and crew, who should have seen the signal-light, were never tested for color-blindness, there is one chance in twenty that the officer or sailor whose duty it was could not distinguish *green*, and one in seventy-five that he would confound this color with *red*. We know how the matter ended. The English admiralty decided that the English vessel was free from all blame, and the French admiralty declared that the French vessel could not be in any way criminated. No one thought of attributing the mistake to the very probable one of color-blindness."

I lately had curious proof of the color-blindness of a sea-captain, who, I understand, has now retired from active service. He was in the habit of working worsteds to while away the monotony of a sea-voyage. These worsteds, however, always had to be picked out for him, and the colors marked, to avoid his making mistakes.

Dr. Daae of Kragerö, Norway, in a lecture on color-blindness, given April 10, 1878, before the Medical Society of Christiana, says,—

"We must admit that the possibility of confounding the signal-lanterns in general is not so great on the railroads as on the sea. On the roads the glass of the lanterns, at least within the limits of each country, has a somewhat definite red or green color, which even those quite color-blind learn to distinguish by the difference in the intensity of the light. The signals, moreover, come at stated times and places, so that it is known where they are to be expected; and thus they can be seen and distinguished at leisure, as it were. Not so on the ocean. In the lanterns of the various vessels the color of the green or red glass varies considerably. The green glass varies also more in intensity than tone. Now let us suppose no signal-light has been seen for some little time, when suddenly a red or green one appears, and but one. The question is then, Is this a red or green light? The vessels are close, and instant decision is necessary. Or several lights are seen, and the ship we are in is sailing before the wind, and hence bound to keep out of the way. Most old sailors can remember cases where those on board were not agreed as to the color of a lantern.

"But how can having rules for the marine of one country only be of avail? On the ocean vessels from all parts of the world pass each other. When two vessels meet, it will help but little if the officers and crew of but one vessel have normal color-perception. If there are color-blind on the other vessel, collision may occur.

"As to the railroads, it is not of such importance that the requirements as to color-blindness should be the same in all countries. If one country has one set of regulations, and another a different one, whilst the third requires no examination, it concerns only the individual country itself. But, as to the marine, it is necessary to have an international law."

The test for color-blindness now being so simple as to be readily carried out by the surgeons attached to vessels, especially naval medical officers, there can be no great difficulty in having an international commission meet, and frame the laws which shall govern all the navies and merchant-marine of the great maritime nations at least. It would then be as readily recognized that every officer and man must be as able to perfectly distinguish the red and green lights as to know where they belong, and what they mean.

CHAPTER XVI.

CAN THE RAILROAD AND MARINE SIGNALS BE CHANGED?

I HAVE given the statistics of the frequency of color-blindness in Europe from many observers, and in this country from my own tests. Its frequency, also, among railroad employés and sailors has been proved by European research; unfortunately not yet in the United States. I do not think any one will now doubt that from two to five per cent of the men absolutely daily employed on the railroads in this country are probably color-blind. This granted, we are at once asked, Why not, then, use some other colors besides red and green? and, when this is answered, why not use *form* instead of color, or the grouping of several white lights, &c.?

I was long ago convinced theoretically of the possibility of substituting form for color by day on the switches, and equally of the *impossibility* of substituting any other colors for red and green as night-signals. Experiment and observation have now convinced me practically that the railroads *can* use form instead of color by day, and can *not* substitute form for color by night. Red and green are the colors which we must select as being most in contrast, and also for many practical reasons in reference to the glass, &c. This I have repeatedly shown at scientific societies. Experiment also has proved to me that red and green must be used as night-signals on the sides of vessels. This matter is, however, too important for me to simply give my own unsupported opinion. A color-blind has gravely discussed with me the necessity of changing the signals to meet his difficulty, saying, "It was not right to throw a man out of his employment for a congenital defect, incurable." We have no better authority than Professor Holmgren, who explains and discusses this question of other colors or form, &c., so thoroughly and so practically, that I must quote his remarks *verbatim*. As to the modification of the signal system, he says, —

"If congenital color-blindness is incurable, — or at least if we know no actual remedy for it, — it is necessary to devise some other method (while retaining the color-blind in the employment of railways) of guaranteeing the communications against any mistakes they might commit with regard to signals. It is seen by what precedes that these errors can and must occur in the use of the signal-colors generally adopted, — *red*, *green* (and *yellow*). The color-blind has only two primitive colors; whilst the normal-eyed, according to the Young-Helmholtz theory, has three. But the usual railroad signal-colors are just those primitive ones which neither the red nor the green blind can perceive. This choice seems therefore unfortunate. Wilson is of the same opinion. If red and green color-blindness are the kinds of complete or partial blindness which are most generally seen, it would seem that the difficulty might be considerably diminished, if, in place of using the actual colors, those should be selected best suited to these kinds of color-blindness, although they might not suit the third kind of partial color-blindness, or violet-blindness, which, according to the experience acquired up to the present time, relatively very seldom occurs.

"Undoubtedly the principle we have endeavored to establish would not be radically enforced; but the practical result at least would be comparatively nearly accomplished. As the color-blind has but two principal colors, or two classes to which he can refer all the colors, it is evident, that, to select two colors that he can recognize and distinguish without the least hesitation, it would be necessary to select one from each class. In this way it is always possible to bear in mind that each kind of color-blindness will always be able to find two colors distinctly defined, but not more than two. It is therefore necessary, first, to ask how far two colors for signals could satisfy the demands of railways and the navy. As regards railways, it is claimed, and it may be conceded, that in case of necessity, and perhaps without too great inconvenience, two colors might be made to answer. It is certain that three colors are a great improvement upon two.

"It is scarcely necessary to discuss this point, since it is only with railroad-signals as with all other signs of communication, — the more numerous they are, the more serviceable are they, and the more complete can be the communications they give. The color-sense is the best proof of this; for certainly the normal-eyed, with three principal colors, has a more complete and acute impression from the manifold colors of the external world than the color-blind who has but two fundamental colors.

"Let us admit, however, that two colors would answer, and that it were desired to sacrifice the advantage of three colors for another advantage, — namely, that of retaining in the service of railways the color-blind: there will still remain the necessity of making a good selection of these two colors. This is more easily said than done. The choice must be so made that one color may be selected from each of the two groups in which all the colors are classed according to the system for the color-blind. Now, it is found, as we have already seen in the instances of the principal colors of the red and green blind, that, amongst the seven colors of the rainbow perceptible to the normal observer, four — namely, red, orange, yellow, and green — belong to one class, and three — especially blue, indigo, and violet — to the second. Consequently, one of the colors must be red, orange, yellow, or green; and the other, blue, indigo, or violet. It should very naturally be our object to give the preference in the selection to the colors which most strongly affect the eye at the time of the comparison. Now, the most intense colors of the spectrum — that is to say, the most vivid colors which enter into the white light of the sun — are yellow and blue, one of each of the two groups. We then select them, the more willingly that the light of the lantern is, without any preparation and to a very high degree, yellow, though it is not homogeneous. But we are far from being so fortunate with regard to blue. We here encounter a difficulty, on the contrary, which induces us to doubt whether a change of colors will accomplish the desired end.

"On all colored surfaces — flags, paintings, semaphores, &c. — employed by railways to reflect during the day the sunlight or daylight, the proposed colors answer perfectly without any doubt, and, in all probability, no color-blind individual of the kinds specified would nominally make mistakes of judgment. But the night-signals are quite another matter, and are by far more important for many reasons. This is, therefore, why we prefer to attach here so much importance to them, as during the day a multitude of different circumstances might give warning of danger, while during the night the colored light is the only signal which indicates it.

"The colored lights used for night-signals are made, as all know, by placing colored glass before the flame of a lantern. The use of Bengal lights as regular signals could scarcely be introduced into practice. Now, a colored glass produces a colored light, because, of all the kinds of light radiated from the flame, but one kind (or at least mainly one kind) is allowed to escape, while all the others, or a greater part of the others, are absorbed by the glass. Thus blue glass, according to its thickness or degree of coloring, absorbs all the other kinds of light emitted by the flame of the lantern, allowing only the blue rays to escape. But, unfortunately, as is well known by direct experience, the flame of the lantern emits comparatively but a small amount of blue light when rape-seed oil and photogene, or generally any of our ordinary sources of artificial light, are employed; and this is why all appear yellow or red when compared with the light of day. Under such circumstances blue glass can naturally transmit only a small amount of blue light; and the light of a blue lantern must, consequently, always be very feebly luminous.

"Of course the intensity of the light will greatly depend on the thickness of the glass. But what is gained in intensity by a thin glass is lost in color; for, whilst thin glass increases the intensity, through it will pass, besides the fewer blue rays, also the red and green. Hence the blue rays become, in an inverse ratio to the thickness of the glass, more like those from an ordinary lantern, and therefore, to a certain degree, white light. The light is in consequence very weak, since only enough red and green light passes through the glass to balance the blue rays.

"What we have just said of blue applies equally to indigo and violet. The proposed changes of the colors of signals furnishes, therefore, but two colors in place of three; and then one is a very feeble light, so that it is difficult to see it far off when sufficiently colored. This state of things scarcely holds out much inducement to introduce a reform of this nature. And it seems the more dangerous that this change of colors in the signals would cause those with normal sight amongst the *personnel* to run the same risk that the really color-blind do: I mean that they would be forced tô distinguish and judge the night-signals alone by the intensity of the light. The safety of the service, as we have shown, would gain nothing, and it would be difficult to find a conscientious man desirous of continuing his work under these circumstances. Such a reform in behalf of the color-blind would, *de facto*, shut out a much larger number of normal-eyed.

"We have heard that blue lights are used on the American roads. This we are not able to deny, but must first be assured that all the American employés can distinguish the signals there used, and then learn all the details of the railroad accidents which have happened in that country.

"The result of all that we have just said is, it seems to us, that the proposed change of the signal colors is not very practical, and such would be the case with any other choice of two colors. It must at least be conceded that the new signal-colors would be to every normal observer worse than those now in use with us, as with nearly all nations: in brief, if they were adopted, it would diminish the public safety. We must add, that, by adopting them, the principle we have explained is not taken into consideration, according to which it is necessary to use a system of signals adapted to all kinds of color-blindness, since the violet-blind are not able to distinguish between yellow and blue. The proposed change should therefore be rejected, it seems to us, on every practical consideration.

"(2d) *Colorless Light and Darkness, Black and White.* — It has been seen that it is impossible to hope for colored signals suiting every one, color-blind or not. It becomes necessary, therefore, to try to devise a plan for establishing a system of signals independent of colors, and based upon the introduction of a colorless light of different degrees of intensity. We have already discussed the most important of the points in reference to the intensity of light. While there is nothing more sensible to our sight than the relative intensity of two lights placed side by side (when the absolute intensity does not exceed certain limits), in the present case the only comparison involved is made from memory, so to speak, which is equivalent almost to an appreciation of the absolute intensity of light. We are so far from being able to judge of this, that, in spite of a deeply felt need and constant efforts, science even has not succeeded in discovering suitable measures to apply to it.

"It is, however, necessary to acknowledge here that a system of signals based only on two extremes of intensity of light — namely, on light and darkness, white and black — ought to suit the normal observer as well as the color-blind. Moreover, such a system ought to satisfy all exigencies, provided it is practically applied, and that two signals only are sufficient. A white and black flag, &c., would fully suffice during the day: but such would unfortunately not be the case at night; for a black light is a contradiction of terms, and it would be necessary, consequently, according to this system, for the night, when signals are of the greatest importance, to be limited not to three, but to one signal only, unless the absence of all signals could be considered as one. Here it might be well asked, whether the better system is not that which is based on the alternations of darkness and light; that is, movable signals or eclipsed signal-lights. But we will not enter a field unfamiliar to us. We cannot, however, but have a sensation of dread at recalling the various artificial means railroad management would have to depend upon for the purpose of retaining or accepting the color-blind in service. As far as we know, no system has yet been discovered, based upon the principles alluded to above, which could advantageously take the place of the one actually in use.

"(3d) *Form, Movement, Number.* — If we do not succeed in finding a suitable system of signals, based on the differences of the quality and quantity of light, there remains but to appeal to some arrangement in space, if absolutely limited to the visual sense.

"Of our other senses in reference to recognizing signals, we might, besides the eye, appeal to the ear. Both can receive impressions from a great distance. But for our purpose the ear is still less adapted than the eye; and the former can only be regarded as secondary for certain definite purposes, or at short distances. For example: in foggy weather the whistle and bell are used, &c. Many different ways suggest themselves of varying the signals by form and arrangement in space: large brilliant surfaces arranged in different forms; several small lights grouped in different positions with reference to each other; lights simply disposed, but differing in value as signals according to their number, or else illuminated figures of simple colors, and produced by different movements, and so on. A practical difficulty seems to be connected with such a system: the signals require the illuminated surfaces to be large enough, or placed at distances considerable enough between the luminous points, to appear distinctly afar off. Now, the larger such a figure, having the outlines marked with luminous points, the greater the risk that a portion of it be hidden by other objects intervening between it and the eye. These two inconveniences must be apparent, particularly if these surfaces and illuminated figures have to be placed at every point where colored lanterns are found; as, for example, on locomotives and cars. Moreover, it will be very difficult to place these signals at all points of the road where accidents may happen. These doubts are perhaps groundless, and possibly better not expressed, as being out of our range.

"It is rather our purpose to discuss this point generally, and examine it scientifically. We would say, therefore, that our eye can more readily detect difference in color than difference in form. The reason of this is very plain. The retina alone, of all the several parts of the eye, must be reached by the light, to give us a definite form or definite light. For the light to reach the retina, all parts of the eye in front of it must be transparent. When this alone is the case we can perceive the color of an object or a light; but if its *form* is to be appreciated, not only must the light reach the retina, but it must affect it strongly and definitely to give us a clear picture of the object. The difference, as we see, is great. The whole dioptric apparatus of the eye is necessary for the form of an object to be perceived, whilst such apparatus is superfluous for simply color-perception. The greater the number of the active agencies necessary to accomplish a certain work, the greater the sources of error in the accomplishment of such work. All organic diseases of the cornea, the crystalline lens, or the vitreous humor, hinder the perception of the form of an object, but not of its color. The advantage as respects color-perception from this is all the more when we remember that the most finished dioptric apparatus of the eye is relatively imperfect; and this imperfection is still further increased by many anomalies. What would a sailor do who had to determine the form of an illuminated object by the help of a poor spy-glass, the glasses of which were dirty, broken, or badly ground? Probably he could not do it; whereas he could decide the color of the light in spite of his poor instrument, which would simply reduce the brightness.

"If the system of signals were based upon form, and all persons discharged from the service of railways, who, in consequence of an imperfection of vision, could not clearly and decidedly distinguish these signals at a distance, the proportion of such would be larger than that of the color-blind. To form an idea of the different capacities of the normal eye in the various senses just mentioned, we will recommend a very simple experiment. Take something, — colored paper, for example; make some plain figures, such as letters, one of which must be attached vertically to a large black or white surface. To prevent any distraction from subjective influences, let some one else select and attach this letter, while the observer stands at such a distance, that, even with the eye directed toward it, but a single object can be seen. If the letters are small, it is not necessary that the distance should be very great. Then, if the symbol be slowly approached, with the eye fixed on the colored surface, the following observations in the order in which the different impressions succeed each other will be made: When the letter is first perceived, neither form nor color can be distinguished. Nothing is seen but a point or patch darker than the background, if that be white; or lighter, if it be black. The first attribute remarked, as the distance diminishes, is its color. When the color is very distinct, it is necessary to approach considerably nearer before the form is perceptible; that is to say, before this letter can be read, and its name given. This simple experiment clearly shows that the eye, as far as it is possible to compare its capacities in different directions, is first sensible to the relative intensity of light, then to color, and finally to form. It would be necessary, of course, to consider various circumstances relative to the choice of color, form, &c., if the experiment should be made with exactness to serve as a basis for a scientific demonstration. What we have said suffices, however, to point out what direction a reform in the signals should take, granting that any such change is desirable. If a signal system could be found and practically introduced which depended on light and dark, then it would be preferable to the present in use. If such fails, then we must consider the present as the most practical, because based not only on the principle of the difference in the quality of light, — that is to say, on color, — but also because just those colors have been chosen which practice has proved to be best suited for the purpose. Experience also seems to have decided in favor of this system; since, in spite of the substitutes proposed with a view to retain the color-blind, it has up to the present time maintained its ascendency, so to speak, throughout the entire world."

As I have already said, our very practical American people have gradually discarded the use of all but red and green lights on the railroads, with but few exceptions. On the sea, of course, the use of other than red and green signals is impossible.

CHAPTER XVII.

NECESSITY AND DIFFICULTY OF CONTROL.

ARE there no measures now taken in the United States to avoid danger from color-blindness? will here at once be asked of me. I would much like to have been able to report on the some two hundred railroads of the United States in respect to any examination of their employés as to color-blindness. It is, however, a *delicate* question. From what I have learned, I conclude that here and there railroad superintendents keep it in mind; and when, from accident or otherwise, suspicion is aroused in reference to an employé, the latter is tested by the superintendent with the flags or lanterns used on the road. This suffices. No medical man — and much less an expert — is called upon to decide. If, anywhere in this country, there is at this time any thing like a systematic test for color-blindness of the *personnel* of the road, I shall be agreeably surprised to learn it. There may be — but I do not know of any — salaried *railroad surgeons* in the United States, whose duty is wholly with the road, and who could learn to test for color-blindness. Even when a test of an employé has been reported to me as made, I have had no proof that it was not simply lack of good eyesight, and not lack of color-perception. I shall be only too happy to be corrected by the management if I am wrong in stating that the railroads of this country are not more protected from the danger of color-blindness than were the roads of Europe before the very recent successful systematic efforts on the part of those from whom I have quoted in this volume. I believe practically nothing is at present sure to protect the community in this respect.

In the merchant-marine service I very much doubt if it is any better. I have been told by naval officers that care is taken in this respect so far as to look out that the men make no mistakes as to the port and starboard lights; but I have not learned that any systematic scientific examination of the naval *personnel* is carried out by the surgeons of the navy. I believe I am right in saying this also of the army. But both army and navy surgeons are eminently qualified to learn and use the present methods of testing for color-blindness, the danger from which they can equally appreciate.

The government can, and no doubt soon will, carry out proper examinations for color-blindness in the army and navy. General national laws can also be enacted as to the merchant-marine; international will come in time as a matter of necessity. The difficulties with the railroads are, however, very great. Here the interests and safety of the community have to contend with ignorance, prejudice, pecuniary considerations, and incredulity born of supposed immunity from danger. These corporations have no surgeons attached to their roads, who, in their interests, could carry out proper examinations to both protect themselves and the community. Even when interest is awakened from acknowledged danger justly feared, railroad managers are very likely to turn to any one calling himself a medical man, and rely on his statement as to his ability to examine and pass judgment on their employés. Then, when they are satisfied from his reports that they are safe, and accident happens, color-blindness is proved in the employé before the court and jury, and at once undeserved miscredit is thrown upon the surety and usefulness of such examinations. It is therefore without hesitation that I would caution as to the choice of those to be engaged in testing railroad employés for color-blindness. The life-insurance companies of the country recognize this most thoroughly,— so much so, that examination for life-insurance is almost a specialty.

We can scarcely hope for such practical good results as were shown in Sweden, where, by the simple efforts of one scientific man, all the railroad employés of the country were in a few months tested, and laws to govern the future made and enforced; yet exactly the same is possible in this country as there. Either the state governments or the state railroad commissioners can require thorough examination of all employés for color-blindness, or the railroad managers can do it themselves. It is with some natural curiosity that the solution of the problem will be watched. In one of these ways this safeguard to travellers must come, since they will learn the danger they incur as quickly as the railroad corporations the danger they subject them to, not to speak of possible damages recoverable after an accident due to color-blindness. Not only must railroad employés and mariners have good eyesight, but they must be proved to have normal color-perception.

Professor Holmgren is at the head of the control in Sweden; and his practical knowledge and experience render, of course, all he says of great value to us about to commence this work here in the United States. He states as follows: —

"No half-way measures are allowable. All employés with defective chromatic vision must be removed from posts of danger. They should be required to distinguish the signals by their color as the normal-eyed can. The violet-blind may be allowed on the road. This defect is so rare as to be scarcely ever met with. There are, of course, positions on the road not requiring the reading the signals; but it is a bad plan not to be able to call on any employé in an emergency. Any method of testing for the elimination of the color-blind will be in place which is *tuto cito et jucunde,* the carrying out of which gives the best results in the quickest time, and is open to the smallest amount of difficulties and misunderstandings. It must not fail to detect a color-blind, or prove that an employé is normal-eyed. Whilst there must be no question of thoroughness, it is to be remembered there are hundreds to be examined, and but little time can be given to each individual. We cannot have heavy or costly apparatus to be transported. These points are to be considered in reference to any method."

"Testing should be only in the hands of those who understand it. On the roads and in the marine the surgeons have the scientific knowledge necessary to carry out examinations. On board ship the sailors could be at least roughly tested by the captain. There are cases where a specialist would need to be employed to decide whether color-blindness existed or not, as an ordinary surgeon would shrink from answering because not in position so to do. So, also, a specialist would be called upon to decide whether the defect was simulated."

"There is a difference to be made between those in, and those seeking, service. The latter we can have time for individually. The former, when a general examination is undertaken, requires from the numbers great care and decision. A thorough examination would seem to insure safety; but acquired color-blindness must be remembered. And if, as is claimed, color-blindness may grow better, it also may grow worse: hence the necessity of continued vigilance, and watching for cases from disease or injury, in addition to the thorough examination for all congenital cases. The possibility of an employé claiming to have been made color-blind by accident, after having been received into service and passed his color-test, is a matter also to be thought of. Color-blindness from railroad injury has been found by Dr. Favre for instance. The rights and claims of the road, or rather the public and the individual, are often nicely balanced, and great circumspection is necessary. Severe diseases like typhus, as well as injuries, and also the abuse of spirit and tobacco, cause color-blindness. Hence, after accidents, the *personnel* interested should be again tested, and always any drinking men or heavy smokers quite often looked after."

"After every railroad accident or collision at sea, dependent in whole or part on misunderstanding colored signals, not only must the men directly at fault be tested, but also all those used as witnesses. The necessity of this is self-evident. It would be absurd to punish any one because a blind man says he saw him break a rule, or let a man go free because a blind man says he saw him obey the rule. The same as to color-signals: no witness should be admitted who is not proved to be free from color-blindness. This is so plain that discussion of it seems useless; but it is not recognized by the guardians of the law. The whole question of color-blindness or not, when claimed or denied, must fall within the province and decision of the specialist alone."

"Granted now that tests are introduced, and thorough examinations carried out on our roads, what is to become of the color-blind? The defect, we know, exists in all degrees of severity. Whilst there will be no doubt of the necessity of dismissing the large majority, the decision as to the others can be determined by the examiner consulting with the management, and explaining the character and degree of the trouble. The possible danger of the incompletely color-blind being called upon to decide colors quickly, *must never be put out of sight*, and this *may occur whatever his position on the road.*"

"We would again repeat that it is the interest of the management, as well as of the public, to remove absolutely all difficulties and dangers arising from color-blindness. This end cannot be considered as attained so long as a single color-blind employé remains in service. When all color-blind are eliminated is the reform first commenced. It is no less necessary to carefully test periodically those with doubtful color-sense allowed to continue in service, to find if they are better, or worse; and these periodical examinations are necessary as long as any with but imperfect color-sense are retained, and the question remains undecided whether their defect on the one hand may improve or be cured, or, on the other, become worse or develop later."

"To settle positively these questions, periodical examinations must be made, 1st, of all with defective color-sense, once so proved; 2d, of those who have been injured; 3d, of the whole *personnel*, in order to detect any who have become color-blind without perceptible cause. How far these periodic tests should be carried out depends, of course, on how thoroughly the original examination has been, and how strict our laws of rejection have been."

"From what has been said, we see the absolute necessity of the government and railroad administration being thoroughly acquainted with the color-sense of their employés, and the thorough testing and elimination of all color-blind, as also the preventing the admission of any such hereafter into service. Whatever stand-point is taken, there rests the very serious importance of the strictest examination of the entire *personnel*. To carry such out with success, it is of course, first of all, necessary to have a practical method of testing that fulfils its purpose in every possible direction. We lay all the more stress on this point, since we believe that it has been principally the want of such a method of testing which has hitherto prevented the reform desired and urged by us."

CHAPTER XVIII.

METHODS OF TESTING FOR COLOR-BLINDNESS.

Trusting that by this time my readers are convinced of the necessity of testing all railroad employés and the marine *personnel*, we can now turn to the question of the test itself. On this, of course, depends our certainty in detecting and eliminating the color-blind. The whole recent widespread control of the chromatic defect on land and sea in Europe has come undoubtedly from Professor Holmgren having introduced a test for color-blindness, so simple, so perfect, and so applicable to the desired purpose, as to render its use imperative, and its success a matter of necessity. My readers, I think, will understand the subject better from hearing what he has to say, as they have already seen from my numerous quotations from him. As professor of physiology, and from an extended acquaintance with the color-blind and great experience in testing for the defect, just what he has to say in his recent work as to methods is here most valuable. And I introduce it all the more willingly, as my own personal experience as well as that of many others entirely convinces me of his correctness, shrewdness, and practical knowledge. He says, —

"It has been shown that color-blindness, different as it is from the normal color-sense, cannot so readily be detected as might be supposed. We must, in fact, regard it as one of the peculiarities of the defect, resulting from conditions already discussed, that it so often escapes detection.

"As the true nature of color-blindness became known, and the peculiarities of the persons so afflicted recognized, various methods were devised for its diagnosis. There are already several which vary either in the principle on which they are based, or in the application of that principle. These are two important points, and any error affecting either of them must necessarily lead to a false deduction. Moreover, if a method fulfils both of these calls upon it, yet it must also have still other qualities, such as we may fairly require of any practical means of examination which is to assist us to our desired end. It must, namely, be reliable, and of quick and ready application.

"The great majority of people are inclined to believe that the best method of testing the railroad *personnel* for color-blindness would be the use of the signals employed, — namely, the lanterns and flags, — as being the most direct, easiest, and suitable. This, to every practical man who has made no special study of color-blindness, is so obvious as to be a recognized fact. Any control which we are here concerned with has only the aim of preventing the mistaking the signals by the responsible *personnel*. What more simple, is asked with seeming right, than to be assured that the railroad employés can distinguish the signals? What other method can quicker bring us to our desired end? and how can we reach it more readily, since these signals are in use on all railroads? At first sight it would seem as if there was no answer to this, and that we must regard any control as sufficient which proved that all the *personnel* could distinguish the colors of the signals. But there is another condition necessary. The examination must not only prove that the men are able to distinguish one, two, or any definite number of lanterns and flags, so or so often, but that they can distinguish all flags and all lanterns under every condition; in a word, that their color-sense is as normal as we have a right to demand. We do not deny that any one thoroughly familiar with color-blindness and its practical detection may successfully use this method with the lanterns; but it is tedious, inconvenient, and of itself gives no certain result. Paradoxical as this may sound, we shall have to confess that such a method is inadmissible, from many well-grounded reasons. It is therefore our duty to substantiate this objection, especially as this method seemingly answers its purpose, whilst in reality it quite defeats it.

"The railroad signal-colors ordered are red and green, without special *nuances* of the colors being designated. This latter, fortunately, is not insisted on, as the railroad managers could not comply with it, since the colors vary in shade, or *nuance*, from many causes. It will be conceded that the *personnel* must be able to distinguish, not only the most commonly used shades, but they also should be able to clearly see red and green colors in general. This is not difficult for the normal-eyed, but simply impossible for the color-blind. It may be proved by testing the color-blind with selected lanterns; but even then the method will be found very inconvenient. The color-blind, as has been shown, acquire from practice a peculiar capacity for distinguishing colored signals. How and what this is has been explained, and that their seeing the colored signals is based only on conjecture. Testing, therefore, with lanterns becomes but a hazard between the examiner and examined, where the latter may readily often win, and where the former bears all the loss if the examined afterwards fails but once. Of course the examiner is sure to win if the play is continued long enough; for, if we know beforehand the examined is color-blind, we can, sooner or later, cause him to make a mistake as to the color of the lanterns. But if we do not know that he is color-blind, and are testing him to decide this, then we shall soon find how unadapted this method is, and how unpractical. Naturally much depends upon just how it is employed. For instance, let us suppose that the usual colored lights are shown to the examined, one after the other, and he is asked their color or meaning, whilst from his answer his color-sense is to be decided on. Now, as we have already shown, the color-blind *may* decide rightly; but we need hardly add that the normal-eyed may fail from carelessness, inattention, or even from *lapsus linguæ*. Hence a color-blind is passed as normal, and the reverse: so in this form the method is not practical. To attain certainty the test must be continued, and repeated till the examined's color-sense admits of no doubt. But how often must we repeat in order to be sure? How often must mistakes be made to prove color-blindness? or how often may they be made, and the defect still be considered not present? It is of course impossible to decide these questions. Certainty naturally increases with the number of trials: but the method is still untrustworthy; and it is depending too much on the knowledge and experience of the examiner in reference to color-blindness to expect a decision from him based on such tests. This method of testing with railroad-lanterns takes, of course, even if supposed sure, a great deal of time, and therefore is inconvenient and unpractical in the examination of hundreds of persons at once. The method is also inconvenient as, from the principle it involves, — namely, the detecting the color-sense of the *personnel* by the objects their duty requires them to recognize, — the test must be made on the railroad itself. A practical method of testing, however, should be one capable of being used in any place.

"We have therefore concluded that testing for color-blindness by railroad-lanterns is for many reasons impracticable, and to be discarded. It is worse with the flags: attempting to use them would cause the examining surgeon to overlook the majority of color-blind employés. After what has been said, it is not necessary to discuss this further. We admit, of course, that the method will succeed better in testing those about to enter the service, and as yet unfamiliar with the signals: but, if such an examination resulted unfavorably, there would be no just ground to refuse the applicant if it is believed that color-blindness is curable; and we do not clearly recognize the distinction between correctly *seeing* the colors and correctly naming them. We can give no better advice to those who are not convinced of the truthfulness of this, than to try it themselves. They will soon find, that, for testing a person for the first time, lanterns and flags are useless.

"We grant, on the other hand, that testing with colored

lights is quite practicable when we want to examine employés already found somewhat deficient, and desire to decide whether they can remain in service or not. In this case it is much better, instead of the usual colored lanterns, to have a large number of colored glasses which can be placed before the light, or lanterns of varying shades of color. Then any one who will work methodically will convince himself and others that the views we have expressed and defended as to color-blindness are correct; and, as to less faulty chromatic sense, its true effect in recognition of the signals will be duly appreciated. For instance, persons with feeble color-sense, to distinguish small colored surfaces, must come much nearer to them than the normal-eyed; whilst those who are completely color-blind cannot tell the ordinary lights with certainty, even when close to them. Many color-blind are even unable to say there is a light, when very feeble, behind a dark-red glass. A very definite result is obtained by letting two color-blind signal each other with lanterns I have had specially constructed. They then make the most marked mistakes. This is a very good plan to convince a sceptical railroad official, as well as the color-blind themselves. From the result of our investigations, we deduce the following as applicable to every test of color-blindness: the examination is not to ascertain the relation of color-sense to certain signals, whatever these latter may be, but to decide plainly and surely whether a given person is color-blind or not, or whether the color-sense is deficient or normal.

"The test is to find out the character of the color-blindness, not by ascertaining all its peculiarities, but simply one or more, which quite serves our purpose. This is all needed, and only exceptional cases require further examination. Now, there are a number of methods which combine more or less the essential characters we need in a practical test. Without discussing them all, we will here notice only a few points which will enable us to apply some rules to govern our decision as to which means of examination to employ. There is hardly any which could not be used, and, if we could carry it out with the necessary knowledge, would not serve our purpose as a method of control, at least when repeated trials could be made. On the other hand, there are methods which, used alone, would never, or but seldom, give us positive results, or which are so tedious and inconvenient as to be quite unpractical. To this class must be referred all those which, like the test with the lanterns, let the examined look at various colors or colored objects, and then demand of them their names.

"This decision is based on what we have already expressed, and also upon our own experience in reference to the way and manner in which the color-blind learn the names of colors, and the success practice gives them. But we do not want to learn the degree of skill a person can attain in naming colors, but how he sees them; in other words, the character of his color-blindness. The great difference between these two powers cannot be too well recognized, and on this ground alone we must again recur to the subject. Just how a color-blind sees a color it is not possible to decide; for it is a subjective sensation. On the other hand, we may form an opinion as to the character of his color-sense by the confusion or the mistakes which he makes in putting colors together, which, to the normal-eyed, are essentially different. Hence any method, to answer all demands upon it, must be based upon the *comparison* between different colors, and the confusion the color-blind make in this comparison. An example will render our idea more clear, and show the importance of it. Suppose, for instance, we have a green-blind. Now, experience shows that such a one confuses the shades of three colors, which are very different to the normal eye; namely, purplish red, green, and gray: or he regards them as exactly similar. Theory shows the reason of this very clearly. The green-blind has not the receptive or percipient organ of green. Purple, green, and gray pass with the green-blind for really one and the same color, which, however, from what he hears, receives under different circumstances the separate names. The consequence is, that he also calls this color sometimes by one and sometimes by the other name, or always calls it by one and the same name,—often by the name he first attached to it, or most often hears. If we test such a person by letting him name the colors, then, in accordance with the theory, the characteristic signs of green-blindness must in turn, and after many trials, show themselves. Without guidance from the theory it is difficult to obtain any clear and correct conception of the color-sense of a green-blind. If he uses all the three names, he will often be right, and as often wrong. In the first case he will readily be thought normal-eyed, and in the second what Goethe said will certainly occur, — 'one gets into the greatest perplexity, and fairly dreads becoming crazy.' If the green-blind carefully uses but one of the names, it will be one of the three, 'purple' (falsely called '*red*'), 'green,' or 'gray,' which he applies to all. Suppose now he uses the name 'green:' then, according to a method depending on the naming of colors, we should conclude that he sees purple and gray badly, but green distinctly. His color-sense will of course be regarded as abnormal; but no one would suppose he was green-blind, since he seems to see that color perfectly. Yet this green-blind will be regarded as such if he used the term 'red' (purple) or 'gray.' We trust this example will remove all doubts as to which of the two points of view is the correct one. Without further defending it, we hold the fact proved, that any practical method of examination must be based on the *principle of comparison*."

From what Professor Holmgren has laid down, we can readily understand why certain methods are not practical as well as not scientific. These methods we must therefore briefly criticise before explaining his. Let us first remember what has been said as to any method which calls upon the examined to name colors shown them, — to those unacquainted with color-blindness, apparently, the simplest and most suggestive. To all such methods we may apply Professor Helmholtz's criticism: "As to the examination of the color-blind, simply asking them to name this or that color will naturally elicit but very little."

Several ways of employing "simultaneous contrast" have been proposed and carried out. Dr. Stilling of Cassel used colored shadows. If we hold before a lamp a piece of colored glass, and allow the light thus colored to fall upon a white screen, this will then appear colored. Now, holding a pencil, for instance, before the screen, we shall have a shadow cast on the colored surface. This shadow will, to the normal eye, appear of the complementary color of the glass before the lamp; whilst to the color-blind the shadow will appear colorless or black or gray. On this principle is constructed Dr. Cohn's chromasciopticon, as also the chromatoscope made by Waldstein. Such tests are not as practical even as they sound, though Stilling showed how we could get the colored shadows by daylight. I would refer to Dr. von Reuss's article in support of my statements. Holmgren's more practical use of the shadows I describe below.

Another method of using simultaneous contrast is based on the experiment of Ragona Scina, and carried out by Cohn and by Pflüger. If we bend a piece of white cardboard to a right angle, and then fasten to the adjacent surfaces a little piece of black cloth, we can hold a plate of colored glass, with one edge resting in the angle of the paper, about dividing the right angle made by the cardboard: now, looking down from above through the glass, we see the horizontally placed piece of black cloth of the color of the glass; but we shall also see the reflection of the vertically placed piece of cloth, and this will appear of the complementary color of the glass. These do not, of course, so appear to the color-blind.

A test, based on H. Meyer's law of simultaneous contrast, has been proposed by Weber and Pflüger. This is well given in the English translation of "Bezold's Theory of Color," by Mr. Köhler. Black letters printed on colored paper, when covered with thin tissue paper, show through this of the complementary color. A gray stripe on a colored ground, when gazed at, takes the complementary color of the ground.

Any other methods of producing simultaneous contrast may of course be employed; but they are useless, as requiring of the examined color-names.

Successive contrast, or complementary after-images, has been suggested by Schirmer and by Cohn. If we look steadily a few seconds at a colored surface on a gray ground, and then quickly remove the colored surface, the ground will appear of the complementary color. We here again must depend on what the examined say they see.

A method of testing for color-blindness will at once suggest itself in the use of the spectroscope. Hirschberg has recently arranged one in which we have two spectra, one over the other, but in reversed order. Movable slits allow us to choose two colors, which appear just alike. The mistakes of the color-blind in doing this show their defect. Stilling proposed the use of the spectra of certain metals, — natrium, lithium, thallium, &c.; and interesting results have been thus obtained.

Rose's color-measurer should be here also mentioned, and Brücke's schistoscope, — only useful, however, for scientific examinations.

A method of testing has been proposed by Forster's perimeter. This is used by ophthalmic surgeons in determining loss of chromatic sense over certain portions of the retina. Small spots of color are brought up from the circumference towards the centre of the field of vision, and we can thus map out the chromatic visual field.

In 1871 Professor Holmgren directed attention to what he called the quantitative disturbances of the color-sense, or incomplete color-blindness. Professor Donders of Utrecht, in 1875, carried out this idea in a method of testing which gave us, not only the fact that the examined was color-blind, but also in what degree. This is described in a subsequent chapter as used on the Holland railroads.

Drs. Dor and Favre have modified Donders's method; and the former published lithographic plates of the colored disks, of definite sizes, on a black background. For this there is great difficulty in obtaining the proper printed colors, both as to uniformity, purity, and saturation.

Suggestions of Professor Holmgren have been carried out by Dr. Stilling in a method of testing for color-blindness which has the advantage of not calling upon the examined to name colors. In accordance with the now well-known laws of color-blindness, letters are printed in colors on a colored ground: these the color-blind fail to see, as there is no contrast to them between the letters and the ground color. Dr. Stilling has, in his more recent editions of this test, very ingeniously overcome, in a great degree, certain difficulties; but there are other practical ones which cannot be overcome. There is no comparison between it and the scientific simplicity of Holmgren's. It may be used as an additional method by those thoroughly acquainted with color-blindness theoretically, and practised in testing for it. Experience has proved this to those who have attempted to use Stilling's cards in testing large numbers, and uneducated people.

Mr. J. Clerk Maxwell, in 1855, proposed a method of judging of the chromatic sense by colored disks revolving on a top. They were so arranged that the various colors could be combined in any proportion. We can thus let a person *compare* colors, and prove their chromatic defect by their variation from the normal-eyed. Landolt proposed a modification for the quantitative determination of color-blindness. In 1870 Dr. Woinow proposed the use of a revolving disk, the inner circle of which was one-half each of black and white, giving us gray when revolving. Three rings outside of this were composed of equal parts of two of the three primary colors, — red, green, violet. To a person blind to the color not represented in one of the rings, this ring will appear gray for reasons I have previously given. Later he modified his disk, as he accepted four primary colors. The inner ring is now to be red and violet (or blue); the outer, green and violet (or blue); the third is left out. If the outer appears gray, like the centre, then we have green-blindness; if the inner, then red-blindness; if both, then red-green-blindness.

More than forty years ago Professor Seebeck of Germany described his testing a number of color-blind by methods of comparison of colors. He used some two hundred pieces of colored paper, and allowed the examined to sort these, putting together what looked to them alike. This was the first time a true method was used; and he obtained very valuable results, having shown that there were different kinds of color-blindness, and different degrees of each kind,—a most important fact, as I have previously described.

In 1855 Professor Wilson of Edinburgh published the first monograph in book-form on color-blindness. In testing various individuals he used little bundles of colored worsteds, letting them sort them out, and put together those seeming alike. The principle was the same as Seebeck's, and a true one of comparison, the examined not being obliged to name any colors. He says,—

"Candidates for appointments where good eyesight is required are not likely to exaggerate their defects of vision. Whenever, therefore, any hesitation in distinguishing colors is manifested, it should be further tried by giving the party under examination parcels of differently colored cloth, paper, glass, and the like, and requesting him to assort them according to their colors. Reds, greens, browns, and lilacs should form an essential part of these parcels, but not to the exclusion of other tints and shades. No person markedly color-blind will, I am persuaded, escape detection if tried in this way; and the kind and number of mistakes which he commits will measure the extent of his color-blindness. The mode of examination thus explained is within the reach of railway superintendents and shipmasters, and will serve every practical end. But where railway servants, sailors, soldiers, or others, undergo preliminary examination by a surgeon, a more minute examination might be made, and in another way."

He refers to the colored disks, spun on a top, of Maxwell. I quote from Professor Wilson to show, first, that, though he used comparison tests, yet he did not seemingly recognize that such alone were of value, as proved by what he suggests. Had the Young-Helmholtz theory of color-perception been then as thoroughly disseminated as now, he would no doubt have appreciated its value in explaining color-blindness. It was not so applied till 1875 by Professor Holmgren, who at the time was unaware of Wilson's results.

The Young-Helmholtz theory of color-perception suggested to Professor Holmgren the value of sorting worsteds in a certain way, based upon the application of this theory to the vision of the color-blind. This method of his, and the manner of using it, I shall give *in extenso* and in his own words, and therefore will here only speak of some other tests which have been copied from it.

Dr. Daae of Kragerö, Norway, has had little squares of worsted worked on a card in rows. Some rows are correct; namely, arranged from the darker to lighter of the same color. Others are arranged of the colors the color-blind especially confound; and they will say, when asked, that these rows are correct. The card is very convenient, not larger than an octavo volume, and the colors arranged to detect red, green, or violet blindness.

Dr. Cohn of Breslau proposed working worsted letters on a ground such as the color of the letter is usually confounded with by the color-blind. These are very deceptive to the color-blind, and they wonder at the normal-eyed's assertion that there are letters on the worsted surface. But the deception is only perfect, and the detection sure, when the color of the letters and the ground-work are just suited to the especial kind and degree of color-blindness of the examined. The test as a modification of Holmgren's has no advantage, and is not very practical.

Dr. Magnus of Breslau has lately proposed a

modification of Holmgren's test by letting the examined pick out from bundles of colored worsteds those which match the colors of the solar spectrum shown them at the same time. This can be used as an additional method by examiners, but is not, of course, as convenient and practical as Holmgren's simple plan.

Professor Donders has recently also proposed and used an arrangement of worsteds. On a little disk of wood one of the colors is wound; and the other, which the color-blind cannot distinguish from the first, is so wound over it as to form rays or a star. A large number of these pairs are chosen, guided by the selection various color-blind make with Holmgren's test; that is, the two worsteds on the disk are such as the color-blind say look to them quite alike. A color-blind is therefore detected in not being able to select those which to the normal-eye present contrasting colors.

I have thus given Holmgren's discussion of the principles of a correct, scientific, and sure test for the detection of color-blindness, and briefly explained what tests have been proposed, because the whole subject is new to us in the United States, and the future control of color-blindness, and assured safety from its dangers thereby acquired, so greatly depend upon the employment of an absolutely certain method, thoroughly and understandingly, by competent examiners.

CHAPTER XIX.

HOLMGREN'S METHOD OF TESTING. — EXAMINATION AND DIAGNOSIS.

JUSTICE to Professor Holmgren demands that I should here explain what he has done in reference to these various forms or methods of testing for color-blindness, and the study of color-sense. He has been over the whole subject before the recent observers I have mentioned, who have attached their names to this or that special modification. His method of examination with the worsteds — to be given in his own words in this chapter — is therefore to be considered as a natural development of his special studies.

March 31, 1871, he published his views on "Color-Blindness and the Young-Helmholtz Theory of Color."[1] He there discussed this theory, and the methods heretofore used in testing color-blindness. He also gave the explanation of the perimetric examinations afterwards carried out by him. By experiments with Maxwell's rotating disk he found the true difference between red and green

[1] Om Färgblindhet och den Young-Helmholtz'ska Färgtheorien, 1871.

blindness, explaining seven cases of complete color-blindness, — five red and two green. He seems to have first shown that green-blindness, as a distinct form, in conformity with Young's hypothesis, did exist, and proved it by exact experiments. In this, time has shown him to be correct.

Nov. 3, 1871, he published "On Forster's Perimeter and the Topography of the Color-Sense."[1] This contains a description of the perimetric examinations and the results thereby obtained, especially the three separate zones of the field of vision of Woinow, in relation to color-perception.

He used the point of fixation as the centre — the physiological centre — in contradistinction to the blind spot, — the pathological centre as he terms it. He here describes a series of perimetric examinations of the color-blind, beginning with the normal color-sense, and following up to complete color-blindness. He also first gives here a description of what he called incomplete or partial color-blindness. This is important to notice, as Stilling attributes wholly to Donders our knowledge and understanding of this form of chromatic defect; whereas Holmgren had very clearly defined it as a quantitative disturbance of the color-sense.

Incomplete or partial color-blindness, — especially incomplete red-blindness, — he shows, is characterized by two principal points: First, in indirect vision with the perimetric examination, the field of vision differs from that of the complete color-blind by having a normal central field; but it is unlike the normal color-sense in having a much smaller central field, thus in both ways

[1] Om Försters Perimeter och Färgsinnets Topographi, 1871.

being only a quantitative difference. Second, in direct vision at the point of fixation, partial color-blindness differs from complete; thus, with good illumination, sufficiently large colored surfaces can, at short distances and with careful fixation, be correctly distinguished in the sense of the normal-eyed. It is different from the normal, however, in that the discernment of colors is uncertain, and resembles the complete red-blind when the light is poor, the distance considerable, or the object small, or when indirect vision is called upon to assist. Now, these points have been scientifically carried out and formulated by Professor Donders since then; but they were understood and described in principle by Holmgren as early as 1871.

From his perimetric examinations he concluded that the three color-perceptive elements have from the centre outwards different extensions, so that they all three occupy the central field; whilst in the middle zone only green and violet perceptive elements exist, and in the outer zone only one of the latter two. This he thought to be the green, as most peripheric; but subsequent examinations proved it to be the violet.

He also in this article expressed the belief that the property of a specific sensation for green in any degree is inseparable from the property of the sensation for red. This afterwards became the basis of Hering's theory.

Oct. 31, 1873, he published "On Theories of Color-Blindness."[1] This is a continuation of his previous work giving his theoretical ideas. It criticises Fick's theory, and endeavors to reconcile

[1] Om Färgblindhetens Theori, Oct. 31, 1873.

the facts so far established with Young's theory of color. The difference between Fick's views and Holmgren's is, that the former refers the material process of color-perception to the peripheric retinal elements, whilst the latter would equally divide it between these elements and the central apparatus in the brain. He also criticises R. Schirmer's article on congenital and acquired anomalies of color-perception, in which Schirmer gives a series of pigment colors which have eccentric fields of vision of varying size. He holds, that, in examining the central as well as the eccentric field of vision, the proper selection of the grades of color has been neglected. He gives, therefore, an idea of those which are equivalent; that is, pigments which, *ceteris paribus*, correspond to the same visual fields, and are recognized at the same distance from the point of fixation.

Holmgren also gives some cases of complete green-blindness, the characteristics of which are especially shown in this article. There are, besides, some improved methods of carrying out the perimetric examinations described.

In 1874 Professor Holmgren published an article "On the Theory and Diagnosis of Color-Blindness."[1] This contains the theoretical and practical groundwork for his method of detecting color-blindness, since published and given here in full. He develops it theoretically from the Young-Helmholtz theory, and practically from Seebeck's method. He published a plate with colored letters, in this article, on the same principle. He also

[1] Om den Medfödda Färgblindhetens Diagnostik och Teori. Nord. Med. Arkiv., B. vi. No. 24–28.

then warned against the misuse of the table, and took the same position which he now holds in reference to all such arrangements of material, and in defence against imitators. This plate of colored letters clearly shows it was the basis on which so much *invention* has been since made.

He also further discussed the true subjective color-sense of the color-blind. He proposed means for rendering the color-perception of the normal-eyed like that of the color-blind, so that they would see colors like the latter. This he accomplished with colored glasses and colored solutions, as has since been done by Delbœuf, as described in a previous chapter.

Returning to the two commonest forms, — namely, red-blindness and green-blindness, — he gives further proof of the existence of the latter as a distinct and independent form, analyzing three additional cases of complete green-blindness.

Finally, he treats the question of the color-visual field of the color-blind, proving that they have as many distinct visual fields as primary colors. He gives in two plates colored perimetric visual fields of the color-blind.

The method of testing as developed from his investigations I will now present as originally given by him. The description may seem unnecessarily extended, and, to the general reader, quite uninteresting. It is, however, for the benefit of those who are in the future to examine employés in this country. Experience with testing for color-blindness will prove its value, and the necessity for its seeming minuteness. Neglect of its study and directions has given rise to much confusion and waste of time on the European roads, the proof of which will be hereafter given.

PROFESSOR HOLMGREN'S METHOD OF DETECTING COLOR-BLINDNESS AS DESCRIBED IN HIS ORIGINAL WORK.

"1. —*A Short Sketch of the General Principles of the Method.*

"Theoretically our method most resembles those of Seebeck and Maxwell, as it is based upon a *comparison* between different colors. It therefore first seeks to discover the chromatic *perception* of the subject, disregarding the *names* he gives to the colors, as generally it is not necessary he should designate the names. Our method resembles Seebeck's most in this, that it does not require a special apparatus for preparing the necessary tints for the examination: it assumes there will be a supply of objects of different colors provided in advance. It agrees again with this method in not allowing, as Maxwell's does, the person examined to remain passive, and simply give his opinon of the resemblance or dissimilarity of the shades indicated, but requires him to discriminate and select the shades, and in consequence reveal by an act the nature of his chromatic sense.

"But practically our method differs essentially from Seebeck's. His certainly gives, in a certain sense, more complete results than ours, by requiring the subject to thoroughly classify, in accordance with their reciprocal resemblances and dissimilarites, the various differently colored objects placed before him. A complete table of his whole system of colors is the result of this. Our method, on the contrary, requires the person examined to select, amongst a large number of variously-colored objects, those alone which resemble the sample shown him by the examiner. The difference is evident. Seebeck's method is, without any doubt, preferable when the nature of the color-blindness in the aggregate is to be considered; that is, so long as this is yet unknown. His method then gives a more complete idea than ours of the nature of the color-blindness. But, for our actual purpose, the main question is to discover a defect, with the entire nature of which we are acquainted in advance. Our practical mission, then, is evidently to discover, if possible, some certain sign which will enable us to accomplish this end by the shortest possible route.

"If a single proof which would detect the color-blind as certainly as if he revealed to us his entire system of colors were discovered, this would undoubtedly be the method preferred to any other, as it would accomplish the object much more quickly and easily. This is the case with our method. We are far from denying, in general, the value of a thorough examination; but we will say that it *may* sometimes be superfluous. Its practical advantage will not be very great if at the cost of a great loss of time; and it may even be prejudicial, if, under a multitude of details, it conceals what is essential, — in a word, prevents our 'seeing the forest on account of the trees.' All this may be applied to Seebeck's method, when the object in view is the one of which we are in pursuit. Our method again endeavors to seize as rapidly as possible one or two essential characteristics while neglecting all the others. A single caudal feather of the peacock reveals whence it came; a single flower or fruit, the plant whence it was plucked; and the genus man is recognized if we can but see a face. It is only when the face is mutilated, the flowers, fruits, and caudal feather are defective, that in certain cases it is necessary to have recourse to other characteristics.

"Our method rests upon these principles: it also offers the same security as Seebeck's. But, as regards the time necessary to accomplish the examination, it bears nearly the same relation to that of the learned German that a minute does to an hour. This may seem a very trifling matter at the first glance, but is in reality of immense practical importance when a multitude of persons are to be successively examined. A simple calculation shows us in fact that an examination requiring one day by our method would require two months by Seebeck's.

"It is but just to acknowledge that it was only by weighing the results obtained by Seebeck's method, and following the Young-Helmholtz theory, as well as the principles we have indicated as indispensable to a practical method, that we have succeeded in formulating our own method, such as we shall explain it in what follows. We also will remark that it is very simple, and easily mastered; but we think this is likewise often the case with all that is useful and practical, and that simplicity offers great advantages. We prefer this method because it seems to us more than any other to fulfil the conditions we have pointed out as necessary to a practical method; namely, certainty, rapidity, and convenience. The only inconvenience of any moment, besides those it has in common with a greater part of the others, is, that it requires daylight. It *can* undoubtedly be used by artificial light (electrical and calcium lights, and certain arrangements of lamp-lights with blue glass); but this causes much loss of time.

"After this rapid sketch of the general principles of the method, we will proceed to give its details, and shall not fail to mention generally the reasons why, amongst several possibilities, we have selected this or that process.

"2. — *The Material and its Arrangement.*

"Our method demands neither costly apparatus nor a special place for the examination. The only necessary elements are a number of variously colored objects. It consists in taking one from a number of objects promiscuously thrown together, and asking the person examined to select from amongst them all the others corresponding with the first in color. With regard to the colored objects, it of course matters little in principle what their nature is, as, in the main, the method never changes, no matter what the kind selected. But, practically, the choice is by no means a matter of indifference. Among the ordinary objects suggested, and also used for the purpose, are pieces of colored paper, glass, or silk, or Berlin worsted, &c., the last of which seems to us the best, for the following reasons: One of the chief advantages of Berlin worsted is, that it can be procured in all possible colors corresponding to those of the spectrum, and each in all its shades from the darkest to the lightest. Such selections may be found in trade, and are easily procured when and where desired. It can be used at once, and without any preparation for the examination, just as delivered from the factory. A skein of Berlin worsted is equally colored, not only on one or two sides, but on all, and is easily detected in a large pile, even though there be but one thread of it. Berlin worsted is not too strongly glaring, and is, moreover, soft and manageable, and can be handled, packed, and transported as desired, without damage, and is conveniently ready for use whenever needed.

"These advantages are wanting in the other colored objects suggested for use. Colored paper or silk may be used when light or dark, dull or bright colors are wanted. But they both have these inconveniences: they must first be cut into suitable pieces, and they are troublesome to handle. Moreover, they are easily concealed from view; and it is necessary to stretch them carefully on a large surface to enable them to be seen without trouble. They are often glaring. They reflect, besides their particular kinds of light, a quantity of white light, which is a prominent defect, as it misleads the color-blind, who, as we know, judge of colors by the intensity of light,—that is, the quantity of light; and he consequently estimates differently the color of a brilliant surface, according to the position in which it is found with regard to the eye, &c. The paper is often colored on only one side, and this gives rise to much trouble, as it is necessary to turn the pieces from one side to the other to see them in their true colors. Finally, from being so much handled, the pieces of paper or silk soon become tumbled and faded.

"Colored glass, which must be in pieces, is not suitable, from the fact that it is difficult to procure it in sufficiently great variety. It is, besides, troublesome to transport, easily broken, and finally inconvenient for using, because necessary to be held against the light of day, or a luminous source, in order that the color may be seen. The advantage of being able to use them by any kind of light does not counterbalance their inconveniences.

"Although these are not all the objections, the preceding will suffice to prove the advantages of Berlin worsted. All this applies equally well to wafers, powders, colored solutions, spools of colored thread, pieces of wood, and porcelain, especially painted for the purpose, &c. They can all be, and have been, employed; but none of these objects are, in every respect, so well suited to our purpose as Berlin worsted.

"A selection of Berlin worsted is then made, including red, orange, yellow, yellow green, pure green, blue green, blue, violet, purple, pink, brown, gray, several shades of each color, and at least five gradations of each tint, from the deepest to the lightest. Green and gray, several kinds each of pink, blue, and violet, and the pale-gray shades of brown, yellow, red, and pink, must especially be well represented.

"The choice of the material does not belong specially to our method. In fact, Seebeck suggested the use of Berlin worsted, which was employed by his advice, and still is at present. To us only belongs the credit of originating the manner in which it is employed. According to our method, the examiner selects from the collection of Berlin worsted in a pile on a convenient table, and lays aside a skein of the especial color desired for this examination; then he requires the one examined to select the other skeins most closely resembling the color of the sample, and to place them by its side. The chromatic sense of the individual is decided by the manner in which he performs this task.

"The result of comparison which the examined makes — in other words, the little skein of worsted which he selects and places by the test — shows us in reality what colors seem alike to him, and thus tells us his relative color-perception. The rapidity with which this examination is made does not seem to directly correspond with the nature of the chromatic sense, but to depend wholly upon the character of the person examined. One of intelligence, with a quick, practical mind, is examined in less than a minute. In this time, in fact, a normal eye could easily find the four or five skeins of the same color as the sample, and the color-blind make a sufficient number of characteristic mistakes to thoroughly establish the diagnosis.

"It might be supposed that this method could be further simplified, and time thereby saved, by previously grouping the colored objects, or, in other words, showing to the examined a number of colored objects arranged in certain system, and asking of him which look alike, and their names. Here the worsteds would have no special advantage over other colored material, and could be replaced by objects with bright surfaces not necessarily movable. On such a proposed table the various colors may be placed without any order, or in a definite order in accordance with their similarity. Thus they may be grouped according to the color-perception of the normal-eyed or the color-blind, and, in the latter case, in different groups corresponding to the different forms of color-blindness.

"The grouping of colors which I proposed was on this principle, and it is printed in the 'Nordst Medicinskt Arkiv.,' 1874, and carried out in the plate published with this book. The plan is a good one where we are dealing with educated and intelligent people, and many color-blind may be thereby detected. To be at all complete, and generally practical, this method must have a much larger number of shades. Experience shows that the color-blind is often uncertain as to the similarity between two colors, depending less upon the color than on what to him is the most important distinguishing mark; namely, the intensity of the light, or the degree of saturation. And, as to equal intensity of two colors whose similarity he would find, he is so particular, that the test may be just too much or too little. We must add that all color-blind of the same class are not as particular as to intensity of light or degree of saturation; and, moreover, it is impossible, on plates which are multiplied, to get exactly the necessary colors, whilst the price increases with the number of colors. The difficulties were therefore enough for us to abandon this method. The worst is, however, that the supposed gain in time is more than counterbalanced by lack of conveniences and other difficulties. In short, the loss is greater than the gain.

"These remarks hold good, not only in reference to this form of test proposed by me in 1874, but also to all colored tables which have so far been published. A proof is, the worked worsteds of Dr. Daae, and the repeated attempts of Dr. Stilling to construct colored plates. As is known, neither have succeeded in solving the difficulties, although careful and ingenious attempts have been made to conquer some of those I have spoken of. These tables, from the very nature of the subject, can only have a limited employment as an *additional* test, but are for the examination of masses wholly unserviceable. Experience has perfectly proved this to me, and will the same to every expert. The new editions, unfortunately, are not changed in this respect.

"By such a colored plate, or any similar arrangement of immovable colored objects, the very work is done which should have been by the examined; namely, the grouping of colors seemingly alike. If, however, this is not done, and the colors are mixed up, then we cannot let them be grouped in accordance with their similarity. The value of this method is, that the objects are movable, and can be mixed and sorted anew.

"Careful consideration will show the importance of this fact. The object of the test is to ascertain a subjective sensation from an objective expression. Now, man has but one means of expressing his subjective sensation to another; namely, by muscular action. The organs of speech and the limbs are the apparatus of motion best answering this purpose, and most used for it. Of the most movable, the tongue and hand each is the representative of its group; and they are the most pliable of all organs. Both equally indicate the different actions by which we impart our thoughts to others; namely, by words and acts. It is scarcely necessary to indicate, that, as a rule, it is the latter (the hands) which we rightly have greater confidence in than the spoken word. This is substantiated in testing the color-blind. We have seen how readily they are detected when forced to act, whilst we must equally remember that the names they give colors are often exactly adapted to conceal their defect. If it is in his interest, as here is the case, not to expose his defective perception, but rather to conceal it, he certainly can do this better by speech than by the hands. This is a general law applicable here, if the relations between the perception and denomination of an object are recalled as we have explained them, and the way these two acts are combined in education. On the other hand, it is clear that our method affords the opportunity, in connection with the investigation of the chromatic sense, of learning much of all the peculiarities relating to the use of our senses. This is why we maintain the principle that it is necessary to leave to the activity of the hands the task of revealing the nature of the sensations, and to have recourse to the tongue only for verification when there is need of more information.

"The combination of the action of the eye and hands, which plays in general so important a part in the training and use of the senses, is also of great consequence in this examination. An attentive examiner, especially if he have already acquired some experience, can draw important conclusions from the manner in which the other executes his task, not only and directly with regard to the nature of his chromatic sense, but generally as to his intelligence and character, and especially in some cases as to his previous training and exercise in the use of colors, and his skill in recognizing them. The examination affords us also the opportunity of making psychological observations, which contribute, in a great measure, in giving us a clear idea of the nature of the chromatic sense.

"A practised surgeon can often detect color-blindness by the first gesture of the examined, and make his diagnosis before the end of the trial. He can, according to the manner in which the task is performed, form a judgment of a feeble chromatic sense in instances which are proved correct by the final result. He also can and must see whether the result is erroneous simply on account of a misunderstanding or a want of intelligence, just as he can see whether the really color-blind succeeds, in a certain degree, from much previous exercise or a considerable amount of caution. In short, the method supplies us with all necessary information; so that, by an examination made with its assistance, a defective chromatic sense, no matter of what kind or in what degree, cannot escape observation. It also calls upon the examiner to watch the examined very carefully, and note his every motion. Different persons act very differently, and cause the surgeon trouble of more than one kind. People of medium intelligence, whether they are color-blind or not, give least trouble, provided they do not feel called upon to be too shrewd. The examination is most difficult with people of small intelligence, or of feeble and uncultivated color-perception, or when we have a color-blind already tested who desires to escape detection, or when the examined has not had good school-education. Practical rules for these special cases are given later.

"The principle of our method depends, as we have said, on the test calling for the selection of but one color among many. It may be asked what need of such a number of colors? Would not a smaller answer? We reply that the color-blind avoids detection with more difficulty, and the diagnosis hence is more readily made, the greater the number of the various colors. The normal-eyed readily selects the right ones from the mass; whilst the color-blind, although the right ones are directly before him, picks out the wrong ones, thereby disclosing the character of his defect. Therefore the greater the number of colors the better, of course, within certain limits.

"What color shall we take for our sample? This is of importance; for we must of course decide on some one color. Experience, as well as the Young-Helmholtz theory, teaches us that more than one color may serve as the sample in searching for a sure and definite characteristic of defective chromatic sensation. All colors do not, however, meet this equally well: hence it is worth while to establish certain rules as to a correct choice.

"The faculty possessed by the eye of distinguishing colors, and that of defining the degrees of light and color (of "saturation") are relatively very different; but these special faculties have this in common, that they have their maximum activity in a certain intermediary region of absolute intensity of light, and their minimum at the two limits of this region. Just as we experience the most difficulty in distinguishing between the shades of intensity of light by a very feeble or very strong illumination, so it is difficult for us to distinguish colors slightly or strongly luminous, or the deepest and the lightest. It is therefore necessary to select as a suitable color for discovering a feeble chromatic sense either the lightest or darkest shades. The well-defined kinds and degrees of a defective chromatic sense confound only colors of mean intensity. But in this case, also, it is a question what tones of color to choose. For my choice I have been guided by the Young-Helmholtz theory, and for the reason that I have proposed my method in support and proof of that theory. As a fact the examination of thousands of persons has convinced me of the excellence of my choice. I have selected, to determine whether the chromatic sense is or is not defective, a light green (dark green may be also used), because green, according to the theory, is the whitest of the colors of the spectrum, and consequently is most easily confused with gray. For the diagnosis of the especial kinds of partial color-blindness, I have selected purple (pink); that is, the whole group of colors in which red (orange) and violet (blue) are combined in nearly equal proportions, at least in such proportions that no one sufficiently preponderates over the others, to the normal sense, so as to give its name to the combination. This is the reason for this choice. Purple occupies a singular position amongst colors: although a mixed, it is, we know a color as well "saturated" as the colors of the spectrum, and might be, from this point of view, classed with them, although it is not found in the spectrum. In fact, it has been regarded as the eighth color of the spectrum, closing the circle of saturated colors. Purple is of especial importance in the examination of the color-blind, for the reason that it forms a combination of two fundamental colors — the two extreme colors — which are never confounded with each other. In fact, from a color-blind point of view, one of two things must happen, according to the theory: either it excites but one kind of perceptive organs, or it excites them all. It appears, then, either like a simple color, — that is to say, like one of the two colors of the combination, — or like white (gray.) Experiment has confirmed this hypothesis. Our sample colors, therefore, are the two complementary colors of each other, — *green* and *purple*.

"In the examination of the chromatic sense of a large number of individuals, it is, of course, of importance to decide quickly, first, whether the chromatic sense of the individual is or is not normal. It is only after establishing the existence of a defect that its nature or degree must be determined. The sample-colors are therefore employed with more advantage in a certain order, as the test must be accomplished as a whole, according to a plan that experience has proved the surest, most rapid, and, finally, most suitable for the purpose.

"*Method of Examination and Diagnosis.*

"The Berlin worsteds are placed in a pile on a large plane surface, and in broad daylight; a skein of the test-color is taken from the pile, and laid aside far enough from the others not to be confounded with them during the trial; and the person examined requested to select the other skeins most resembling this in color, and place them by the side of the sample. In the first place it is necessary that he should thoroughly understand what is required of him; that is, that he should search the pile for the skeins making an impression on his chromatic sense independent of any name he may give the color, similar to that made by the sample. The examiner should explain that resemblance in every respect is not necessary; that there are no two specimens exactly alike; that the only question is the resemblance of the *color;* and that, consequently, he must endeavor to find something similar of the same shade, something lighter and darker of the same color, &c. If the person examined cannot succeed in understanding this by a verbal explanation, we must resort to action. We must ourselves make the trial by searching with our own hands for the skeins, thereby showing in a practical manner what is meant by a shade, and then restoring the whole to the pile, except the sample-skein. As it would require much time to examine each individual in this way, it is advisable, when examining a large number at the same time, to instruct all at once, and, moreover, to ask them to attentively observe the examination of those preceding them, so as to become more familiar themselves with the process. By this, time is saved, without loss of security; for no one with a defective chromatic sense finds the correct skeins in the pile the more easily from the fact of having a moment before seen others looking for and arranging them. He makes the same characteristic mistakes; but the normal observer, on the other hand, generally accomplishes his task much better and more quickly after having seen how it must be done, and this is the advantage of our method.

"The colored plate is for the purpose of assisting the examiner in the choice of his colors, and helping him decide the character of the trouble from the mistakes the color-blind make. We have attempted to represent the colors we are now to speak of. They are of two classes, —

"1st, The *colors for samples* (*test-colors*); that is, those which the surgeon presents to the persons examined; and

"2d, The '*colors of confusion;*' that is to say, those which the color-blind selects from the heap of worsteds, because he confuses them with that of the sample.

"The first are horizontal on the plate, and marked with

Roman numerals; the second are vertical, under the test-colors, and marked with Arabic figures.

"We have already described why such a table cannot be constructed with a small number of colors adapted to all color-blind. It is, moreover, often difficult — even impossible — to accurately give the brilliant colors the worsteds have. The test-colors, with the exception of II., answer the purpose; but the others not so well, from the difficulty we have spoken of, and because all color-blind do not choose the same shades of the same color.

"The colored table is not intended to be directly used to test with, though it may serve this purpose occasionally. It is rather to simply assist the surgeon in his choice of the correct test-colors, and help him diagnosticate the special form of color-blindness.

"As to the conformity between the worsteds the color-blind take from the heap and the confusion-colors of the plate, we must simply rely on the tone, and not much on the intensity of light or degree of saturation. In all cases where we have to vary from this rule, we must hold to the relative rather than the absolute saturation. The confusion-colors of our table are only to illustrate the color-blind's mistakes, and this purpose they serve perfectly. Having made this explanation, we will pass directly to the test itself. The following are the directions for conducting this, and making our diagnosis from the results: —

"Test I. — The *green* sample is presented. This sample should be the palest shade (the lightest) of very pure green, which is neither a yellow green nor a blue green to the normal eye, but fairly intermediate between the two, or at least not verging upon yellowish green.

"*Rule.* — The examination must continue until the one examined has placed near the sample all the other skeins of the same shade, or else, with these or separately, one or several skeins of the class corresponding to the 'colors of confusion' (1–5), until he has sufficiently proved by his manner of doing it that he can easily and unerringly distinguish the confused colors, or until he has given proof of unmistakable difficulty in accomplishing this task.

"*Diagnosis.* — He who places beside the sample, one of the 'colors of confusion' (1–5) — that is to say, finds that it resembles the 'test-color'— is *color-blind.* He who, without being quite guilty of this confusion, evinces a manifest disposition to do so, has a *feeble chromatic sense.*

"*Remark.* — We must remember that we might have taken more than five colors for 'confusion;' but we have here in view, not *every* kind of defective color-sense, but only those important in the business of railways. The number of colors on the plate is therefore sufficient, as these are the most important and most common.

"As to No. 1, which represents the gray color, we would remark that too much stress must not be laid on the light intensity, or on slight differences in the color-tone. This is especially true of the gray skeins which the examined puts with the sample. If we need determine only whether a person was color-blind or not, no further test would be necessary. If we want to know the kind and degree of his color-blindness, then we must go on with another test.

"TEST II. — A purple skein is shown the examined. The color should be midway between the lightest and darkest. It will only approach that given in II. of the plate, because the color of the worsted is much more brilliant and saturated, and more towards the blue.

"*Rule.* — The trial must be continued until the one examined has placed near the sample all or the greater part of the skeins of the same shade, or else, simultaneously or separately, one or several skeins of 'confusion' (6–9). He who confuses the colors selects either the light or deep shades of blue and violet, especially the deep (6 and 7), or the light or deep shades of one kind of green or gray inclining to blue (8 and 9).

"*Diagnosis.* — 1. He who is color-blind by the first test, and who, upon the second test, selects only purple skeins, is *incompletely color-blind.*

"2. He who, in the second test, selects with purple only blue and violet, or one of them, is *completely red-blind.*

"3. He who, in the second test, selects with purple only green and gray, or one of them, is completely *green-blind.*

"*Remark.* — The red-blind never selects the colors taken by the green-blind, and *vice versa.* Often the green-blind places a violet or blue skein side of the green, but only the brightest shades of these colors. This does not influence our diagnosis.

"The fact that many green-blind select in this test, besides gray and green or one of these colors, also bright blue, has led to misunderstanding. Some have from this concluded that red and green blindness may exist together in the same individual; others have thought that these two kinds of color-blindness were not readily distinguished by my method. The former conclusion is not correct. The two kinds have great similarity in close unanimity with the theory, but differ in innumerable slight variations. They are nevertheless, in view of the theory, to be considered as two sharply defined species.

"The second conclusion can only arise from not understanding and not using the method correctly. The especial purpose of this method must here be kept constantly in view, and that is to find a characteristic of the defective color-perception of the examined. This characteristic, or sign, with green-blindness, is the confusing the purple with gray or green, or both. This confusion is the point to be determined: all else may be neglected. A complete color-blind, who confuses purple with gray or green (bluish green), or both, is *green-blind, do what else he may.* This is the rule, and it will not fail the careful and observant examiner who understands the application of the test. On the contrary, it is often possible, in marked cases of incomplete color-blindness, to decide which kind we have by the way the examined acts with his hands.

"We do not mean by this that the diagnosis is always very easy. Practice and knowledge are necessary. Moreover, as we have often said, there is a long series of degrees from incomplete color-blindness to normal vision on the one side, and, on the other, to complete color-blindness. There must naturally be a border line where differences of the two kinds of color-blindness cease to be recognized.

"The examination may end with this test, and the diagnosis be considered as perfectly settled. It is not even necessary, practically, to decide whether the color-blindness is red or green. But to be more entirely convinced of the relation of complete color-blindness with the signal-colors, and especially to convince, if necessary, the railway employés and others who are not specialists, the examination may be completed by one more trial. The one we are going to mention is not necessary to the diagnosis, and only serves to corroborate the investigation.

"TEST III. — The *red* skein is presented to the subject. It is necessary to have a vivid red color, like the red flag used as signals on railways. The color should be that of II. *b* of the plate, rather towards yellowish red.

"*Rule.* — This test, which is applied only to those completely color-blind, should be continued until the person examined has placed beside the specimen all the skeins belonging to this shade or the greater part, or else, separately, one or several 'colors of confusion' (10–13). The red-blind then chooses, besides the red, green and brown shades, which, (10–11), to the normal sense, seem darker than red. On the other hand, the green-blind selects opposite shades, which appear lighter than red (12–13).

"*Remark.* — Every case of complete color-blindness discovered does not always make the precise mistakes we have just mentioned in the preceding examinations. These exceptions are either instances of persons with a comparatively inferior degree of complete color-blindness, or of color-blind persons who have been exercised in the colors of signals, and who endeavor not to be discovered: they therefore usually confound at least green and brown; but even this does not always happen.

"ADDITIONAL NOTE. — We have not given rules for discovering *total* color-blindness, because we have not found any cases of this kind. If any such should be found, they will be recognized, according to the theory, by a confusion of every shade having the same intensity of light.

"*Violet-blindness* will be recognized by a genuine confusion of purple, red, and orange in the second test. The diagnosis should be made with discrimination. The first test often shows blue to be a 'color of confusion.' This may, in certain cases, be the sign of violet-blindness, but not always. We have not thought it advisable to admit defects of this kind: only the most marked cases, that other examinations establish as violet color-blindness, should be reckoned in the statistics. Finally, to acquire a desirable uniformity, it is necessary to add, that, in the preparatory examination, it is my habit to indicate in the journal, especially kept for that purpose, cases of *complete color-blindness* by 2 (2 R., 2 G., 2 V.), those of incomplete blindness by 1, and those of feeble chromatic sense by 0.5 (0.5 R., 0.5 G., 0.5 V.)."

Professor Holmgren has subsequently published a further explanation of this method of testing for color-blindness, which is not in the Swedish, French, or German edition of his book, nor in the abridged translation of the Smithsonian. I therefore add it here in full, as it is very important for examiners:—

" *The Detection of Color-Blindness among Large Numbers.*

"Those who, in the collection of material for scientific research or for the practical purpose of control among railroad employés and sailors, have to test the color-sense of large numbers of persons, in order to separate the color-blind from the normal, and ascertain the former's kind of defect, will have found the great value of a method which is rapid and sure in its working. This is very satisfactorily fulfilled by my method with the worsteds as originally given. But, to gain still further time,—that is, to increase the rapidity of the examination without detracting from its surety and practicability,—I have lately somewhat simplified the method of working, whilst retaining the same principle, thereby gaining a third or more of the necessary time.

"As my method has been so favorably received, and its use spread so rapidly and so widely, I think it right to give a brief explanation of this modification for the benefit of professional men.

"The worsted method, from the many colors and the movable character of the material, is very readily applicable to any special case. It can, as no other, be variously modified to meet circumstances. We are here dealing with practical contrivances of more general value, which, simple as they may seem, were only learned by long experience. They partly relate to the worsteds, and partly to the particular way of carrying out the test itself.

"I. The right choice of colors for the collection of worsteds to be used helps not a little to shorten the examination. All who are practically acquainted with my method have had their patience tried by the want of readiness of the normal-eyed in picking out the lighter of the green skeins corresponding to the sample from the other green shades of the bundle. In my book I had to devote many pages to this point. As I there said, it is the normal-eyed who cause most loss of time, from their peculiar misappreciation of the green colors, which is of no importance for the main object, and generally to be corrected. The color-blind, on the other hand, make no such errors, but other very different and characteristic mistakes, and generally very quickly.

"There is therefore considerable gained if we can help the normal-eyed, and still not change the conditions of the test for the color-blind. This may be done by leaving out of the bundle of worsteds all the green colors, except the lighter ones belonging to Test I. In this primary test the choice for the normal-eyed will be within quite narrow limits; and, as experience has shown, they are quickly through. The color-blind, however, to whom the other colors, or so-called confusion-colors, resemble the green, has as great a choice as before.

"The removal of the superfluous greens is therefore simplifying the method, and an improvement from the saving of time. We lose also nothing from the certainty of the color-blind's distinguishing himself from the normal-eyed. We must, however, not fail to remember, that, though this renders the method more precise as to the practical point, yet it also limits it. Opportunity for observing certain other points is lost. For instance, we have reduced to a minimum the chance of watching the evident difference in the intelligence, practice, and education of the examined, all which possesses a certain psychological interest.

"When, as in railroad employés and sailors, we are concerned alone with rapidly detecting the commonest forms and degrees of color-blindness, — namely, complete red and green blindness and incomplete color-blindness, — we may of course, also, leave out the bright-blue worsteds, and, with Test II., the bright-violet colors. But in Test II. we must, for the green-blind, leave all the grades of the bluish-green confusion-color, No. 9 of the plate. I will here speak only of the green colors, because they are of most importance, and sufficiently indicate the principle of the simplification.

"II. As to the carrying-out of the test, it could not be quicker than the selecting at once from hundreds of persons the color-blind from the normal-eyed. Such an examination of a mass of people is conceivable, but not practical, because the necessary surety and certainty, as well as the classification of the color-blind, demand a separate examination of each individual.

"This simplification, however, allows of a larger number of persons together being prepared for the test. A principle of the method is the fact that the examined does not have to answer any question, but is simply compelled to show the character of his color-sense by a definite action. This of course implies his being instructed as to precisely what he is to do. Just how this is done, and the test conducted, has no small effect on the rapidity of the whole examination. If each person is thoroughly instructed as to what he is to do, he finds it extremely simple, and rapidly makes the test, whether he is color-blind or not.

"The certainty of the test is not interfered with whilst its rapidity is increased by giving the preparatory instruction to a large number together. It adds to rapidity, if all the examined, or as many as possible, see each individual tested. We need not fear that the color-blind can learn any thing by seeing what the normal-eyed do. The effect of the examination is all the more striking and convincing when a number have regularly gone through with the test correctly, and then one comes who has for some time stood among the lookers-on, and makes the characteristic mistakes of the color-blind. This is always the case. On the other hand, a normal-eyed may thus learn to imitate the mistakes of a color-blind. In testing numbers thus, it would, however, but rarely happen that any one was interested in simulating color-blindness. Even in this case counterfeiting the color-blind is readily detected by the subsequent control examination, and hence quite harmless.

"With these preliminary remarks, the practical rules for quickly testing large numbers for the common forms of color-blindness may be briefly given as follows: —

"1st, In the first test, we leave out of the bundle of worsteds all the greens, with the single exception of those to which the test-color I. belongs (*vide* the plate), and which should consist of about five grades or shades.

"2d, When using the second test, we put in the bundle or near it the bluish greens of various intensities, corresponding to the confusion-color No. 9.

"3d, Before commencing, let some fifty stand round the table on which the worsteds are placed, or be so arranged that they can see what takes place on the table. Then call attention to the test as follows: —

"4th, We hold up the five green worsteds before the examined, and tell them to carefully observe them, so as to readily and quickly pick them out from all the mixed-up colors. Then we place test I., the brightest of the five, to one side, and mix the others well in the bundle. With our own hand we rapidly pick these out again, and lay them with the first to one side: in other words, we perform the test just as it should be, and this we can repeat as often as is useful in hastening the examination.

"5th, After this preparation, we let the examined come one after the other to the table, and repeat the test they have seen done. The others must keep quiet, and neither by laughing, calling out, or signs, interfere with the one being tested.

"6th, When any has shown himself color-blind by this test, then, for the differential diagnosis, Test II. will be used. Test III. need not be at all.

"7th, As in general the test is rapidly made, a feeble sense of color is shown by great slowness in the manifestation.

"We may thus with perfect certainty test a hundred or more individuals in an hour, especially soldiers or those under discipline.

"Finally, I would remark, that, with this method of testing, we need not speak a word, of which experience has convinced me. We may test the dumb without even knowing their sign-language. This method, therefore, recommends itself above all others for testing uncivilized people whose language is unknown to the examiner. Such examinations, which I have already carried out to a small extent, will be of interest in reference to the question of development of the color-sense in general."

I have thus given Holmgren's precise description of the worsted-test as he carries it out. My own experience has been to lead me to employ the seemingly longer method with the larger number of greens. Therefore I add here the exact description given in the original in full of the way of conducting it. To those of my readers who may consider it superfluous or unnecessarily extended, I would say, try and go on with the test alone amongst those with whom a mistake on your part would be fatal, and you will gladly turn back and carefully study this following chapter, with thanks to Holmgren for it.

CHAPTER XX.

SPECIAL DIRECTIONS FOR CONDUCTING THE TEST.

"The method, as we have said, plays an important part in an examination of this kind, not only from the principles upon which it rests, but also from the manner in which it is used. The best plan for directing how to proceed is by oral instructions and *de visu;* but here we are obliged to accomplish this by description. Now, this is always defective in some respects, especially if we wish to be brief. What has been said would evidently suffice for an intelligent and experienced physician; but it may not be superfluous to enter still further into detail to provide against any possible difficulties and loss of time. The object of the examination is to discover the nature of a person's chromatic sense. Now, as the fate of the one to be examined and that of others depend upon the correctness of the judgment pronounced by the examiner, and that this judgment should be based upon the manner in which the one examined stands the trial, it is of importance that this trial should be truly what it ought to be, — a trial of the nature of the chromatic sense, and nothing else, — an end that will be gained if our directions are strictly followed. It is not only necessary that the examiner carefully observe them, — which does not seem to us difficult, — but that he also take care that the individual examined does thoroughly what is required of him. This is not always as easy as one might suppose. If it were only required to examine intelligent people, familiar with practical occupations and especially with colors, and with no other interest connected with the issue of the examination than to know whether they are color-blind or not, the examination would be uniform and mechanical; but it is required to examine people of various degrees of culture, all of whom, besides, have a personal interest in the issue of the examination. Different people act very differently during the examination for many reasons. Some submit to it without the least suspicion of their defect; others are convinced that they possess a normal sense. A few only have a consciousness, or at least some suspicion, of their defect. These last can often be recognized before the least examination by keeping behind the others, by attentively following the progress of the trial, but, if allowed, willingly remaining to the last. Some are quick; others, slow. The former approach unconcernedly and boldly; the latter, with over-anxiety and a certain dread. Some have been perhaps already tested, and practised themselves in preparation for the trial; others have never been familiar with colors. Among those already tested may be some color-blind. Some of these latter are uncertain about their mistakes, and act with great care; whilst others again are practised in distinguishing the signals and hence conclude that their color-sense is perfect. They make the trial quickly, and without thought; of course regularly making the mistakes characteristic of their special form of color-blindness.

"The majority, however, desire to perform their task as well as possible; that is, to do what the normal-eyed does. This of course assists in testing them, provided it does not lead to too great care, as then the testing the color-blind is more difficult; the trouble being that much time is thus wasted. Only a very small part have a contrary desire; namely, to pass for color-blind, though normal-eyed. We will speak of these later, and now only concern ourselves with those who stand the test in good faith with the desire to appear normal, though perhaps color-blind.

"The trial generally goes on rapidly and regularly. We will only mention those hinderances and peculiarities which most frequently occur. The examiner must watch that no mistake is made from not understanding. The names of the colors need never be used, except to ascertain if the name learned hides the subjective color-sensation, or to find the relation between the name the color-blind employs and his color-perception.

"The person examined who thinks more of names than the test itself (this being generally a sign of school-learning) selects not only the worsteds of the same shades, — that is, those of the same color to his eye, — but all which generally have the name of this color: for instance, in the first test I., not only the green like the sample, but all that are green; and with the second test, not only the purple (and what are generally called red), but all which *look* reddish, scarlet, cinnabar, or sealing-wax red. This is of no importance; for those who only do this have scarcely such defective chromatic sense as we are concerned with. He is either normal-eyed or violet-blind. Simply as a test of violet-blindness in the interest of science, we can go on with the trial, and ascertain how far the grouping of the two colors was due to a confusion of names or to defective color-perception. Otherwise this examination does not concern the practical point we aim at.

"Under any circumstance it is better to correct the mistakes just mentioned, when arising from misunderstanding, and even necessary, in reference to mistakes we explained with the first test. It might be said that it was sufficient if the examined confounded the sample-color with green only; that it was indifferent whether he distinguishes carefully between the various kinds of green. But, in fact, this is not so unimportant. We must give full value to the determining whether the infraction of the rules arises from misunderstanding, or lack of practice with colors, or, finally, from a true chromatic defect. To include all that is green would render the test tedious and unpractical. In fact, no little judgment has been exercised in the selection of the very lightest shade of the green proposed as a sample-color; for it is exactly what the color-blind most readily confounds with the colors (1–5) of the plate. If the subject were allowed to depart from the narrow limits established by the trial, it would include every shade of green; the result of which would be that he would prefer to select all the vivid shades, and thus avoid the dangerous ground where his defect would certainly be discovered. This is why it is necessary to oblige him to keep within certain limits, confining him to pure green specimens, and, for greater security, to recommend him to select especially the lightest shades; for, if he keeps to the darker shades, as many try to, he readily passes to other tones, and loses himself on foreign ground, to the great loss of time and certainty of the test. What we have just said of green applies also, of course, to purple.

"The principle of our method is to force the one examined to reveal himself, by an act of his own, the nature of his chromatic sense. Now, as this act must be kept within certain limits, it is evident that the examiner must direct him to a certain degree. This may present, in certain cases, some difficulty, as he will not always be guided, and does either too much or too little. In both cases the examiner should use his influence, in order to save time and gain certainty; and this is usually very easily done. This intervention is of course intended to put the examiner in the true path, and is accomplished in many ways, according to the case in point.

"We will here mention some of the expedients we have found useful:—

"(A) *Interfering when the Examined select too many Colors.*

"It is not always easy to confine the one examined within the limits of the method. He easily slips in the first test, for example, a yellow-green or blue-green skein among the others, and, as soon as there is *one*, others follow usually; and it thus happens that in a few moments he has a whole handful of yellow-green, a second of blue-green, a third of both these shades at the same time. Our process has assisted us in more than one case of this kind.

"(*a*) When the person examined has begun to select shades of one or several other colors than those of the sample, his ardor is arrested by taking from him the handful of skeins he has collected, and asking him whether his eye does not tell him there are one or several which do not match the others, in which case he is solicited to restore them to the pile. He then generally remarks that there is some obscuration, and proceeds in one of the following manners:—

"1. He rejects, one after the other, the foreign shades; so that the correct remain, which is often only the sample-skein. He is shown what mistake he has made. Names are used to remind him that one class of green may be yellow green; and another, blue green: and, to induce him to avoid them, he is advised only to select skeins of the same shade as the specimen, although they be lighter or darker, and have neither more yellow nor blue than that. If his first error arose only from a misconception or want of practice in handling colors, he begins generally to understand what he has to do, and to do properly what is required of him.

"2. Or else he selects and rejects immediately the skein of the sample itself. This proves that he sees the difference of color. He is then shown the skein as the only correct one, and asked to repeat the trial in a more correct manner. He is again put on the right track as just before; and the trial proceeds rightly, unless the error arose from a defect in the chromatic sense. Many seem, however, to experience a natural difficulty in distinguishing between yellow green and blue green, or the dull shades of green and blue. This difficulty is, however, more apparent than real, and is corrected usually by direct comparison. If the method requiring the name of the color to be given is used, a number of mistakes may be the result. If a skein of light green and light blue alone are presented to him, asking him to name them, he will often call blue green, and green blue. But if, in the first case, a blue skein is immediately shown him, he corrects his mistake by saying this is blue, and that green. In the last case it happens so *mutatis mutandis*. This is not the place for an explanation. It must suffice to say that the error is corrected by a direct comparison between the two colors.

"There is, according to the theory, one class of the color-blind — violet-blind — who, in consequence of the nature of their chromatic sense, and, therefore, notwithstanding the comparison, cannot distinguish blue and green. But our method has nothing to do with this class of the color-blind, because such are not dangerous on railways.

"(*b*) *Another Process.* — If the one examined place by the side of the sample a shade, for instance, of yellow green, the examiner places near this another shade, in which there is more yellow, or even a pure yellow, remarking, at the same time, that, if the first suit, the last must also. The other usually dissents from this. He is then shown, by selecting and classing the intermediate shades, that there is a gradation, which will diverge widely if logically carried out as he has begun. The same course is followed with colors of the blue shades, if the blue-green were first selected. He sees the successive gradations, and goes through with this test perfectly if his chromatic sense is correct.

"To ascertain further whether he notices these additions, or the tints of yellow and blue in the green, we can take ourselves the yellow green and blue green to ask him if he finds this to be so. We can judge by his answer of his sense with regard to these shades, and the object of this investigation is accomplished.

"It results from all this that many who are finally considered to have a normal chromatic sense may occasionally cause embarrassments. In the main, the normal observer of this kind causes greater loss of time than the color-blind. It is astonishing to see with what rapidity the color-blind betray their defect. At least it is found, in the majority of the cases examined by us, that the first skein of wool selected from the pile by the color-blind in the first test was one of the 'colors of confusion.'

"(B) *Interfering when the Examined select too few Worsteds.*

"Those who evince too great slowness also require the interferences of the examiner in another manner. We can lay aside here those cases in which, at the sight of the complex colors of the heap of wool, the examined finds it difficult to select a skein resembling the sample in a collection where all the particular colors seem to differ from each other, and in consequence declares immediately that he can find none resembling the specimen. It is replied that an absolute resemblance is not demanded, and that no one asks impossibilities; that time is limited, many are waiting, &c. But there are people who — from natural slowness, from being unaccustomed to such business, from fear of making mistakes, and especially if previously examined and suspected of color-blindness, or from many other motives — proceed with the greatest caution. They do not even wish to touch the wool; or they search, select, and replace with the greatest care all the possible skeins without finding one corresponding with the sample, or that they wish to place beside it. Here then are two cases: on one hand, too much action with the fingers, without result; on the other, too little effort. The examiner is forced to interfere in both cases.

"(*a*) At the time of a too great manual action, without corresponding practical result, the examiner must be careful that the eye and hand act simultaneously for the accomplishment of the desired end.

"Some people forget that the hands should be subservient to the eye in this trial, and not act independently. Thus they are often seen to fix their eyes on one side while their hands are engaged on the other. This should be corrected, so as to save time and avoid further labor. When, from the manual activity of the one examined, or by the unobserved aid of the examiner, all the correct skeins, or only a portion, are found in the pile, it is wise to stop, and invite the former to cross his hands behind his back, to step back a pace, and quietly consider all the skeins, and, as soon as his eye has met one of those for which he is looking, to extend his hand and take it. The best plan is to advise him to look first at the sample, and then at the pile, and to repeat this manœuvre until his eyes find what he is looking for.

"This stratagem generally succeeds when nervousness from over-anxiety causes his hands to tremble; but it is not always easy to induce him to keep his hands behind his back until the moment for taking the skein in question.

"(*b*) In cases of great caution, the trial is hastened, if the examiner come to the assistance of the other by holding above the pile one skein after the other, and requesting him to say whether it resembles the color of the sample or not. It will be advisable first to select the skeins that a color-blind person would approve. If he is so, he will approve of the selection, and the question is settled; if not, he rejects them, not without a characteristic smile, or with an expression of wounded dignity. This also enlightens us as to his chromatic sense. But even the color-blind may, in such a case, refuse what is presented, especially if his caution is premeditated, and he suspects that a snare is intended. It is found quite frequently that he rejects the correct shades likewise presented with the others. This is not the case when one, having a normal chromatic sense, is slow and deliberative when subjected to the test under this form. He has an eye alive to the correct colors.

"One process, in cases of this last kind, is to select false samples, which are placed quite near the correct one, by the side, above, or below, to attract the attention of the examined from the right side. It is necessary so to proceed that the true sample be displaced when the others are drawn out, so that the person examined may see it move. It does not, however, always happen to catch his eye. The best means is then to make him examine the whole, with his hands behind his back, and invite him to freely make his choice. But, whatever the process, it is necessary, in every case where one has been assisted in selecting a certain number of skeins which he has found analogous to the sample-color, to make a rule not to conclude the trial without examining into the effect of the aid accorded. It is necessary to hold in the hand the approved package, and ask if he is satisfied, or if he would desire any change. If he approve the choice, the diagnosis is established. The same course must be pursued with the defective chromatic sense, that the trial may be made with or without assistance. To be thorough, the name given by the color-blind to the colors in question may be likewise asked.

"In cases where any one suspected of color-blindness has remained some time to see the trial of others, and where, as often happens, he has remarked the samples belonging to a required green shade, he may of course profit by it in his own trial. But this can be prevented by furtively concealing one or two of these samples. If he seem to be disposed to confound green and gray, it will be very easy to entrap him. If we do not succeed, even when assisting him, in entrapping him in this snare, the hidden samples may be put back into their places, to be convinced that the trial is correct.

"From the above, it is seen that many artifices may be necessary in our examination. It may be regarded as an advantage of our method that it has at command a great variety of resources. We have by no means mentioned all;

and yet many who have only read this description will probably reproach us with having devoted ourselves too much to details which seem to them puerile. But we believe that those who have examined the chromatic sense of a great number of persons, and acquired thereby considerable experience, will think differently.

"We are convinced that time is saved by such artifices, and a more certain result obtained; whilst a practised surgeon, who has become to a certain degree a *virtuoso*, will accomplish his object quicker and surer by such artifices than one who neglects them. Recent experience fully confirms this. All those who have familiarized themselves with my method, and have had experience with color-blindness, and of whose competence there can be no doubt, report, without exception, that it is to be fully depended on, — the most practical and the best. Therefore the single unfavorable opinion I know of — namely, that of Dr. Stilling [1] — can only arise from neglect of the simplest rules of the method. He thus appears to have wholly overlooked my first and most important test, and admits his inability to decide between the names and the color-confusions of the examined, which is so readily done by my method. Moreover, he used the *plate* in my book to test for color-blindness, in direct opposition to my expressed directions, and the principles of this mode of trial. This will suffice to explain to every intelligent person Dr. Stilling's erroneous and confused ideas as to the application and carrying-out of my method. The lack of value of a judgment based upon such a misapplication and wrong use of the method is self-evident.

"An advantage of our method we showed to be, that those who were to be examined could be present and see each individual tested, without this interfering in the least with the certainty of the result. The individual test is even hastened thereby. The color-blind, and even the normal-eyed who are not familiar with colors, are generally rather shy about being tested in whatever way it is done. As ours, however, is carried out, they have more reliance. The majority are even amused. The old adage holds true here, that it is easier to find fault than to do it yourself. The surgeon,

[1] Die Prüfung des Farbensinnes biem Eisenbahn und Marine-personal. Cassel, 1878, 1st edition.

who watches not only the examined, but also those around, can often see from their faces how closely the latter observe the person being tested when he takes out the wrong colors, as also when he neglects the right ones under his eye. This gives those looking on confidence and assurance, till their turn comes, when they appear as uncertain as before they were confident. There is in this something attractive, stimulating the interest, and hence not without benefit.

"From this we see that our judgment of a person's color-sense is made, not only by the material result of the examination, the character of the worsteds selected, but often also by the way the examined acts during the test. We should mention a very common manner of persons on trial, which, in many cases, is of great diagnostic value. Often, in searching for the right color, they suddenly seize a skein to lay it with the sample ; but then notice it does not correspond, and put it back in the heap. This is very characteristic; and, if an examiner has often seen it, he can readily recognize it, and be assured that it is an expression of difficulty in distinguishing the differences of the colors. We frequently see this in the first test, with shades of greenish blue and bluish green. Here it means nothing important: quite the reverse, however, when it concerns the gray or one of the confusion-colors 1–5. Uncertainty and hesitation as to these colors, which the color-blind do not distinguish from the sample, even when directly comparing them, is positive proof of mistake, implying defective chromatic vision, like the complete color-blind. No doubt the form of chromatic defect which we have called *incomplete* color-blindness exists in several kinds and degrees. This is not the place to further discuss our experience on this point; and, for the practical purpose we have in view, it is not necessary. As we have explained, there are, among these, forms gradually approaching normal color-sense. How they appear has been described. We designated them as *feeble color-sense*.

"It is, perhaps, not easy to detect this special form by any other, or even our own, method: therefore we give the following as a means of so doing. The only way of getting at the point is one we gave in the early chapters of our book; namely, the determining at what distance the examined could distinguish a small colored surface. For, in fact, we have to do with a feeble color-sense, which does not *prevent* the distinguishing of the colors, but only renders it difficult. We may suppose, in comparison to the normal color-sense, the *feeble* is due either to a weaker response to excitation on the part of the color-perceptive organs of the retina, or a relatively smaller number of these organs. In either case this method would give us the same result, judging from our experience in testing the eccentric portions of the field of vision with the perimeter.

"The method we here speak of shows us also the effect of habit and practice on the color-perception, and it is worth while to dwell on this point. It happens not seldom that a person who by test No. I. has been noted 'incomplete color-blind,' after they know of their mistake and have practised in distinguishing colors, will so comport themselves at a second trial that we have to simply mark them as of 'feeble color-sense.' This fact might support Dr. Favre's idea that defective chromatic vision may be improved. This possibility, however, does not militate against our hypothesis from the theory, as to the nature of feeble color-sense. It does not change our stand-point in the question. We have the same sometimes with test No. II., explainable by what we have said; namely, that, between the complete lack of chromatic sense and the incomplete, there was a series of gradations, and that just here practice would affect the result of examinations.

"All the examples here spoken of but prove that many seeming trifles and stratagems are of value in making the examination, — amongst others the keeping the sample a little way off from the heap of worsteds, as also the removal of every thing which can cause the examined doubt and uncertainty. We must not, therefore, let them do what many want to; namely, hold a number of the worsteds in the hand at once. We must make the person being tested place each skein, as he takes it up, either with the sample or back on the pile. Many who are not clear whether the skein is like the sample or not, instinctively put the shades most resembling the test-sample at the side of the pile towards it, and thus gradually form a little bridge, whose security they would not undertake to vouch for. No such half-rules must, however, be allowed.

"*Deciding whether the Examined are fitted for their Duty.*

"The method of scrutiny here described is able to detect, as we have seen, not only complete or incomplete color-blindness, but a feeble chromatic sense. Moreover, it has been proved that there is a perfect gradation, from complete color-blindness on the one side to the normal chromatic perception on the other. The question then naturally arises, from our practical point of view, whether it is possible to draw a dividing line between the kinds and degrees of defective color-vision which would except those who could not cause any inconvenience to the railway service, and, in case of an affirmative answer, where such limit is to be found.

"It must first be remembered, that, in the existing state of things, these questions neither can nor ought to be settled in the same manner in every case, since the examination is intended for individuals of two different classes, — 1st, the aspirants for railway employment; and, 2d, the employés, or those already in service.

"It will be readily understood how great is the difference of the cases, in deciding what may be the result of the examination. We have already given our views on this point. Justice here calls for an essential distinction, supposing that the test has been always made with sufficient accuracy. Hence we must pay especial attention to both of the above classes when deciding whether an employé is fitted for his duty.

"(A) *Those who are Applicants for Railroad Service.*

"We must bear in mind that in Sweden, according to the regulation in force there for the management of state railways (followed also, as far as we know, on the private lines), it is required, that, in order to be admitted, each applicant 'prove by a certificate from a physician that he is exempt from any kind of infirmity, disease, or defect of conformation that could be prejudicial to the exercise of his functions;' and also, that among these defects of conformation, in connection with signals, are reckoned the defects of the chromatic sense, to which the managers have especially directed the attention of the physicians attached to the lines.

"According to the principles we have stated, the greatest severity should be observed in this case; or, in other terms, the least defect in the sense of colors should be a sufficient ground for rejection.

"We must seek, therefore, to adapt the method of test to this law. The object of a test is to prevent any one from working as a railroad employé who does not have a perfectly normal color-perception. We have already sufficiently explained the evils arising from contrary action in case of admission to railroad-work. The border between normal and abnormal color-sense, like that between the normal and abnormal in all analogous fields, is purely conventional, and can never be sharply defined. In this case, however, it is necessary, and our experience shows, that, so long as the question of improving color-blindness is an open one, we must consider as over the border the slightest chromatic defect that our method can detect, or the slightest degree of incomplete color-blindness; that is, feeble color-perception. In consideration of the insignificance of the trouble, our demand seems hard; and yet we think that it is not too severe. On the contrary, it is quite possible that hereafter still stricter rules will become necessary.

"Our practical work is greatly simplified by drawing this boundary-line. We hold as fixed that the surgeon is not to be asked to decide whether a man is fit for the service or not, but simply to state the kind and degree of the color-blindness of the employé referred to him. The decision of an intelligent person is then immediate and decisive, whether he gives all the examined a written certificate, including the color-blind, or refuses this to the latter. The statement of the slightest color-blindness in the first case, as also the refusal to give a certificate in the latter, are both equal to refusal.

"(B) *Employés already in Service.*

"We must here ask ourselves if we must not modify the limit we have just traced, in order to carry out the principle we stated before; namely, that it is necessary to adopt less severe rules as to the elimination from the service of those who are already employed. We here encounter great difficulties: and it will be seen that it is not possible to settle the question summarily; that is, that a sharply defined limit cannot be traced. In such cases the physician should always, when he discovers a defect in the chromatic sense, give a certificate which will indicate its nature. These indications include, as we have already said, the diagnoses *complete red-blindness, complete green-blindness, incomplete color-blindness, or a feeble chromatic sense.*

"Our method adheres strictly to the theory; but, on account of the transition-forms, the diagnosis cannot always meet the very exact demands of the theory. If we class with complete color-blindness only those cases in which one of the three elements of the visual apparatus is wholly wanting or completely paralyzed, and with incomplete color-blindness only those cases in which none of the three are wholly wanting, but simply the receptability of one is very much reduced, we shall have to group many cases of the latter class with the first. On the other hand, we shall often have to consider the lower grades of incomplete color-blindness with feeble chromatic sense. We must, however, recall cases of a person — especially if subsequently practised — being at the first examination marked as completely color-blind, whilst a second time they appeared only incompletely color-blind; and others where a person was at one time incompletely color-blind in the fullest sense of the word, whilst at another only feeble color-sense could be shown. In such cases the record should state, in addition, 'incomplete color-blindness,' approaching complete red or green, or incomplete color-blindness of slight degree, &c.

"The same strict rule should be applied to those already employed as to those seeking service, and all discharged who show any lack of color-perception. This would certainly most surely protect the railroad service from danger. Such a general law, however, has its difficulties, especially as we must recognize, in respect to the danger of confounding the signals, a great difference between complete color-blindness and a feeble color-perception. The different cases of incomplete color-blindness vary also in degree. To draw a line here, and say beforehand who shall be dismissed and who retained, will be as easy in regard to the first as difficult in reference to the latter; for we are convinced that every case of complete color-blindness of both kinds, as well as every case of incomplete of the higher degrees, should be immediately dismissed. But, as regards those who may be retained, it is clear that the first question concerns those who, at the time of the trial, were regarded in the diagnosis only as having a feeble chromatic sense, and then those who in the first test merely confound gray with the sample-color. But we do not venture to lay this down as a principle; for, if it should be proved that these individuals can generally distinguish the light of colored lanterns with sufficient accuracy, this does not prove that it is so in every case, and especially not at every distance required in the service. This is why we know nothing better to advise than to refer all such cases to competent specialists, as long as the transition period of which we have spoken lasts.

"It may be asked, How will the specialists themselves proceed? To answer this, however, would require a much more extended scientific discussion of the various methods than we have proposed here to make. We would only give some hints. A specialist who is familiar with this subject has all known methods at his disposition; and, if these fail, he need but invent others. As, however, I have been in the position of the specialist in reference to the reform on the railroads of Sweden, I will here say how I have proceeded.

"In the examination of doubtful cases submitted to my judgment, I determined according to several of the methods mentioned in one of the preceding chapters. In general, these persons were all subjected to a trial according to the methods of Seebeck and Maxwell, and an examination by means of the visual perimeter and of colored shadows, as well as the lanterns of my invention and colored glasses. These last means have capacity especially in view; and they are very suitable for the object, when it is desired to investigate those who have been already discovered, by my method of Berlin worsteds, as having a defective chromatic sense.

"The light of colored lanterns and illuminated surfaces generally, conveniently arranged and methodically used, may serve especially in such cases to enlighten us as to the faculty of the person examined for appreciating colored signals. Our experiences of this kind have shown us that the majority of color-blind railway employés, however much practice they have had, are utterly incapable of recognizing and distinguishing the regulation colors of lanterns, especially when they are employed in the shades which are not most commonly in use in the service. This applies not only to the completely red and green blind, but also to the incompletely blind. These last require the most circumstantial investigation, and it is not to be assumed that the lower degrees can stand the trial. They may often, it is true, distinguish the signal-lights at a short distance with sufficient accuracy; but they do not succeed at a comparatively greater distance. As the places where the trials are usually made do not command such distances as railways for observing signals, signal-lights cannot of course be used for these trials. They are replaced by small illuminated surfaces, which, seen from a suitable distance, produce exactly the same effect as lanterns at a great distance. Such surfaces are made by placing a screen, with a suitable opening covered with a colored glass, before the flame of a lamp.

"We have, however, said enough in reference to means to be employed in such cases. We had no thought to enter into the details of them further, and doubt whether this would on the whole be advisable. The reason of this will be apparent from the following chapter."

CHAPTER XXI.

EFFORTS TO CONCEAL OR TO FEIGN COLOR-BLINDNESS.

"WE have announced that none of the kinds of color-blindness we have in view in this work could escape discovery by our method. But this, of course, assumes that the subject does his best in the trial, and acts in good faith. If it happen that one persists, either in concealing a conscious color-blindness or for some other motive, in not giving the least information by act or word, it is evident that the examination must fail from this simple reason, and that it is impossible to draw any positive conclusion with regard to his chromatic sense. The examiner may in such a case mention unconditionally in the certificate that the one examined refused to submit to the usual examination.

"It is not difficult to say how it is necessary to act with regard to such persons. It should, in fact, be the interest of each one possessing normal sight, desirous of entering the service of railways, &c., to endeavor to be competent in every respect, and consequently to give manifest proof of his sense of colors. The color-blind alone have any interest in concealing their defect: therefore they endeavor to escape the trial. Every candidate who will try to avoid the prescribed trial must therefore be considered and treated as color-blind. Such obstinacy on the part of an employé must be considered and treated as an infraction of the regulations.

"But cases may arise also in which those possessing normal sight will feign color-blindness, and act as if they were so affected. This may occur when some one wishes to receive a pension before the time, or else to escape punishment consequent upon an unexpected accident. These are just the very cases that put the method and perspicacity of the examiner to the test. The examination then assumes the character of a kind of criminal inquest, where the judge and the accused must give all the attention of which they are capable to their reciprocal acts and expressions, to try to entrap each other. The one examined tries to prove that he is color-blind, while the examiner endeavors to prove that he has normal sight. The prospect of coming off victorious in so singular a contest rests, in the last resort, with him who best understands the nature of color-blindness, and has most experience in the manner in which the color-blind act. To enable the pretender to deceive the examiner, it is absolutely necessary that he surpass the latter in knowledge of color-blindness. There is in this an element of success to the examiner, as it would be extremely rare to find a railway employé or sailor who would, under the circumstances mentioned, be subjected to an examination by a person inferior to himself in knowledge. It is clear, in fact, that an examination so difficult, so minute, and involving so much responsibility, should be confided to the most competent person possible. But it is, on the other hand, very improbable that a case should occur where it would be necessary that a learned and experienced specialist would have to submit to an examination.

"In the first place, examinations of this kind must rarely occur; and, when they do, it must be at least in the most difficult cases, — that is to say, after an accident, — under circumstances where the one examined has not had much time to study his part. It will generally be seen then that he has not a profound knowledge of the nature of color-blindness, but imagines it to be a difficulty or incapacity to distinguish signal-colors or colors in general. He will therefore be governed by this idea; and either he will perfectly distinguish every other color, so as to mistake only the signal-colors, or else he will believe he must confound no matter what color. But, as we have seen, each kind of color-blindness follows laws as fixed as the normal sense. Such a strategem will not fail to violate them, and the individual will be caught in the very act.

"But there is absolutely nothing which opposes the supposition that this individual may have a certain knowledge of the nature of color-blindness, or, at least, that he may have an idea of its regularity with regard to the confusion of colors. He may have studied the proofs we have cited; and, owing to the exercise and observation of the color-blind, he will know how to perform them in a manner suitable to the object in view. The examiner has always, however, the choice of other sample-colors; and the Berlin-worsted method affords a large choice. If that does not suffice, and the individual has learned from the truly color-blind to classify the whole collection of worsteds according to their chromatic sense, — that is to say, that he can stand the trial according to Seebeck's method, — and if he is so thorough in his part that there is no means of making him depart from it by abrupt or contradictory questions, the examiner may employ for the examination a number of other known methods, but probably unknown to our individual. It must not be forgotten here that it is generally easier to discover faults committed by others, than to avoid being guilty of them one's self; and one must be profoundly familiar with his borrowed part not to be guilty of inconsistencies. With regard to feigning a certain kind of color-blindness, we know by our experience, with regard to this, that it is a very difficult thing, and scarcely ever succeeds before an attentive and experienced examiner. All these circumstances are advantageous for the examiner; but his superiority is not limited to this. For if it should happen — an extremely improbable thing — that a pretender were familiar with all the known tests and methods, and besides had not less practice than talent in executing them as accurately as the color-blind, the examiner has, nevertheless, the power of inventing, owing to his special knowledge, new tests, and of varying those already known.

"When speaking of the examination of those already in service, and the rules to govern us here, we called attention to the necessity of acting with great caution in doubtful cases. The test for color-blindness should then be carried out by a competent specialist; but the details of the several methods he would use we purposely omitted. Still less do we think it well to give details in reference to the trial of those simulating color-blindness. It rarely happens that a writer or professor has cause to withhold the very fullest knowledge of any special department of knowledge. Our case is, however, an exception; for every further detail is but putting another weapon in the hands of the malingerer, and thereby contributing to diminish the chances of success of the examining surgeon. In such case it is not only wise but right to keep silence. It may even be doubted whether too much has not already been said. We thought it, however, proper to say what we have, in order to convince others that it is very possible to expose a malingerer pretending to be color-blind. It would be very unfortunate if the author ities had the slightest doubt on this point. It is not improbable that the facts we have given have caused one or another to give up the difficult *rôle* of a *pseudo*-color-blind.

"Of course such examination requires the greatest care and foresight, and must be thoroughly and perfectly carried out before a decision is given. This is justified by the interests at stake. Although such a test should only be put in the hands of a thoroughly competent person, yet it is but right that a decision involving so much (fine or imprisonment, perhaps) should not be left to a single individual.

"Besides the precaution, which must not be neglected, of conducting the examination in the presence of expert and competent persons, there is an especial means, which, while being certain of preventing all fraudulent attempts, judges the accused in the usual manner; that is, by the testimony of two persons. These two witnesses should be two color-blind of the same kind as that feigned by the examined. If these two individuals are first subjected separately and independently of each other and the *pseudo*-color-blind to the same trial as he, let the results be noted down carefully, and then the whole three together; and it will then soon be seen how the case stands with the suspected individual. The two color-blind will, in this manner, give the necessary testimony without resting upon the discretion of the examiner. This manner of proceeding must, however, be employed with caution and discrimination, as the conformity between two color-blind of the same class is not absolutely perfect in every respect. The result must therefore always be made to harmonize by the explanation of the examiner."

CHAPTER XXII.

METHOD OF DECIDING THE PRECISE AMOUNT OF COLOR-BLINDNESS BY HOLMGREN'S CHROMATOSKIAMETER, OR COLOR-SENSE TESTER. — PROFESSOR DONDERS'S METHOD OF DETERMINING QUANTITATIVELY COLOR-PERCEPTION.

One of the additional methods of detecting color-blindness is of value for examiners to be acquainted with. It is based on the true principle of comparison, no names of color being required of those examined. It also, like the method of Donders, enables us to express in figures the *amount* of the chromatic defect in each individual case. The apparatus is arranged to enable us to use colored shadows. It is not very expensive, and can be used by day or night. To further test railroad employés or others, after having decided on their color-blindness by Holmgren's worsteds, it will be, as I said, of great value to examiners, and also serve the purpose of physiological experimenters. It has the advantage of giving constant results independent of the examiner. These results can be readily understood by the laity, and the test applied before them. As Professor

Holmgren says, "the apparatus may also be used in determining the absorptive power of various colored glasses," &c. It must be understood that it is a means or method for the *expert* alone to employ. I will here give the author's full description of it. He has tested it thoroughly with the many color-blind found on the railroads and elsewhere in Sweden. It is not described in his book, and first appeared in a pamphlet in Swedish. The following is from a condensed description in German, given by Professor Holmgren himself: —

"I would devote a special chapter to the discussion of the conditions of colored shadows, and the importance of the light by which they are produced. I have found it very difficult, if not impossible, to get a shadow which reflects no light. Without light the shadow in simultaneous contrast has no color.

"I hold here also, as always, that every method for the detection of color-blindness must depend on the principle of *comparison* of different colored lights or surfaces. In this sense the colored shadows can be used as any other colored surfaces if they are produced by two lights, or, what amounts to the same, by two from the same source. We may thus use the light of a single lamp, by letting one portion pass through the colored glass to the object causing the shadow, and the screen on which the shadow is cast; whilst another portion of the light, by means of a mirror near the glass, is thrown upon the same object. We thus have two shadows on the screen of complementary color. One is illumined alone by the light through the colored glass, the other wholly by the light of the lamp reflected from the mirror; whilst the rest of the surface of the screen is illuminated by both. Now, as we move the mirror to or from the lamp, we can regulate the relative luminosity of the shadows. I have constructed such an apparatus, which I would call a chromatoskiameter. In the centre of the apparatus is a petroleum-lamp with a round wick. The lamp is on a stand, from which project two horizontal movable arms. On these arms are the rest of the apparatus. The colored glass, the pencil to cast the shadow, and the screen of white porcelaine on which the shadow is cast are arranged on one of these horizontal arms at a fixed distance from the flame. On the other arm is the mirror which can be moved to or from the lamp. The arms are marked on the sides with a millimetre scale, supposed to commence in the centre of the flame. Thus the distance of the several parts from the lamp can be read off on the scale.

"In employing the instrument, I have used a red glass, which allowed only spectral red to pass, and a green, which passed mostly the middle spectral green, but also some other light, — no red, however. In using the instrument to detect color-blindness, we must grade it by trial, and determine its constants for the glass used. We must, for this purpose, find for each glass the distance the mirror must be from the flame to cause the two shadows to appear alike to the normal eye; that is, of the same degree of brightness each of its own color. This distance of the mirror for my eye I found, for the *red* glass, to be 40 centimeters; for the *green*, 35 centimetres, — a difference of 5 centimetres. To find this position of the mirror is much easier with the color-blind than the normal-eyed, for the simple reason that for the former, when the shadows are of the same degree of brightness, they are generally of the same color. The distance of the mirror for him is quite different from that of the normal-eyed, and so characteristic as to detect him thereby. It is also very different in different cases. All the cases examined can be separated into two distinct series, corresponding to the two forms of color-blindness I have described; namely, red-blindness and green-blindness. The distance of the mirror with red-blindness (the average of 25 cases) was, —

For the red glass	=	73.2 centimetres
For the green glass	=	27.6 "
Difference (R. G.)	=	45.6 centimetres

With green blindness (from an average of 35 cases recorded) the distance of

The green glass was	=	48.5 centimetres
The red glass was	=	28.7 "
Difference (Gr. R.)	=	19.8 centimetres

"Incomplete color-blindness may also readily be detected by differences of the mirror's distances from that for the normal eye. For the very slightest grades of chromatic defect this method is not so good to be used alone, since such forms of the trouble are apt to be confused with a lack of knowledge or understanding in reference to appreciating the relative luminosity of the shadows.

"In the original article the examination of 135 cases of various grades of color-blindness was recorded. This method, as is seen, is based wholly on the principle of *comparison*. It is not, however, the comparison of two colors, but that of the intensity of two lights of different kinds. It has this practical advantage, that the color-blind, who are very sensitive to differences of luminosity, can readily find the right position of the mirror. Theoretically there is also the advantage that it shows the chromatic defect to be a lessened sensitiveness for a special kind of light, — one of the primary colors.

"In the respective distances of the mirror from the flame, as read off from the scale, compared with the distance for the normal eye, we have in every case a relative measure of the reduced sensitiveness. Now, as the mirror is movable, and can be altered in position till the *luminosity* of the two shadows is alike to the eye of the person examined, the intensity of the unaltered lamp-light on one shadow will serve to measure the intensity of the light on the other shadow, which has passed through the colored glass, and become more or less homogeneous. As the zero-point of the scale is in the flame, greater numbers or distances of the mirror must correspond to lessened sensibility to light of the color of the glass. This quite agrees with the numbers above given for red and green blindness; the first showing abnormal want of sensitiveness for red, and the latter for green light. This agrees again with the Young-Hemholtz theory, and also, as well, with the results of my tests with the worsteds. The cases referred to were first tested with the worsteds, and the diagnosis confirmed by examination with the chromatoskiameter.

"The characteristic confusion of colors of the color-blind does not necessarily imply a great reduction of perception for any one of the primary colors. They are explainable by a disturbance of the color-sense in the individual case, whereby the sensibility for one of the primary colors, independently of its real value, is reduced in comparison with sensibility of the other two. This explains a large number of the cases tested with this instrument. Hence it is of value to test each case with two complementary colored glasses. The difference between the distances of the mirror for each expresses the value of the defect to be ascertained.

"The absolute distance of the mirror has of course only a relative value, does not immediately represent the intensity of the illumination of the shadow; that is, the sensitiveness of the eye examined. This, however, we can deduce from a formula I will here give. Taking the above figures as representing the average distance of the mirror, the sensitiveness of the normal eye (the intensity of the lamp being unity)

For the red light = 0.115.
For the green light = 0.137.

The average sensitiveness of the red-blind

For red light = 0.048.

The average sensitiveness of the green-blind

For green light = 0.088.

Or, if we regard the normal color-sense as a measure for the sensitiveness,

Normal color-sense = 1.00.
Red-blindness = 0.42 (R.).
Green-blindness = 0.64 (Gr.).

By the value gained from the distance of the mirror, applied to normal color-sense, we may calculate the absorptive power of the glass. The absorption by the glass, expressed as loss of light, is thus: —

For the red glass = 42.5 centimetres.
For the green glass = 43.1 centimetres.

"Thus, by using a larger number of suitable colored glasses, we can study not only the normal chromatic sense, but also the various forms of color-blindness. The principle of the method does not, however, restrict us in practice to colored shadows; but it may be extended to any colored lights or surfaces. Therefore it would be well, upon the same principle, to employ the spectral light in the study of the color-sense and its defects.

"I have here confined myself to the use of two glasses, principally because these experiments were directed to the detection of color-blindness among the *personnel* of the Swedish railroads, where, of course, we were concerned with the red and green only. These examinations have at least proved the existence of green-blindness as an independent typical species, in accordance with the Young-Helmholtz theory, hitherto but little regarded, or ignored. This is directly opposed to the idea that red and green blindness are but one and the same thing, called red-green-blindness.

"As to the practical use of this method, I regard it only as one of the category I have called *methods of control*, and in my original article have given the reasons why it is not comparable with my worsted method as a preliminary test, which I still regard as the best of any at present proposed."

Another method of quantitative determination of color-blindness was carried out by Professor Donders on the Holland railroads. It has not been given in English, and I present it for the benefit of our examiners in this country. Like this one of Holmgren's, it is an *additional* method.

PROFESSOR DONDERS'S METHOD OF QUANTITATIVELY DETERMINING COLOR-PERCEPTION.

"Approaching slowly a small colored object, the normal eye detects the color but little later than the light. We shall not, however, seek long before finding a person who sees the color much later than he sees the light. On this is based my method of examination.

"For testing with reflected light, disks of colored paper are used, 1, 2, 5, or more millimetres in diameter. Each one is separately glued to a little piece of black velvet; and, in like manner, pieces from the white, red, and green signal-flags. These little pieces of velvet, with the colored disks on them, can with slight pressure be made to adhere to a larger piece of velvet a metre square, fastened upon the wall, and on which one or more can thus be exhibited as we desire.

"Color-perception K is in the inverse proportion to the amount of light; that is, equal to the square of the distance *d*, at which the colors are recognized, and inversely proportional to the square of the diameter *m*. Let D represent the distance at which the normal eye sees color, of $m = 1$ (that is, disks of one millimetre diameter), and we have

$$K = \frac{1}{m^2} \cdot \frac{d^2}{D^2}.$$

This formula gives for the normal eye $K = 1$, and for every other eye $K < 1$.

"In the formula of visual acuteness $V = \frac{d}{D}$, the distances are simply d and D (not d^2 and D^2), because the distinguishing a printed letter is in proportion to the visual angle in all directions. Moreover, in this formula D is regarded as constant. This is because, in the varying light of an ordinary room, with fair light, the visual power is near its maximum. This does not hold in the same degree in reference to distinguishing color. The lack of light is of course partly compensated for by the greater sensibility of the retina and the wider pupil; but, with increasing daylight, the perception of most colors also increases very considerably. Therefore it is important for the examiner to determine each time his own D, and take this into consideration. In deciding the visual acuteness (form-perception), we take into account diminished illumination when it materially reduces our own visual power. This is all the more necessary with color-perception, since the same colors are not to be obtained exactly alike everywhere; and those obtainable are not always recognized at the same distance. Moreover, from use they lose their brightness. We may, however, accept as a general law, that bright, saturated colors, one millimetre in diameter, when placed on black velvet in a good light, will be seen by an eye with normal visual acuteness (ametropia being corrected) at a distance of *five* metres.

"This method supposes that the examiner has normal color-sense, which is readily determined by comparison with others. It is also necessary that, before testing, both the examined and examiner should have been in the room for a time with equal illumination. Decreasing daylight reduces all colors, but not all equally. Blue, for instance, requires of all the colors the least light to be recognized when we pass from a darker to a lighter locality; the most light, on the other hand, when we go from a lighter to a darker locality.

"For transmitted light, the flame of a candle may be used, such as is employed in England to determine the candle power of gaslight. This is placed behind a blackened wooden screen, in which is an opening, 25 mm. in diameter, covered with ground glass. In front of this hole a rotating metal disk is arranged, pierced with holes, 1, 2, 5, 10, and 20 mm. Just behind the opening in the screen is a rotating disk with holes, — one clear, the others containing red and green signal-lantern glass, as also other colors, which we can, by turning, bring in front of the hole in the screen. The candle is arranged to slide along a scale, thereby giving us its distance from the screen. The red glass is one that passes mostly red rays, up to orange, but no others. The green is one which passes a part of the rays from yellow to bluish green, and a little of the red.

"During the examination, daylight is to be so far excluded from the room as to only render recognition possible close to. We can then determine the distance A, at which, for the normal eye for white and colored light, with $m = 1$, $D = 5$ metres. At this distance D in the formula will keep the nearly constant value of 5 metres.

"With the candle and the finely ground glass employed, the white candle-light will give us $A = 1.75$ metres, the red glass will give us $A = 0.65$ metres, the green $A = 0.25$ metres. In this test with transmitted light, care must be taken to keep the opening in the direction of the candle. The examination is otherwise conducted in the same way as with reflected light. If the examined is color-blind, then the degree of brightness for the several colors is not the same in respect to A, and they decide the color from this difference in the brightness. This is shown if we vary the value of a, when those who are uncertain call the color alternately red or green. When using the largest opening, and bringing the flame close to the glass, there are but few persons who fail in recognizing the color if close to. In this numerical determination to also decide the recognition with stronger illumination, we need only make our formula $\frac{a^2}{A^2}$, where a is the distance of the flame from the glass found necessary, and A its normal distance. The power of color-perception will then be

$$K = \frac{1}{m^2} \cdot \frac{d^2}{D^2} \cdot \frac{a^2}{A^2} = \left(\frac{1}{m} \cdot \frac{d}{D} \cdot \frac{a}{A}\right)^2$$

Taking $\sqrt{K} = \frac{1}{m} \cdot \frac{d}{D} \cdot \frac{a}{A} = L$, it follows, as L is found by observation, that the power of color-sense $K = L^2$. It is more practical to hold to L, and, in general, to remember $L = \sqrt{K}$. With reflected light $\frac{a}{A}$ is eliminated, and, with transmitted light generally, $a = A$; so that, as a rule, we may confine ourselves to the formula $L = \frac{1}{m} \cdot \frac{d}{D}$, and, if we use the one millimetre opening, to the formula $L = \frac{d}{D}$.

"It is interesting to observe how the examined gradually passes from doubt to certainty. We show him a single test at five metres' distance. He sees the little disk, but not its color. A step nearer, and he ventures to call it "red." Another step, and he doubtfully says, "No, green." Finally, he says "red" again, and at last decides more positively for this color. Just where he became certain is readily determined. Or we put a number of the disks of varying diameters together on the large piece of velvet, and, pointing to each with a stick, ask its color quickly. With partial color-sense it readily appears how, in approaching, first the larger disks, and then the smaller, are rightly named; whilst with less color-perception only the larger are told close to, and where there is complete absence the color of even these is not recognized. We may thus determine the numerical degree of color-blindness with sufficient accuracy.

"The disk must not be steadily gazed at. The examined must turn his eyes aside, and step nearer, at once giving the name of the color pointed out. If the answer is not immediate, then again a step, with the eye removed from the object, and the question repeated. By steady gazing, the complementary color may be called up in the eye, and the decision rendered difficult."

In a letter to me of Feb. 23, 1879, Professor Donders says, —

"I think I may have given too brief a description of my method. Dr. Daae did not understand that it was not the preliminary, but only the secondary, examination in which transmitted light was used, and where the distinction of colors had already been proved imperfect. Dr. Stilling says, that, continuing to fix the eye on the disk, the secondary image of complementary color is developed, not aware that I expressly said that I allow only one or two seconds for giving the name of the color. Others speak of the great difference of the daylight, and forget that I prescribe that every observation is to be made at the same time by the examined and the examiner, the latter noticing at what distance (indicated at the point where the examined sets his foot) he distinguishes the color; and, if this is not five metres, then it is to be put in the formula as four or three, or whatever distance it is found. The determination or calculation is not thereby rendered longer or more difficult."

I considered it proper to introduce here Professor Donders's replies to the criticisms made on his method, since, as we see, they arose from a misunderstanding, or neglect of his directions for conducting this quite practical test, and which was carried out on the Holland roads, as I have formerly described. I also give the whole explanation of the test, as it is the one required to be used at present by the five ophthalmic surgeons now authorized to examine candidates for railroad service in Holland.

CHAPTER XXIII.

LAWS OF CONTROL OF COLOR-BLINDNESS NOW IN FORCE IN EUROPE. — LEGISLATIVE ACTION OF THE STATE OF MASSACHUSETTS.

HERE in the United States, either the several State legislatures, the State railroad commissioners, or the individual railroad corporations, will be sooner or later called upon by the community to establish and carry out some regulations controlling color-blindness among the employés: therefore it becomes of considerable importance for all parties interested to know how this control has been effected in Europe, and the precise manner of conducting the test. In order to answer this, I have corresponded with many surgeons in Europe, and, through their instrumentality, am able to here give the at present provisional laws in reference to most of the European states.

The European governments have not stopped to frame laws, but immediately carried out the examinations, and are subsequently considering the precise regulations for the future, &c. It will be also seen that the governments have provided for the elimination of all color-blind from their own railroads and navies. The private companies, where independent of their government, have followed its action. In what I have to say as to these laws, &c., there is much of vital importance for us in the United States about to commence this control. I would call the especial attention of my readers to the prudent and practical action of the Swedish Government, in comparison with that of the German states, in putting at the head of the control one who was as competent to conduct it as he was to originate the method of testing.

Professor Holmgren kindly furnishes me the following in reference to Sweden: —

CIRCULAR OF THE ROYAL SWEDISH RAILROAD DIRECTORY TO THE SUPERINTENDENTS.

To the Superintendents.

The royal directory would hereby call the attention of the respective district-surgeons to the fact that the lack of power to distinguish the several primary colors excludes entrance to railroad service: therefore persons seeking service must be tested for any such lack of visual power.

As it is of importance to be assured that the officials now in service can distinguish correctly the colors used in signals, the chiefs of sections, by means of the usual flags and lanterns, or other means they may find best adapted, are to ascertain if those under them are incapable of recognizing these colors. The results of such examinations are to be reported to the directory, and any suggestions in reference to dismissals which may seem necessary.

Surgical assistance will not be necessary with this last-named trial.

C. O. TROILIUS.
C. LIMNELL.

STOCKHOLM, Sept. 16, 1876.

Professor Holmgren writes me, —

"Having called the directory's attention to the fact that these rules in reference to those already in service were not sufficient, but that a thorough examination by the railroad-surgeons should be made, for which the surgeons must learn my method, the following circular was issued:—

CIRCULAR.

To the Superintendents of all the Districts.

The directory hereby orders a surgeon from each district, next Tuesday the 24th at 12 M., to meet Professor Holmgren in Upsala, to there learn from him his method of testing for color-blindness among the employés. Any other of the surgeons of the district may also attend the professor at this time for the same purpose.

A pass is to be issued both to those surgeons who are sent to this meeting, and to those who desire to attend, in accordance with the seventh clause of the travelling regulations.

C. O. TROILIUS.
C. LIMNELL.

STOCKHOLM, Oct. 16, 1876.

To the Superintendents.

Since, in accordance with the directions of Sept. 16, 1876, a number of the railroad-surgeons have learned from Professor Holmgren his method of examination for color-blindness, the directory hereby prescribes,

That this examination shall be gradually carried out among the railroad *personnel* by the surgeons, in accordance with Professor Holmgren's method.

That the surgeons who may not have already learned this method shall instruct themselves, either directly from Professor Holmgren himself in Upsala, or through those who attended his lecture on this subject.

That they report to the directory the result of their examinations, together with such suggestions as were required by the circular of Sept. 16; and, when color-blind are found in positions where the distinguishing the colors is important, they are to immediately make the necessary reports and remarks which the circumstances require, without waiting the termination of the tests.

C. O. TROILIUS.
C. LIMNELL.

STOCKHOLM, Nov. 9, 1876."

The directions of the superintendents to the surgeons were as follows, for an example: —

To Railroad-Surgeon Professor C. B. Merterton, *Upsala.*

The following from the directions of the royal railroad directory is communicated for your information and government: —

That the railroad-surgeons are to test all employés for color-blindness by Professor Holmgren's method.

That those surgeons who may not be acquainted with this method are to at once inform themselves, either from Professor Holmgren in Upsala, or from some of the surgeons who have heard his explanations and lecture on the subject.

That a report of these examinations is to be made as soon as possible.

In reference to the *personnel* of the traffic-department now employed, all station-masters have orders to transmit you lists of the whole *personnel* under them; and you are to record in the proper columns such remarks as the examination calls for.

C. J. Hemmarskord.

Stockholm, Superintendent's Office
of the Fifth Traffic District, Nov. 13, 1876.

"This is all official which relates to the railroads. It is, however, seen that all necessary is practically accomplished. 1st, Those entering the service must be tested for color-blindness, and all showing the slightest lack of color-perception refused. 2d, All those now employed are to be tried, and the color-blind either dismissed, pensioned, or given employment where the recognition of the colored signals is not necessary. I have acted as chief of control, and tested over again all those who were found defective by the railroad-surgeons.

"You will thus see we have been very practical. Without first making any laws, we carried out the reform quite simply under my personal supervision. I still act as the head of the control of color-blindness; and, now that we have gained a thorough practical experience, we shall this year establish laws to govern the railroads and the marine." (In letter of January, 1879, of Professor Holmgren to me.)

The Swedish navy and mercantile marine have not been neglected; and I will here give a transcript from the laws in reference to the former, as prepared by Professor Holmgren. In reference to the mercantile marine, Professor Holmgren writes me of date March 5, 1879: "I have been unable as yet to forward you the laws concerning the con trol of color-blindness in the merchant marine. The government has not yet given its sanction. They are thorough, definite, and strict." It must be remembered that all these laws of Sweden and the other European countries, as here given, must be considered as only provisional, and to simply serve the present purpose of *immediately* carrying out the test and the control of color-blindness.

ORDERS IN REFERENCE TO NORMAL COLOR-PERCEPTION AMONG THE PERSONNEL OF THE IMPERIAL SWEDISH MARINE AND ARMY CORPS.

1st, Upon his majesty's recommendation, the sect. 54 of the laws of the Naval School require that every cadet must, besides other qualifications, possess normal power of vision, together with normal color-sensation.

[*Remark.* — This is already so far carried out, that every cadet, on entering, is tested as to his color-perception. — F. HOLMGREN, January, 1879.]

2d, In the general orders to the pilot directory it is required, "That all in the pilot-service, ordinary and extra officials, shall, as soon as may be determined by the pilot directory, be examined, to find if they have normal color-perception. Those who do not have the power of distinguishing the colors are to be noted in the list by the pilot directory. After the examination the number of color-blind in each district is to be recorded, and sent in to the chief of the marine department, accompanied by such suggestions for action as may be considered necessary."

Given at the Palace, Stockholm, Nov. 18, 1876, by imperial order. FREIHER F. W. VON OTTER,

Marine Minister.

[*Remark.* — These examinations have been already carried out, and the results sent in to me. — F. HOLMGREN, January, 1879.]

3d, *The Regulations of the Imperial School of Navigation of June* 1, 1877, *Sect.* 16, 2.

Every applicant to enter the navigation department of the school must bring a physician's certificate as to the condition of his color-perception. A fault in color-perception will not prevent the reception of the candidate.

[*Remark.* — This last must be soon stricken out, or altered. — F. HOLMGREN.]

4th, *Royal Orders to the Chief of the Military Personnel of the Imperial Marine.*

1st, That all the *personnel* of the seamen's and boys' training-ship shall, at the next general review, pass the surgeon's examination as to their power of color-perception. Those who fail shall be duly recorded on the crew's manifest, and a notice of the number of color-blind in each company be reported by the mustering-officer to the chief of the marine department.

2d, That all the men of the Imperial Marine Corps, and boys of the navy, who have not been examined in accordance with the 1st regulation, shall be tested under sect. 284 of the Regulations of the Marine, 3d part, of the required medical supervision. The company report, when the examination was before the man went on board, and the commander, when this test was after he was on board, shall take note of the same, to be reported in the former case to the proper military head, who will report to the chief of the marine department; in the latter case, the commander, who will follow the rules under Rule I., here given.

3d, The special directions in reference to the medical examination, in accepting the recruit, will be given hereafter.

Given at the Palace at Stockholm, Nov. 18, 1876.

FREIHER F. W. VON OTTER.
H. P. LILLIEHÖEK.

[*Remark.* — The examinations ordered in 1 and 2 are long ago carried out, and the results handed in to me. In reference to No. 3, a committee of military surgeons has, in connection with the other regulations of acceptance and continuance, for both the army and navy, formulated the rules to be followed under No. 3. This has been since published, and is now only awaiting royal sanction. It is as follows. — F. Holmgren, January, 1879.]

5th. — 1*st Part, Sect.* 7.

The naval service calls for no especial bodily condition other than the physical condition required in the line, except the addition of assured normal color-perception. (*Vide* the Addendum.)

Addendum. — Special Examination, Sect. 19.

In reference to normal color-sense, care is to be taken that no one is admitted into the naval service whom the examination proves to be in any degree red-blind, green-blind, or partially color-blind.

The test for color-perception is to be carried out by Professor Holmgren's method, by which partial color-blindness is determined from the confusion of the light green, or first sample, with gray, brownish gray, yellowish green, pale red, or pale grayish purple (1, 2, 3, 4, or 5).

Red-blindness is determined by confusing, with the purple (II.), blue and violet (6 and 7); green-blindness, by confusing, with the purple, green and gray (8 and 9). Compare "Color-Blindness in its Relations to Railroads and the Marine," by Frithiof Holmgren.

Sect. 21. For these examinations, the following apparatus, &c., is necessary, enclosed in a box; viz., a copy of the above-mentioned book, and a collection of the worsteds.

The following are in general the regulations of the Norwegian Government of date May 7, 1877: —

1st, By order of the civil department, all railroad employés are examined by Professor Holmgren's method.

2d, By order of the navy department, the pupils in the navy-officers' school are to be tested for color-blindness, as also all enrolled in permanent service.

3d, It is now under advisement to require pilots to be tested for color-blindness; but regulations are not yet arranged and carried out.

Several private Swedish steamship companies have ordered examinations of their crews.

Through the efforts of Dr. Favre, the *personnel* of the French Transatlantic Steamship Company are subjected to a test for color-blindness. The British Cunard Steamship Company requires the surgeons of the ships to test the men for color-blindness. Colored glass is provided; but the special method is left to the individual medical officer. If, as has been lately stated in print, the men are subjected only to this test with colored glass or colored lanterns, we must, from all that has been shown and proved, consider that there has been no test as to the true color-sense of the *personnel*. Asking the names of colors or of colored lights, &c., will not tell us just how the person examined sees these lights, &c. Steamship companies, therefore, when they think they have done all necessary to protect the lives and property intrusted to them, may thus, from want of a perfect method of testing, be simply gathering into their crews men whose chromatic defect is most dangerous, and who could not obtain employment when a perfect test was applied.

The instructions as to the examination of persons seeking employment in the Bavarian railroad service are, —

I. As to the physical capacity of each individual, their visual power is to be tested, and also their color-perception; the result to be recorded in the report.

II. The test for color-blindness is to be conducted with the accompanying worsteds, which the applicant is to sort by colors, and designate.

Only those who can distinguish the differences of color are to be recorded as free from color-blindness. All other cases are to be noted with the remark, for example, — "Distinguishes red (or green) with difficulty."

The sanitary inspector-general of the railways of Northern Italy replies, —

"In answer to your question on color-blindness, my reply is, that although no printed regulation formed by the administration for our railways exists, which excludes color-blind men from being taken into the service, that contingency is guarded against by instructions given to the sanitary inspectors of the company, commissioned to examine the candidates for employment on the railways, which are to this effect: that, as to the visual faculty, they be able clearly to distinguish the different colors, both by natural and the artificial light of the lamp used on the trains and in signal-boxes, at the maximum distance of normal eyesight. These instructions have been, since the last few years, very strictly adhered to in the employment of new engine-drivers, stokers, and signal-men, — in fact, of all who have part of the great responsibility of the safety of the trains. Owing to this, and to the fact, that, when the least doubt arises as to the perfect state of the eyesight of one of our employés (due to age or sickness), he is at once subjected to a medical examination, we have as yet had to lament no accident on any of the lines under our direction which could in any way be attributed to color-blindness."

The minister of public works of Belgium proposed the following questions to the Royal Academy: —

1st, Is color-blindness a congenital defect? and can it be acquired? In the latter case the administration would *periodically* test its agents.

2d, What is a practical and efficient method of determining whether an employé fails in chromatic sense?

The committee of the academy replies, —

> "They are convinced that color-blindness may arise from a severe disease, contusions or wounds of the head, the abuse of tobacco and of alcohol. A periodic examination of the active *personnel* is therefore advised. . . . The examination of those suspected of color-blindness should consist in making them sort, according to their colors, worsteds or silks, chosen especially for this purpose. The color-blind hesitate in such a choice as this, and arrange most unexpected matches. It is the method carried out by Professor Holmgren. . . . A change or modification of the signal-colors used has been proposed; but Professor Holmgren has well answered how impracticable this would be."

I have noticed elsewhere (p. 134) the suggestions of this committee as to attaching colored glasses, &c., to the engines, to assist color-blind engineers or stokers.

Dr. Favre states that the examination for color-perception has been in force on the Lyons railroad since 1858. In March, 1870, the following special questions were put to the surgeons of this road: —

1st, How many candidates have you examined? and in how many years?

2d, Since when have you tested in reference to colors?

3d, How many color-blind have you found?

4th, What form of color-blindness have you found most frequent?

5th, Have you observed color-blindness from accident or injury? How often? How long did it last? What were the circumstances of the case?

6th, Have you written on the subject of color-blindness, congenital or traumatic?

The reports and statistics thus gathered I have elsewhere included. In 1876 Dr. Favre reports the Dombes et Sud-Est and the Midi roads as carrying out this test.

In 1877 the director-general of the Holland railroads called upon Professor Donders of Utrecht to carry out the examination of the employés for color-blindness. This was done, and the results I have already given. Professor Donders drew up the instructions for the guidance of the twelve surgeons deputed to carry out the details of the first examination, and a final official report was sent in to the director-general.

I have received from Professor Donders the printed blank required hereafter to be filled out in the case of every railroad employé. Every candidate for service must pass an examination by one of five ophthalmic surgeons in Amsterdam, Rotterdam, Anheim, Utrecht, and Leyden. These surgeons' names and hours for examinations are printed on the back of the blank, the face of which reads as follows: —

NETHERLANDS RAILROAD COMPANY. — The undersigned states that the sight of —— is sufficient (*a*) for the employment of engineer or fireman; (*b*) for the employment of station-master or those who may fill his place, assistants, haltmaster, director, first conductor, conductor, porter, brakeman, switchman, ranker, bridgekeeper, linekeeper, or linekeeperess.

THE OPHTHALMIC SURGEON.

The 187 .

(Signature of the examined to be given in the presence of the surgeon.)

N.B. — In case the candidate desires employment under *a*, *b* is to be stricken out, and the reverse.

There is required, for *a*, eyes and eyelids healthy externally, without habitual congestion or inflammation; field of vision, not limited in either eye; acuteness of vision, normal; refraction, normal; color-perception, at least four-fifths according to Donders's method. For *b*, eyes and eyelids externally healthy, without habitual congestion or inflammation; field of vision, not limited in either eye; normal acuteness of vision in one eye; normal refraction; color-perception, at least three-fifths; with the other eye, acuteness of vision at least one-half; color-perception, one-half.

These examinations are required by the royal official regulations of Jan. 31, 1879, published in the "Nederlandische Staats-Courant" of March 3, 1879, chap. v. art. 85: —

"All employés must be able to read and write and possess normal power of vision, so far as this is required for the proper performance of their duty.

"Employés who, by the decision of the minister of the department of industry, commerce, and the navy, are considered unfit to perform their duty, are, at the request of the minister, to be discharged by the managers of the railroads."

Regulations were also proposed to the government by Professor Donders in reference to the navy and merchant marine; and they are now accepted and enforced, as seen from an order in the same official paper: —

"The minister of the department of industry, commerce, and the navy, referring to art. 2 of the royal decree of Feb. 17, 1879 (Staatsblad, No. 37), in regard to the carrying out directions for the examination for a warrant as mate in the merchant marine, as directed by royal order of May 5, 1877 (Staatsblad, No. 98), has decided to require, —

"1st, In the test for visual acuteness and color-sensation ordered in the article, the following: —

"*a* — Normal vision without correcting glasses with one eye, and at least one-half of normal vision with the other eye.

"*b* — Both eyes must be without manifest hypermetropia of a degree above D 1.00, and in one eye at least nominal vision.

"*c* — Visual field not limited in either eye.

"*d* — Eyes and eyelids externally healthy, without habitual congestion or irritation.

"*e* — Color-perception perfect for transmitted light in one eye, and at least one-half in the other; according to Donders's method.

"2d. The report and declaration of the expert, as required in the above, shall be considered valid for one month only from the time the test is made.

"TAK VAN POORTVLIET.

"GRAVENHAGE, Feb. 27, 1879."

By the same order three ophthalmic surgeons are appointed as the experts for these examinations in Amsterdam, Rotterdam, and Leeuwarden.

In England, Parliament has never enacted any laws in reference to the control of color-blindness among railway employés or the navy and mercantile marine, so far as I can at present ascertain. The individual railroad corporations have, however, taken steps in this direction in regard to their men. Professor Wilson says, in 1856, "I am happy to say that the publication of my papers has induced the Great Northern Railway Company to require that in future all their porters shall be tested as to their freedom from color-blindness before they are admitted."

A terrible accident at Arlsey, Dec. 23, 1876, called out replies from railroad-surgeons to newspaper articles in reference to this point of control. In "The London Times" of Jan. 1, 1877, Mr. S. L. Mason writes, —

"The risks incident to the peculiar physical defect known as color-blindness, railway managers have long been alive to. On our leading lines, without exception, precautions are taken against the employment of men subject to that disqualification. In Mr. Seymour Clark's time, when

I was connected with the Great Northern Railway, this matter was scrupulously attended to, and, no doubt, is so still under the present able management. At the date I speak of — ten years ago — no porter, even though destined to work in a goods-shed, would be certified as eligible for appointment by the board until his eyesight should have been subjected to certain prescribed tests, among which was the discrimination of colors, especially those used in railway-signals."

Other testimony was given in "The Times," "The Lancet," &c., that railroad employés were tested on several different lines by Mr. Oliver Pemberton of Birmingham, Mr. C. Puzey of Liverpool, Mr. Page of Carlisle, and Dr. Jaspar McAldin. In the medical discussions, however, it was shown that the tests applied to detect color-blindness were very faulty and wholly inadequate. In consequence of the use of methods requiring only the color-name of objects or railroad-signals, the surgeons were deceived into the idea that color-blindness was not as frequent as Professor Wilson had shown it to be. The public fears excited at the time of the Arlsey accident were thereby unfortunately quieted. No better proof is needed of the necessity of a uniform and certain test being applied to employés than the facts and discussions of the Arlsey accident.

Dr. D. Argyll Robertson of Edinburgh kindly writes me of date March 9, 1879, —

"I trust that the following facts, which I have ascertained through the surgeons to the North-British (Dr. Dunsmure) and the Caledonian (Dr. John Duncan) Railway Companies, may be of service to you. I may mention that these are the two chief railway companies in Scotland; the North-British possessing 930 miles of railway, and the Caledonian 753 miles.

"NORTH-BRITISH RAILWAY. — Since about 1865 or 1866, when Dr. Dunsmure directed the attention of the manager of the company to the subject, both engine-drivers and stokers are invariably examined as to color-perception before being engaged. The men are tested by means of a board with ten different colors upon it. Three men have been rejected on account of color-blindness since examinations were instituted.

"CALEDONIAN RAILWAY COMPANY. — Before any one is employed as signal-man or guard, he is first examined by a doctor, and especially as to his sight, and power of distinguishing colors. Only about one in a year is rejected on account of color-blindness.

"All engine-drivers are tested as regards perception of color when they are passed from 'firing' to 'driving,' and no case of color-blindness has yet been met with. This, however, is probably due to the circumstance that the men are aware that they are to be tested, and do not persevere as stokers if they considered they were not competent to pass as drivers. . . . There is no legislation here enforcing such examinations."

Abundant proof has been given in this volume of the inadequacy of such tests as are thus shown to be at present used on these Scotch roads, as well as on the various English roads, from the evidence of the surgeons connected with them. No wonder so few color-blind are detected. A simple act of Parliament enforcing universally such a test as Holmgren's or Donders's would insure safety, as the medical officers of the roads are perfectly competent to properly carry out such examinations.

"*Order of the Handelministerium of Prussia, March,* 1877, *published in the Official Paper of the Government of the Interior*, 1877.

"In consequence of the frequent occurrence of cases of so-called color-blindness, and the great dangers which may arise from the same on the railroads, it is recommended, —

"1st, That persons in the outside railroad service, such as station officials, pointsmen, signal-men, engineers, stokers, brakemen, and conductors, be first tested as to their color-perception before being employed.

"2d, That all those not engaged in the above-mentioned positions be tested for color-blindness, in order to eliminate the red or green blind from positions where the recognition of the colored signals is requisite.

"3d, This examination is also to be made of convalescents where it is requisite; namely, after typhus-fever, injuries of the head, severe contusions, and the like, as also in general to be repeated every five years.

"If this examination is to be carried out over a large district by a recognized ophthalmic surgeon, it would necessitate numerous journeys of the officials and employés, and cost much time. It is suggested that it is within the proposal of the imperial direction to consider that any physician, even if he has not made a specialty of diseases of the eye, can carry out this test with sufficient exactness to insure safety: therefore the imperial railroad directory is advised to have the proposed examination conducted by the several district railroad-surgeons."

In accordance with the order of the Handelministerium of Sept. 19, 1877,—

"The examination is to decide whether the person tested can correctly distinguish *red*, *green*, and *violet* by daylight, and also by artificial light, or whether there is the slightest suspicion of color-blindness: therefore the examination must be done by *an ophthalmic surgeon*."

In reference to the regulations and instructions for these examinations, I will quote from Dr. Magnus of Breslau, as what he states is pertinent to all such tests, and therefore extremely important for us here in the United States, where the whole subject is new. He says,—

"The very great necessity of good color-perception on the part of railroad employés, concerning as it does the safety of the public roads, has already excited general attention, thanks to the untiring efforts of Professor Holmgren. And it has led already to valuable practical measures; but yet it has seemed to us, that, precisely on this point, certain reforms are very desirable. The regulations from the authorities for the purpose of avoiding the possible results of the action of color-blind officials are, and rightly so, first directed towards a most careful test of the color-sense of all the employés. All candidates are to be examined, and all those in service equally thoroughly tried for color-blindness. A similar examination of the whole *personnel* is to be carried out every five years. A general examination for color-blindness is directed by the regulations of the authorities. The method and the way and means of conducting this examination are, however, undetermined. The choice of methods is rather left to the fancy of the examining surgeon; or, if a method is advised him, this is not always the same, the several railroad managers varying greatly in this respect. But the result of every test for color-perception is very dependent upon the method employed. Now, the various methods at present used are not of the same value. Some of them, on the contrary, give very unreliable results; whilst others leave but little to be desired in respect to precision. Hence the values of the reports of the several examinations on the various German roads are not the same, but exhibit great and doubtful variations. If we could compare the percentage from the statistics of all the German roads of the extent of color-blindness, we should see within what limits such percentage varies, and how the results of the individual examiners differ. For example, "The Breslau Journal" of Oct. 10, 1878, reports the test of 1,348 employés of one of the roads here, and the finding of but 10 color-blind (or 0.74 per cent); whilst one of my colleagues, who tested the employés of another road, told me he found 4 per cent.

"We see, therefore, that the test for color-blindness, as it is now carried out on our German roads, does not fulfil the object desired. Absolute safety of the traffic, with due regard to the interests of the *personnel*, cannot be gained by such differing and uncertain data. To obtain the great benefit of an obligatory examination of the color-sense of the railroad employés, the varying reports as to the extent of color-blindness must be corrected, and greater unity obtained. This can only be done by one and the same method being required on all our roads. Hence it will be asked, which of the present methods is most practical, and has so stood the test of employment as to be naturally called for in the interest of the safety of the public communications? The answer to this very important question will be governed by a critical analysis of the several methods of testing. In my examination of 5,486 persons I have very particularly considered this very point, and, from my experience, decided that the method of Professor Holmgren of Upsala is the one giving us the most exact results in testing large numbers. It is so superior to the other present methods, in exactness of result and convenience of use, as to render it undoubtedly the best. In such an important question the opinion of a single observer should not, of course, be taken alone, but others' experience also heard and considered. In doing this we shall find similar favorable opinions of Holmgren's method from those who have used it. Thus Dr. Cohn, in Breslau, in his criticism of the several methods of testing, declares Holmgren's to be the best. We hear the same from Professor Pflüger in Berne, and from Dr. Jeffries in Boston. The latter is so convinced of the superiority of Holmgren's method, that he writes me of date Sept. 19, 1878, from Boston, as follows: 'My own experience teaches me the great value of Holmgren's method over all others, and I wish it would be ordered by your Kaiser throughout Deutschland.'

"In interest, therefore, of the safety of railroad travel, we feel called upon to require the following: That the test for color-blindness now obligatory on most of the German roads should be the same and identical throughout the empire, and carried out in the same way on every railroad; and that Holmgren's method, being the most certain and most preferabl, should be alone employed for this purpose."

The value and truth of this quite moderate criticism of Dr. Magnus can best be proved by showing what has been done on a number of the German roads. This I am enabled to do from a lecture given by Dr. E. Gintl, Central Inspector of the Lemberg-Czernowitz-Jassy road at Vienna, April 2, 1878, before the society of Austrian railroad officials. After an introductory sketch of color-perception, &c., and some of the methods of testing for color-blindness, he says, "It will thus be seen, that, for the examination of the employés in general, any of the methods may be used. Stilling's or Holmgren's tables, or the colored charts, or Waldstein's apparatus, are quite sufficient; but, to decide the doubtful cases or the individual colors, only the spectroscopic apparatus of Schmidt and Hausch in Berlin can be employed with certainty, as I have personally proved in the testing of a very large number of persons." He gathered the reports from forty-six railroads, on which 41,444 employés were tested, and 319 color-blind found, — a percentage of 0.769. I here give these reports: —

No.	Name of Railroad.	Date of Test.	Number Tested.	No. Color-Blind.	Per Cent.	Method of Testing employed.	Remarks as to those found Color-blind April, 1878.
	German Roads.						
1	Badische Staatsbahn	...	...	...	...	...	New employés to be tested; old not yet examined.
2	Baierische Staatsbahn	...	...	...	...	...	January, 1878, not yet commenced the tests for color-blindness.
3	Berg-Märkische Bahn	...	...	...	...	...	Examination not yet finished.
4	Berlin-Anhalt	July, 1877,	2,658	12	0.45	Stilling's tables	8 red, 2 blue-yellow, 2 blue-black blind.
5	Berlin-Gorlitz	June, 1876,	77	...	...	Vierordt's spectroscope	
6	Berlin-Hamburg	July, 1877,	465	10	2.15	Stilling's tables	2 red-green; 8 confound only shades of color.
7	Berlin-Potsd.-Magdeburg	June, 1877,	1,735	11	0.63	Colored-paper tables	7 red-green, 1 green-blue, 1 violet-red, 1 yellow-red, 1 violet-black blind.
8	Berlin-Stettin	Sept., 1877,	2,910	3	0.10	Colored-paper tables	1 confounds all complementary colors; 1 orange-blue, 1 yellow-blue blind.
9	Cöln-Minden	Aug., 1877,	4,200	85	2.02	Stilling's tables	Confounds color-tones. No color-blind in strictest sense.
10	Elsass-Lothringen	...	...	...	...	...	Tests not yet finished.
11	Hanover Staatsbahn	July, 1877,	5,107	56	1.10	Stilling's tables; Vierordt's spectroscope	18 confound all complementary colors; 22 red-green, 15 red-blue, 1 left eye red-green blind.
12	Hessische Ludwigbahn	Dec., 1877,	...	...	...	...	Tests not yet finished.
13	Lübek-Büchen-Hamb'g	Dec., 1877,	496	26	1.21	Colored tables and glasses	3 red-green-blind; 3 could not distinguish any color.
14	Magdeburg-Halbstädter,	Dec., 1877,	...	...	...	Colored tables and glasses	Tests not yet finished.

15	Nassau u. Taunus Bahn,	July, 1877,	1,308	6	0.46	Colored tables and glasses . . .	All red-green-blind.
16	Niedermärkische Bahn .	Dec., 1877,	. . .	. .	. .	Stilling's, Vierordt's .	Tests not finished.
17	Obsschlesische Bahn .	Dec., 1877,	. . .	. .	. .	. . . . . .	Tests not finished.
18	Oldenburgische . .	Aug., 1877,	800	14	1.75	Colored-paper tables .	3 red-green; 10 blue-green; 1 yellow-green.
19	Ost-bahn, preuss . .	June, 1877,	6,287	45	0.75	Stilling's tables and colored papers .	29 red-green; 1 blue-orange; 1 violet-yellow; 5 blue-green; 1 blue-yellow; 8 could not distinguish.
20	Pfälzische Eisenbahn .	. . .	. . .	. .	. .	. . . . . .	Tests not finished.
21	Rechte Oder Uferbahn .	Mar., 1878,	880	1	0.11	Green and red glasses, and targets . .	Red-green-blind.
22	Rheinische Eisenbahn .	. . .	. . .	. .	. .	. . . . . .	No report made.
23	Saarbrucken Eisenbahn,	July, 1877,	1,457	8	0.55	Green and red glasses, and targets . .	4 red-green; 1 uncertain in blue; 1 red-blue; 1 uncertain in yellow; 1 without color-sense.
24	Sächs. Staatsbahn . .	. . .	. . .	. .	. .	. . . . . .	No official examination.
25	Thüringische Eisenbahn,	June, 1877,	1,500	3	0.20	Stilling, Vierordt .	1 red-green and red-blue, 2 red-green blind.
26	Weimar-Gera Eisenbahn,	Oct., 1877,	68	1	1.47	Stilling's tables . .	Blue-red and yellow-green blind.
27	Werra Eisenbahn . .	July, 1877,	719	7	0.97	Stilling's tables . .	All red-green-blind.
28	Westphalische Eisenb. .	. . .	. . .	. .	. .	. . . . . .	Tests not finished.
29	Württemburg Staatsb. .	Jan., 1877,	. . .	. .	. .	Stilling's tables . .	From January, 1877, new employés to be tested; old ones not.
	Total . . .	. . .	30,590	268	0.876	. . . . . .	

No.	Name of Railroad.	Date of Test.	Number Tested.	No. Color-Blind.	Per Cent.	Method of Testing employed.	Remarks as to those found Color-blind.
	Austrian and Hungarian.						
30	Oester.-ung Bahnen .	Jan., 1878,	. . .	. .	. .	Colored papers and glasses . . .	Test not finished.
31	Böhmische Nordbahn .	Oct., 1877,	540	1	0.19	Colored papers and glasses . . .	Green-blue-blind.
32	Böhmische Westbahn .	. . .	. . .	. .	. .	. . . . . .	
33	Buschtiehrader Eisenb.	July, 1877,	1,514	3	0.20	Colored yarns, Vierordt's . . .	1 red-green; 2 completely color-blind.
34	Carl-Ludwig-bahn . .	. . .	. . .	. .	. .	. . . . . .	Tests not finished.
35	Franz-Joseph-bahn .	. . .	. . .	. .	. .		No tests yet made.
36	Nordbahn . . .	Aug., 1876,	700	. .	. .	Signal-glasses; Waldheim's chromatoscope, and Vierordt's . . .	Only new employés tested. Uncertainty in deciding tones.
37	Elisabethbahn . .	Dec., 1876,	Not given,	. .	. .	Colored paper, Stilling's tables . .	
38	Kaschau-Oderberger B.	. . .	. . .	. .	. .	. . . . . .	Tests not finished.
39	Lemb-Czernow-Jassy B.	Dec., 1876,	Not given,	. .	. .	Vierordt's spectroskop	Tests not finished.
40	Rudolfbahn . . .	May, 1877,	1,678	1	0.06	Signal targets and glasses . . .	1 red-green-blind. Examination going on.
41	Nordwestbahn . .	Oct., 1877,	. . .	. .	. .	Waldheim's chromatoscope . . .	Given up for practical reasons. 20 did not recognize the violet; 1 did not recognize the green; 1 did not recognize the blue.
42	Oester. Staatsbahn .	June, 1877,	5,601	39	0.70	Colored papers and glasses . . .	5 red-green; 3 green-blue; 4 black-green; 4 uncertain; 1 no color-sense.

43	Sudbahn	. . . .	. . .	. .	. .	. . . . . .	Test not yet finished.
44	Turnau-Kralup Eisenb.	Nov., 1877,	354	1	0.28	Colored papers . .	For all complementary colors.
45	Ung. Nordostbahn . .	. . . .	. . .	. .	. .	. . . . . .	Test not yet finished.
46	Ungar-Staatsbahn . .	Aug., 1877,	1,167	6	0.51	Dr. Gross's colored lamps . . .	2 red-green, 4 green-blue blind.
	Total . . .	. . . .	10,854	51	0.489	. . . . . .	

Contrasting these results with those where a a thorough test gave us as in France 5.77, in Switzerland 6.28, in Sweden 2.15, and in Finland 14.01, and we can readily appreciate the force of Dr. Magnus's criticism, and my remark above, that but here and there can the color-blind employés have been detected on the German roads.

I have also given this long list of railroad examinations, collected by Dr. Gintl, as a warning to our railroad corporations in this country, and to the examiners they shall hereafter employ. The several German railroads' surgeons, not being officially directed to employ Holmgren's method, and unfortunately hearing it spoken and written about in a tone of doubt, naturally chose other methods they individually knew of. Moreover, some of the German physicians who had paid especial attention to this subject, and who had tested some thousands of persons for color-blindness by Holmgren's method, deliberately misapplied it, in absolute contradiction to his express and very explicit directions. Thus, to detect whether a person is color-blind, we have seen that a peculiar shade of green worsted is used, and the examined directed to pick out what looks like it, lighter or darker. A purple (German, *rosa*) is used to decide whether a person is *red* or *green* blind. This latter is *not* to be used to detect color-blindness, but only which *form* of the defect we have. Nevertheless Dr. Cohn of Breslau, in reporting his results to the Heidelberg Ophthalmological Society, 1878, says, "As the very best and the quickest method of first testing for color-blindness, I must again and again recommend the *purple* worsted. It has served perfectly." He also speaks of the colored plate attached to Holmgren's book, and copied in this volume, as being as bad to detect color-blindness with as the purple worsted is good. Now, this plate is only intended, and so most definitely described, to *illustrate* the colors to be used, and the colors of confusion or mistakes of the defective. This ignoring Holmgren's explicit directions as to the carrying out of the test with the green worsted, and then speaking of the colored plate as if that had been proposed to be used by Holmgren, was most unfortunate and misleading. It has naturally led others to follow him without reading Professor Holmgren's book. Dr. Cohn tried Stilling's, as also other methods, but found, as every examiner will, Holmgren's the most convenient and practical.

Thus the reports I have quoted of the German roads show most conclusively that from a faulty method of testing only here and there, so to speak, have the color-blind employés been detected. This is very unfortunate, as it throws, for the time being, a certain doubt over the whole question of the frequency of color-blindness, its danger, the necessity for control, and the elimination of the defective. Moreover, the entire work in Germany will have to be done over again. Probably, from what I lately learn, the correct tests are now being officially ordered, and carried out. Thanks to the energy of Professor Holmgren in Sweden, the affair was there better conducted. The government first ordered the use of the flags and lanterns by the railroad officials to test for color-blindness; but, when Holmgren showed them the uselessness of this, they ordered *his* test, and also required all the railroad-surgeons to learn it of him, and carry it out properly.

From a lecture on color-blindness by Dr. A. von Reuss of Vienna, and a letter of date March 17, 1879, I am able to still further substantiate the criticisms I have made or introduced in reference to the examinations of the German employés.

The Austrian Handelministerium ordered Nov. 18, 1876, that "persons who could not distinguish the signals on account of near-sightedness or color-blindness were not to be admitted into the service." This led to the carrying-out of the examinations as above given with such unsatisfactory results. Dr. von Reuss says, —

> "Why these differ so greatly from the numbers reported by ophthalmic surgeons was readily seen from the original reports sent in to Dr. Gintl, and which he kindly allowed me to see, from which reports the data of the tables were collected. In these reports are mentioned blue-red-blind, blue-black-blind, green-blue-blind, violet-black-blind, yellow-red-blind, &c., and this where Stilling's tables had not been used, which might have given rise to such confusion. This is a proof that the examiners did not know what they were about. The majority of the examinations are therefore useless."

In this lecture Dr. von Reuss reports testing 593 employés, and finding 3.2 per cent color-blind. In his letter to me of March 17, 1879, he says, "I have tested 600 employés of the Elizabeth-Westbahn, and found 3.5 per cent color-blind." He employed Professor Donders's method with the worsteds.

The unsatisfactory results of the examinations by the several railroad-surgeons, due to a want of knowledge and the lack of a uniform and certain test, led to the following order from the Handelministerium: —

ORDER OF THE HANDELMINISTERIUM, OCT. 15, 1878, TO ALL THE RAILROAD CORPORATIONS, RESPECTING PROFESSOR HOLMGREN'S METHOD OF TESTING COLOR-BLINDNESS.

My frequent attention having been called to the work of Professor Holmgren, "De la Cécité," &c., I have obtained professional opinions as to the method of testing color-blindness proposed in it, showing it to be practical and very simple, and perfectly answering the requirements. The method consists in causing the examined to select from a number of skeins of colored worsteds all those corresponding to a pattern shown him. The examiner decides from the manner in which this is done. A normal-eyed will select four or five skeins in a minute, and the color-blind will as quickly make such characteristic mistakes as to render the immediate diagnosis possible. In doubtful cases, and where deception is supposed, a more thorough test must be applied, with, for instance, a spectrum apparatus.

As experience has shown that color-blindness, besides being congenital, may be acquired, safety requires that not only should those entering service be tested as to their perception of the three primary colors, — red, green, and violet, — but that the test should be repeated periodically, and especially after diseases, and contusions of the head.

I desire to call the attention of the corporations to the book above mentioned, and would ask their consideration of the suggestions here briefly made, since, from the necessary apparatus, the examinations of employés has hitherto been expensive and inconvenient; and this method therein proposed greatly simplifies and facilitates the testing for color-blindness.

K.-K. Handelminister CHLUMETZKY.

VIENNA, Oct. 15, 1878.

Jan. 8, 1879, in the House of Representatives

of the legislature of Massachusetts, Mr. Hamilton A. Hill of Boston introduced, at my request, the following order: —

"That the Committee on Railroads inquire whether any and (if any) what legislation is necessary in reference to the employment by railroad companies, in certain responsible positions, of persons affected with color-blindness."

This order was passed by the House, and a public hearing given as follows: —

COMMONWEALTH OF MASSACHUSETTS.

COMMITTEE ON RAILROADS.
STATE HOUSE, BOSTON, Jan. 13, 1879.

The Committee on Railroads will give a hearing to parties interested in an order relative to legislation in reference to the employment by railroad corporations, in certain responsible positions, of persons afflicted with color-blindness, at room No. 10, State House, on Wednesday, Jan. 22, at ten o'clock A.M.

EDWIN W. MARSH,
Clerk of the Committee.

By invitation of the Committee on Railroads I appeared at this hearing, and argued in support of the conclusions contained in this volume. My statements were supported by European statistics, and my own collected in this community, by experiments in reference to color-perception, the exhibition of various tests, &c., and by the practical illustration of the value of Professor Holmgren's method in detecting the chromatic vision of several color-blind who were present at the time. There was no opposition to my statements or conclusions.

As the result of this hearing, the Joint Committee on Railroads reported, Feb. 28, 1879, in the Senate, the following resolve: —

"That the board of railroad commissioners be instructed to consider whether any legislation is expedient or needful with reference to the employment by railroad corporations of persons afflicted with color-blindness."

This was passed in the House of Representatives March 21, 1879, and in the Senate March 24, 1879; receiving the signature of the governor March 25, 1879.

It is thus seen that Massachusetts has been the first State to take action in reference to the control of color-blindness on the railroads. She possesses, of course, no authority on the water. There the General Government must act in concert with other nations. It is now in the hands of the Massachusetts railroad commissioners to carry forward the work of investigation, and report hereafter to the legislature. If they can induce the several railroad corporations to meet the just demands of the community, and eliminate the color-blind from their employ, then a law, subsequently enacted, can be based upon the result of the examinations, and made to meet all requirements of the future. This law of control should also, as in Europe, require the proof by test, of normal visual power for *form*, as well as normal color-sense.

It is to be hoped that the other States will quickly follow the action of Massachusetts. The advantages of a uniform law throughout the country, and a uniform and absolutely certain system of testing for color-blindness, I need not dwell upon here, since it is self-evident from what I have brought forward in this volume. There will be no excuse for such blunders as were made in Europe, now that we have the benefit of them in this country.

I have spoken of my action and its results, in order that my professional brethren in other States may see how my efforts were successfully carried out, and be able to refer to them when themselves undertaking similar work in their own communities.

CHAPTER XXIV.

PERSONAL EXPERIENCE WITH HOLMGREN'S METHOD. — SUGGESTIONS AS TO ITS USE.

THE experience which I have gained in the use of Holmgren's method of detecting color-blindness by the worsteds is, I think, worth here recording for the benefit of my brother ophthalmic surgeons, whom the railroads may hereafter ask to test the employés of their roads. First, as to the choice of the worsteds themselves, since a good deal depends on this: Proper colors can be obtained directly from Fraulein Letty Oldberg, in Upsala, Sweden, for about 5 crowns 63 pfennigs. Such a selection was sent me by Professor Holmgren; and similar ones I have made here, and used in my testing. The colors of the green and purple test in the colored plate in the Swedish, French, and German editions of Professor Holmgren's book, are apt not to be correct, and may mislead any one. This arises from the difficulty of reproducing in chromo-lithography the precise tints, and rendering these permanent.

To learn the test, I would strongly advise, not a simple perusal, but a careful and repeated study of Holmgren's directions and explanations given in this volume. They may at first seem rather prolix; but experience will soon show how valuable his minute directions are, which, when properly studied, will relieve many a doubt, and clear up many a seeming discrepancy in our actual test of old or young. When thoroughly understood theoretically, it will be found quite simple, and readily adapted to test even very young children with; as, for instance, primary-school children. I would advise first commencing with educated adults, and afterwards testing in the schools, where material is more at hand and more manageable. We shall, moreover, meet in the schools of lower social grade just the sort of stupidity and lack of appreciation which we are likely to meet among uneducated railroad employés, sailors, and factory workmen. It is a curious fact, which, I think, all who test large numbers will sooner or later find out, that dulness of comprehension and dulness of perception will almost invariably simulate color-blindness. Many a teacher in our schools has been greatly surprised that I have not marked as color-blind a boy who seemed to them to do about the same as the color-blind, but who had thrown out with the pattern a single worsted, which quickly told me that I had to deal with stupidity, and not a chromatic defect. It has been often very hard to disprove the story the worsteds picked out told, when that story was dictated by mental dulness. The teachers generally found that I selected their brightest scholars as such.

There is besides this a dulness of color-perception, or rather a peculiar slowness in the colors taking effect, so to speak, which is at first confusing to the examiner, unless he bears it constantly in mind, and is familiar with it. It is difficult to describe, but is yet readily recognized. All this adds to the danger of our considering that we have at least partial color-blindness before us, and hence increasing our ratio at the expense of truth. As inexperience and stupidity will most trouble us in the younger classes of lowest social grades, I would advise commencing with the oldest students one can avail themselves of, and then going to the high schools before the grammar-schools. At present I should be inclined to think, that, however seemingly curious and interesting it might prove, the testing for color-blindness, by even so simple a method as this of Holmgren's, in the primary schools, would be time lost, as well as likely to mislead one as to the relative proportion, &c. Moreover, there are students and grammar-scholars enough in all our cities of any size to furnish more than ample material. I ought to add here, however, that I found no difficulty with the several hundred in the grammar-schools who had just come from the primary; i.e., within a few days.

All my examinations were made with Holmgren's test. My purpose was to quickly obtain an approximate estimate of the proportion of color-blind in our community, and at the same time to disseminate a knowledge of the existence of such a chromatic defect and its nature, in order to prepare the way for some action in reference to control on the railroads and in the marine. It has been, except in a few instances of educated adults, wholly impossible for me, at present, to test those

I found color-blind by other methods than Holmgren's. My own experience, however, and the reports from Europe of the gentlemen there at work in this investigation, confirm me in the belief, that, whatever additional method I might employ, I should not probably change my opinion of the individual case of color-blindness. For the purposes I have had in view, my time has been better spent in continued work in our schools, than in stopping to test over again, by additional methods, persons so young as school-children from eight to seventeen years of age. I hope, hereafter, to accomplish more in testing the adult color-blind.

For a time I worked under a disadvantage in reference to classifying the red and green blind, because my purple worsted was not dark enough, owing to the color having faded in the plate in Holmgren's book, and thereby deceiving me. But I supplemented this weak point in my decision by having a red and a green worsted of as nearly as possible the same degree of luminosity, and asking the color-blind which was the darker. Their decision I generally found very quickly made, and adhered to. I also asked them to pick out the *black* worsteds, and found they would select the dark greens or dark reds, according as they were green or red blind. Since I have had the proper shade of purple, this has not of course been necessary. I have, however, frequently carried it out *after* deciding by the purple, in order to see how accurate my previous division into red and green probably was. I have decided I cannot be very far from right, and therefore have given my records as I made them. I did not make up the tables till I had finished, and consequently did not know what the relative proportion of red and green blindness was during the time I was testing.

I have followed Holmgren in making three divisions, — complete red and green blindness, and partial color-blindness. My three cases of violet-blindness I have allowed to stand under partial color-blindness. These I have found the test readily showed. As color-blindness exists in all degrees, so to speak, it would of course be possible, by careful special examination of each case, to express its particular degree; as by Donders's method or by Holmgren's color-sense tester. The percentage of color-blindness, each examiner finds, will be modified by where he draws the line; that is, how feeble must the chromatic sense be to come under the head of partial color-blindness, and also what shall be regarded as feeble chromatic sense, and what only dulness of perception. The greater our experience, however, the more carefully can we decide these points. Holmgren's method with a pretty large number of worsteds has seemed to me to be particularly well adapted for this purpose. I have kept to the original plan of having a large number of green worsteds, finding that for my purposes it worked best; and I was willing to give the extra time, in consideration of the psychological study it afforded me. Professor Holmgren has spoken of this. I am not certain that with young people it is not best, since as much time is wasted by their searching for the three or four greens in Holmgren's modified method, as in throwing out all or a decisive number of the greens when there are many of them. I think, also, it gives the examiner a better chance to watch the play of the hands, from which so much can be deduced.

It may not be amiss if I say I use about a hundred and fifty skeins of worsted, and carry them, wrapped in a piece of white cotton cloth, which can be spread over a table or other surface. On this the colors show well in contrast. When statistics are being gathered, or large numbers must be tested with the smallest loss of time, this plan will save trouble, and thereby add to the total number examined. Even amongst the youngest scholars, — and several hundred were just from the primary schools, — I have not failed to convince myself, and show to the teachers, color-blindness where it existed. It is useless, I think, to argue with those of my European friends who still think they can *always* detect a lack of chromatic power by Stilling's tables or other method. Their number, I believe, will become steadily less when they take hold of Holmgren's test in earnest, and carry it out as directed by him; as has, for instance, my friend, Dr. Magnus of Breslau. My experience teaches me to advise my ophthalmic brethren, or other physicians who will be called upon to carry out the work I have commenced in this country, to waste no time with other methods, but to fully and carefully familiarize themselves first *theoretically* with Holmgren's test, and then *practically* commencing with adults.

CHAPTER XXV.

CONCLUSIONS AND RECAPITULATION.

One male in twenty-five is color-blind in a greater or less degree.

Of this defect they may even themselves be wholly unconscious.

This blindness is red, green, or violet blindness. Total color-blindness also occurs.

This defect is congenital. It exists in varying degrees. It is largely hereditary. It may also be temporarily or permanently caused by disease or injury.

It is incurable when congenital. Exercising the eyes with colors, and the ears with their names, helps the color-blind to supplement their eyes, but does not change or increase their color-perception.

Experiment and experience show that we are *forced* to use *red* and *green* marine signal-lights to designate a vessel's direction of motion and movements, and at least *red* lights on railways to designate danger.

Form, instead of color, cannot be used for these purposes.

There are many peculiar conditions under which

railroad employés and mariners perform their duty, which render colored signals, and especially colored lights, difficult to be correctly seen.

These signals can never be correctly seen by the color-blind. There are such among railroad employés.

There is, therefore, great danger from color-blindness.

Railway and marine accidents have occurred from it.

There is no protection but the elimination, from the *personnel* of railways and vessels, of all persons whose position requires perfect color-perception, and who fail to possess this. This can now be readily and speedily done.

Therefore, through a law of the legislature, orders from state railroad commissioners, or by the rules and regulations of the railroad corporations themselves, each and every employé should be carefully tested for color-blindness by an expert competent to detect it. The test and the method of application should be uniform. All deficient should be removed from their posts of danger. Every person offering himself as an employé should be tested for color-blindness, and refused if he has it. Every employé who has had any severe illness, or who has been injured, should be tested again for color-blindness before he is allowed to resume his duties. Periodic examinations of the whole *personnel* should also be required.

Such regulations are generally in force on the European railroads.

An international commission should be called to

establish rules for the control of color-blindness on the sea, and the carrying out the same examinations amongst pilots, masters, and crews of steamers and sailing-vessels, in the navies and the merchant marine.

BIBLIOGRAPHY.[1]

Abercrombie. Inquiry concerning the Intellectual Powers, 1840, p. 51. — *Aubert and Foerster.* Græfe's Archiv., vol. iii. 2, p. 38. — *Aubert.* Physiologie der Netzhaut: Breslau, 1865. *Alexander.* Græfe's Archiv., xv. 3, p. 103. — *Annuske.* Græfe's Archiv., xix. 3, p. 254. — *Anaxagoras.* Mullach. Frag. Phil. Græc: Paris, 1860, vol. i. p. 250. — *Aristoteles.* De Sensu et Sensili, cap. iii. — *Angell.* Atlantic Monthly, 1870, p. 200. — *Allen, Grant.* Nature, vol. xix., 1878, p. 32; The Color-Sense, its Origin and Development, London, 1878; Mind, January, 1878. — *Andree.* Ueber den Farbensinn der Naturvölker: Zeitschrift f. Ethnologie, Jahrg. x., Heft iv., Berlin, 1878. — *Allgemeine Zeitung,* March, 1878. Allge. med. Central.-Ztg., Jahrg. xlviii., Stuck 6. Farben-Unterscheidungsvermögen der Eisenbahnbeamten.

Benedict. Der Daltonismus bei Sehnerven-atrophie: Græfe's Archiv., Bd. x. 2, p. 185, 1864; Wien Med.-chirg. Rundschau, 1862, Dec., p. 211. — *Boys de Loury.* Aberration dans les Sensations des Couleurs: Lancette française, No. 151, 1843; and Bull. de Thérap., vol. xxv. p. 459, 1843. — *Bronner.* On Daltonism: Med. Times and Gaz., April 12, 1856. — *Boyle.* Experiments and Considerations touching Color: London, 1670. — *Buffon.* Sur les Couleurs accidentelles: Mem. de

[1] This does not include, except incidentally, vision in general, or simply form-perception. The large works on physiology, physiological optics, and ophthalmic surgery, are omitted. The individual titles of an author's articles are not always given, but their place of publication follows his name.

l'Académie des Sciences, p. 147, 1743. — *Bourgeois.* Manuel d'Optique expérimentale: Paris, 1823. — *Brewster.* Edinburgh Philos. Journal of Science, vol. iv., 1837. — *Biot.* Précis élémentaire de Physique expérimentale: Paris, 1842, t. 2. — *Brücke.* Des Couleurs, trad. Franc. par P. Schutzenberger: Paris, 1866. — *Brenner.* Oesterr. Zeitung für prakt. Heilkunde, 1855, p. 300. — *Bezold.* Theory of Color, translated by Koelher: Boston, 1876. — *Brücke.* Ueber das Wesen der braunen Farben: Pogg. Annal., lxxiv. 461, 1848, Bd. cl. pp. 71–93, 221–247. — *Burckhardt.* Verh. der naturf. Gesellsch. in Basel, x. 90–93. — *Becker.* Zur Lehre von der subjectiven Farbenerscheinungen: Poggendorff's Annalen, v. p. 305. — *Bow, R. H.* On Change of Apparent Color by Obliquity of Vision: Proceeds. Roy. Soc. Edinb., vol. vii. p. 155–160. — *Briesewitz.* Inaug. Dissert.: Greifswald, 1872. — *Blaschko.* Der Daltonismus bei Eisenbahnpersonal: Vierteljahrssch. f. gericht. Med. 1874, p. 74. — *Beer.* Bd. ii., p. 428. — *Butter.* Trans. Phrenog. Soc.: Lond., 1822; Nov. 28, Edinb. Phil. Jour., vol. vi. p. 135, 1822. — *Bert.* Perception des Couleurs chez les Peintures: Gaz. des Hôp., No. 9, 1878; Soc. de Biologie, Jan. 19, 1878. — *Brandis.* Goethe's Naturwissenschaft und Morphologie, Heft i. p. 297. — *Bastian, B.* Zeitschrift f. Ethnologie, Bd. i. p. 89. — *Böttiger.* Die aldobrandinische Hochzeit: Dresden, 1810, p. 128. — *Bernstein.* Five Senses of Man. — *Bezold.* Eine neue Methode der Farbenmischung, Sitzung. der math. phys. Classe, Jan. 8, 1878; Ueber die Vergleichung von Pigmentfarben und Spectralfarben, ditto, March 4, 1876. — *Brewin, R.* Shakespeare's Color-Names: Nature, Jan. 30, 1879. — *Blackie, Prof.* Before the Roy. Edin. Soc., Jan., 1878. — *Bertier, T.* Du Daltonisme et plus spécialement de la Dyschromatopsie acquise: Thèse de Paris, p. 44.

Chisolm. Color-Blindness from Neuritis: Ophth. Hosp. Rep., vol. vi. 214, 1865. — *Clemens.* Farbenblindheit während der Schwangerschaft: Archiv. für phys. Heilkunde, vol. xi. p. 41, 1858. — *Clemens.* Daltonisme Non-Congénital: Gaz. des Hôpit., p. 180, 1860; et Ann. d'Ocul., t. xliii. p. 185. — *Cornaz.* De l'Hyperchromatopsie: Ann. d'Ocul., t. xxv. p. 3, 1851. — *Combe.* System of Phrenology: Edinb., 1830; Chambers' Edinb. Jour., vol. iv. p. 118; Trans.

Phrenog. Soc., p. 222. — *Cunier.* Achromatopsie héréditaire depuis cinq Générations: Ann. d'Ocul., t. i. pp. 417 et 488, 1838. — *Cornaz.* Quelques Observations d'Abnormités congén. des Yeux: Ann. d'Ocul., t. xxiii. pp. 42–47. — *Chevreul.* De la Loi du Contraste simultané des Couleurs: Paris, 1839. — *Chevreul.* Remarques sur les Harmonies des Couleurs: Compt. rendus de l'Acad. des Sciences, t. xl. pp. 239–242, 1855. — *Challis.* Theory of Composition of Colors; Philos. Magazine, xii. p. 329. — *Clausius.* Revue des Cours scientifiques, Jan. 20, 1866. — *Chevreul.* Des Couleurs, &c.: Paris, 1866. — *Cutter.* Maladie oculaire de l'Électricité atmosphérique; Gaz. hebd., xxiv., 1849. — *Crinum.* Properties of the Primary Colors, &c.: London, 1830. — *Chodin.* Pression oculaire sur le Percep. des Couleurs: Ann. d'Ocul., t. lxxviii., 1877: Græfe's Archiv., xxiii. 3; Abhängigkeit der Farbenempfindung von der Lichtstärke: Sammlung phys. Abhandl. von Professor Preyer, 1877, 1 Reihe, 7 Heft. — *Colquhoun.* Glasg. Med. Journal in Frorieps Notizen, xxiv. 305. —*Czermak.* Ueber Schopenhauer's Theorie der Farben; Wiener Akad. Sitzungsber., Bd. lxii. pp. 393–341. — *Chevalier, A.* Les Verres colorés employés en Oculistique: Compt. rend. de l'Acad. des Scien., vol. lxxvi. p. 177, 1873. — *Chodin.* Zur Frage von der Farbenempfindungen auf der Peripherie der Netzhaut: 1873, Petersb. Med. Bote.; then Woinow's Objections and Chodin's Reply, pp. 95, 183. — *Cohen.* Ueber Eisenbahnfälle und deren Verhütung, Daltonismus: Nederl. Weekbl., 1874, No. 34, p. 513. — *Clarke.* Lancet, 1872, i. p. 601. — *Cohn, Dr. H.* Der Simultan-Contrast zur Diagnose der Farbenblindheit: Centralblatt f. prak. Augenheil, February, March, 1878; Breslau Zeitung, Feb. 5, 1878; Gestickte Buchstaben zür Diagnose der Farbenblindheit; Centralblatt f. prak. Augenheil, April, 1878; Ueber Beobachtungen an 100 Farbenblinden; Tagebl., d. 51; Vers. deutsch. Naturf. u. Aertze, No. 3, p. 62, 1878; Sitzung der Heidelberger ophth. Gesell., Aug. 12–13, 1878; 1878, Breslauer Zeitung, No. 537; Schles. Gesellsch. f. vaterl. Cultur., Sitz. am 25 Oct., 1878; Centralblatt f. Aug., 1878; Ueber die spectroscopische Untersuchung Farbenblinder, ditto, Nov., 1878, p. 264. — *Cohn u. Magnus.* Untersuchung von 5,000 Schulkindern in Bezug auf Farbenblindheit, ditto, Mai, 1878. — *Charcot.* Gazette médicale de Paris, No. 8, 1878. — *Classen.* Entwurf. einer Physiologie der Licht- und Farbenempfindung: Preyer Sammlung phys. Abhandl., 2d Reihe, 2 Heft, June, 1878. — *Kuhne.* Die farbige Kugeln der Zapfen der Vogel Retina: Centralblatt f. m. W., 1878, No. 1. — *Cuignet.* Ann. d'Oculist, lxvi. p. 17. — *Collardo.* Journ. de Phys., t. xii. p. 86. — *Chantilly, Girod de.* Théorie des Couleurs et de la Vision (pseudonym, G. Palmer). — *Cooper, W. White.* Vision: Cyclopædia of Anatomy and Physiology. — *Charpentier, Dr. A.* De la Vision avec les différentes Parties de la Rétine: Arch. de Phys., No. 6, 1877; also with *Landolt,* in Comptes rendus, t. lxxxvi., Feb. 18, 1870. Gaz. med., No. 9, 1879. — *Chevreul.* Compt. rendu, t. lxxxvii., 1878, p. 576, 707. — *Cohn, H.* Studien uber angeborene Farbenblindheit: Breslau, 1879. — *Craig, Christie.* Shakespeare's Color-Names: Nature, No. 460, vol. xix.

Dalton. Memoirs of the Literary Society of Manchester, vol. v., 1798: Edinb. Jour. Sci., ix. p. 97, 1779. — *Dalton.* Eigenthumlichkeit des Sehvermögens: Frorieps Notiz., No. 737, 1845. — *Decondé.* Daltonisme dichromatique: Ann. d'Ocul., t. xx., 1848. — *D'Hombres-Firmas.* Observations d'Achromatopsie: Ann. d'Ocul., t. xxiii. pp. 42 et 127, 1850; Compt. rendus, 1849, ii. — *Dor, H.* De la Dyschromatopsie: Sitz. der bern. naturforsch. Gesellsch., July 20, 1872; Lyon Méd., t. xvi. p. 201, 1874; et Ann. d'Ocul., 1874, lxxi. p. 104. — *Dalembert.* Mém. de l'Acad. des Sci.: Paris, 1767. — *Dove.* Eine Methode Interferenz- und Absorptionsfarben zu mischen: Berl. Monatsber., March 11, 1847. — *Durand.* Essai de Phys. philosophique: Paris, 1866. — *De Martini.* Effets produits sur la Vision par la Santonine: Compt. rendus de l'Acad. des Sci., xlvii. p. 259, l. p. 544; Compt. rendus de l'Inst., t. l. p. 554, 1860. — *Dolbeau.* Atrophie de la Papille, Leçons de Clinique chirurgicale: Paris, 1866. — *Dobrowolsky und Dr. Gaine.* Pfluger's Archiv. f. Physiol., Bd. xii. p. 432, 1875. — *Dobrowolsky.* Græfe's Archiv., xviii. 1, pp. 53–103; Berl. Akad. Bericht., 1872, p. 119. — *Dove.* Monatsberichte der Berl. Akad. d. Wissensch., April, 1871; Poggendorff's Annal. der Physik., Bd. 143, pp. 491–195. — *Donders.* Rep. Heidelberg Ophth. Soc., 1871, p. 470; Rep. Heidelberg Ophth. Soc., 1877. Quantitative Bestimmung der Farbensinnes, besonders bei Eisenbahnbeamten. — *Deyaund.* Mém. de l'Acad. d. Sci., 1858. — *Donders.* Fall von vollständiger Achromatopsie: Klein Monatsbl. f. Augenheil, 1871, p. 470. — *Donders, F. C.* Die quantitative Bestimmung des Farbenunterscheidungsvermögens: Graefe's Archiv., Bd. xxiii. 4, 1877. Rapport van het Gezichtsvermogen van het personeel. Staatsspoorwegen: Utrecht, 1877. Also in Report nederlandsch. Gasthuis Oogligders, 1878; Dichromatische stelsels. Kon. Akad. v. Wettenschappe te Amsterdam, Dec. 28, 1878; Annales d'Ocalistique, January, February, 1879. — *Daae, Dr. A.* Farbenblindheit und Entdeckung von Farbenblinden; Centralblatt für prak. Augenheilkunde, January, 1878; Statistik der Farbenblindheit, ditto, April, 1878, November, 1878, p. 263; Die Farbenblindheit und deren Erkennung, uberset. von Dr. M. Sanger, Berlin, 1878. Om Farveblindhed: Norsk Magazin for Lageridenskalen, 1878, Heft. vi. p. 81–89; Ueber Farbenblindheit, Deutsch med. Wochens, No. 1, 1879. — *Derby, R. H.* Color-Blindness from Alcohol and Tobacco: New York Med. Jour., 1871. — *Delitzsch.* Der Talmud und die Farben: Nord u. Sud, 1878; Mai Heft., Farbenstudium; Daheim, Nos. 29–31, 1878. Farben in der Bibel: Herzog. Realencyclop., p. 488. — *Delbœuf et Spring.* Recherches expérimentales sur la Daltonisme: Bulletin de l'Académie royale de Belgique, 1878, t. xiv., No. 1 et 4; Revue Scientifique, March 23, 1878, No. 38; Recherches sur la Mesure des Sensations: Bruxelles et Liége, 1873. — *Dreher.* Die Kunst in ihrer Beziehung zur Psychologie und zur Naturwissenschaft, 3d Auflage: Berlin, 1878. — *Dor, H.* Echelle pour mesurer l'Acuïte de la Vision chromatique, Paris, 1878; De l'Évolution historique du Sens des Couleurs, Acad. des Sci. de Lyon, Nov. 19, 1878. — *Dor et Favre.* Nouvelle Recherches, Vision chromatique: Lyon, 1878. — *Darwin.* Philos. Trans., 1786, et Zoonomie. — *De Ville, J.* Manual of Phrenology, London, 1835, p. 108. — *Dieterici.* Die Naturbescreibung und Naturphilosophie der Araber im zehnten Jahrhundert Berlin, 1861, p. 85. — *Darwin.* Cosmos, 1878, pp. 264, 423 — *Dherbes.* Moyen de éviter les Accidents dûs au Dalton isme; Compt. rendu. t. lxxxvii. 1878, p. 502.

Eichmann. Achromatopsie: Med. Zeit. des v. f. Heil kunde in Preussen, No. 47, 1853, p. 224. — *Esquirol.* Maladies mentales: Paris, t. ii. p. 26. — *Eichmann.* Fechner Centralblatt, 1854, pp. 294, 295. — *Earle, Pliny.* Am. Jour. Med. Sci., 1845, April. — *Emmert, E.* Ueber der Farben: Berne, 1872. — *Ewald.* Die Farbenbewegung: Berlin, 1876. — *Eliotson.* Frorieps neuen Notizen, 1839, No. 247.

Favre. Réforme des Employés de Chemin de Fer affectés de Daltonisme: Lyon, 1873. Recherches cliniques sur le Daltonisme: Lyon, 1874. Sur Dyschromatopsie consécutive aux Lésions traumatiques: Lyon, 1875. De la Dyschromatopsie dans ses Rapports avec l'État militaire et la Navigation: Lyon, 1876. Du Daltonisme dans ses Rapports avec la Navigation: Lyon, 1877. Réforme des Employés, &c.: Gazette hebdomadaire, p. 578, 1873. Le Traitement du Daltonisme dans les Écoles: Lyon, 1877. Résumé des Mémoires sur le Daltonisme; Acad. des Sci., 1877. Résumé: Gazette hebdomadaire, June 14, 1878; Acad. de Science, June 3, 1878; Archives générales, 1878, p. 371; Des Mesures sanitaires et des Moyens préventifs nécessités par le Daltonisme: Paris, 1878, p. 32. — *Fronmuller.* Mangelhafter Farbensinn: Memorabil., t. vi. 7, 1862. — *Forbes.* Proceed. Roy. Edinb. Soc., vol. iii. p. 251, 1849; Phil. Mag., 1839, 3d series, vol. xiv. p. 121. — *Fizeau and Foucault.* Ann. de Physique et de Chimie: Paris, 1849. — *Foucault.* Compt. rend. de l'Acad. des Sci.: Paris, 1850. — *Figuier.* Année scientifique: Paris, 1865. — *Faucouneau-Dufresne.* Précis des Maladies du Foie, &c., p. 378, 1856. — *Fick.* Zur Theorie der Farbenblindheit; Verh. d. Physik., Med. Ges. in Würzburg, neue Folge, Bd. v. pp. 158–162. — *Feris.* Du Daltonisme dans ses Rapports avec la Navigation: Paris, 1876. — *Falck.* Santonin: Deutsche Klinik, 1869, Nos. 27, 28. — *Francheschi.* Santonin, 1861; Ann. d'Ocul., p. 199. — *Fick, A.* Farbenblindheit, 1875: Pfluger's Archiv. f. Phys., June 13, 1878, xvii. 3, 4; Gartenlaube, No. 27, 1878, p. 456; Neue Untersuchungen über Farbenblindheit. — *Fechner.* Pogg. Ann. der Phys. v. Chem., 1840, Lond. and Edin. Phil. Mag., 1839, Dec., vol. xv. p. 441. — *Favre.* Traitement du Daltonisme par l'Exercice chez l'Enfant et chez l'Adulte: Lyon Med., 1879, xxv. 1879, and Paris, 1879, p. 16. — *Förster.* Tabak und Alcoholintoxication: Nagel's Jahresbericht f. Opth., 1876, p. 417.

Galezowski. Sur les Alterations, &c., Paris, 1867; Arch. gén. de Med., Sept., 1867; Sur l'Achromatopsie pathologique: Compt. rend. du Congrès ophth., Paris, 1867; Sur les Amauroses syphilitiques, 1867; Du Diagnostic des Maladies des Yeux par la Chromatopsie rétinnienne, Paris, 1868; Cécité par Cause patholog. pour les Couleurs, Ann. d'Ocul., t. lxv. p. 221, 1871; Sur la Physiologie des Sensations colorées de la Rétine, Ann. d'Ocul., t. xlix., 1863, p. 93, Jan., Fev., 1868. — *Goubert*. De l'Achromatopsie, &c.: Paris, 1867. — *Grailich*. Beitrag zur Theorie der gemischten Farben: Wiener, Ber. t. xii. p. 783; t. xiii. p. 201. — *Grandeau et Langel*. Revue des Sciences: Paris, 1865. — *Gladstone*. On his own Perception of Color: Rep. British Ass., ii. p. 12, 1860. — *Guepin*. L'Action de la Santonine: Compt. rend. de l'Acad. des Sciences, li. p. 791, 1860. — *Gouriet*. Gaz. des Hôpit., No. 113, 1861. — *Galezowski*. Rétinité glycosurique: Ann. d'Ocul., t. xlix. p. 93. Étude ophthalmoscopique, &c.: Paris, 1866, p. 47. — *Guillemin*. Les Phénomènes de la Physique: Paris, 1868, p. 406. — *Goethe*. Farbenlehre, 1810, pp. 126–190. — *Giros v. Gentilly*. Theorie der Farben: Lichtenberg Magazin, i. 2, 57. — *Gall*. Anat. et Physiol. du Sys. nerv., iv. 98. — *Geiger, Lazarus*. Ueber den Farbensinn der Urzeit und seine Entwickelung: 1871, Stuttgart. — *Geiger, Alfred*. Zur Entwickelungsgeschichte der Menscheit: Stuttgart, 1871. — *Guillemin*. La Lumière et les Couleurs: Paris, 1874. — *Giovanni*. Santonin, 1868: Jour. de Chimie méd., p. 373. — *Gould, Dr. B. A.* U. S. Sanitary Com. Mem., p. 543, 1869. — *Gunther*. Der Farbensinn des menschlicher Auges in seiner geschichtlichen Entwickelung: Augsberger. Allg. Zeitung, Beilage, No. 62, 1878. — *Gueroult*. Évolution du Sens de la Couleur: Review of Geiger, Gladstone, Magnus, and Javal; Ann. d'Ocul., Mar., April, 1878, p. 193. — *Gartenlaube*. Nos. 4, 1876; 23–29, 1877; 27, 1878. — *Gladstone*. Nineteenth Century, Oct., 1877; Studies on Homer and the Homeric Age, Oxford, 1858. — *Grassman*. Philos. Mag., 1854, 254. — *Gintl, Dr. E.* Ueber den Farbensinn und dessen Einfluss auf die Verkehrssicherheit der Eisenbahnen: Zeitung des Club Oest. Eisenbahn-Beamten, April 27, 30, 1878.

Hays. Impossibility of distinguishing Colors: Am. Jour. Med. Sci., 1840, Oct., 1858. — *Helffl*. Ueber Achromatopsie, &c.; Med. Zeit. des Ver. f. Heilk. in Preussen, No. 20, 1850. —*Helmholtz*. Handbuch der phys. Optik: Leipzig, 1867; Paris, 1867. —*Herschel, Sir John F. W.* Remarks on Color-Blindness: Proc. Roy. Soc., vol. x. p. 72, 1859. —*Hufner*. Farbenblindheit in Santoninrausche: Græfe's Archiv., xiii. 2, p. 309, 1869. —*Herschel*. Metropolit. Encyclop., article Light, p. 507, 1828. —*Helling*. Handb. d. Augenkrankheiten, Berlin, 1821, Bd. i. S. 1–3. —*Hirtzel's*. Zeitschr. f. Phar. No. 6, 1858. —*Happe*. Ueber den physiolog. Entwickelungsgang der Lehre von den Farben: Leipzig, 1877. —*Huddart*. Phil. Trans., London, vol. lxvii., 1777, pp. 260–265. —*Hocheeker*. Ueber angeborene Farbenblindheit: Græfe's Archiv., B. xix. 3, pp. 1–37. —*Harvey*. Edinb. Phil. Trans., x. 253; Edinb. Jour. of Sci., vii. 85. —*Holmgren*. De la Cécité des Couleurs dans ses Rapports avec les Chemins de Fer et la Marine, Stockholm, 1877; Abridged translation by Smithsonian Institute, 1878; Om färgblindhetoch den Young-Helmholtzska färgtheorien, Upsala, 1871; Ueber Forster's Perimeter und die Topographie des Farbensinnes, Upsala läkare fören förhandl., vii. 2, p. 87, also vol. 10, p. 541; *Vide* also Nordist. Medic. Arkiv., 1874, Bd. vi. Nos. 24, 28. —*Hering*. Sitz. d. Wiener Akad., Bd. lxix. Abth. iii. pp. 85–104, 179–218. —*Himly*. Krankh. u. Missb. d. mensch. Auges, 1843, ii. p. 468. —*Holmgren, F.* Om nagra nyare praktiska metoder att upptäcka färgblindhet, Upsala, 1878; Om den medfödda Fargblindhetens Diagnostik och Teori, Nord. Med. Arkiv., 1874, Bd. vi. No. 24–28; Om färgblindheten i Sverige, Upsala, 1878; Zur Entdeckung der Farbenblinden, Centralblatt f. Aug., August, 1878, Sept., 1878; Ueber die farbigen Schatten und die Farbenblindheit, ditto, 1878, p. 213–272; Till Sveriges Läkare angäende färblindheten, Upsala, Oct. 22, 1878; Om Pupillafständet hos färgblinda. Upsala Läk. Förh. Bd. xiv. p. 73. —*Hartshorne, H.* Colored After-Images how caused: Am. Jour. Med. Sci., April 1878, p. 447. —*Hall, G. S.* Perception of Color, Proceed. Am. Acad. Arts and Scien., vol. xiii., March 14, 1878. —*Hirlinger*. Prufung's Tafel für Farbensinn: Stuttgart, 1878. —*Horner*. Die Erblichkeit des Daltonismus, Ophth. Klinik., Zürick, 1876; Monatsblatt f. Aug., July, 1878, p. 321. —*Hirschberg*. Fall eines angeborenes farbenblinden Maler: Centralblatt f.

Aug., July, 1878, p. 156. —*Hays.* Jour. Med. Sci., July, 1878; Review of Color-Blindness. —*Harlan, G. C.* Ditto, Oct., 1878, p. 466. —*Harvey.* Edinb. Roy. Phil. Soc. Trans., vol. x. p. 253, 1826; Phil. Mag., series 1, vol. lxviii. p. 205; Edinb. Jour. Sci. vol. v. p. 114; Bid. Univer., t. xxxv. p. 175. —*Herschel.* Light, Ency. Metrop., § 507, p. 434, 1845. —*Hirschberg.* Tabaksamblyopie: Deutsch. Zeits. f. prak. Med., 1878. —*Henry, Professor J.* Color-Blindness: Princeton Review, July, 1845; also in Smithsonian Repts., 1878. —*Helmholtz.* Handbuch der phys. Optik.: Leipzig, 1867. Populäre wissen. Vorträge: Braunschweig, 1871; Phil. Mag., 1852, p. 519. —*Hardman, E. T.* Shakespeare's Color-Names: Nature, Jan. 23, 1879. —*Hirschberg, J.* Das Doppelspektroskop zur Analyse der Farbenblindheit: Centralblatt f. Augenh., Feb., 1879, also 1878, p. 248; also Verhandl. der physiol. Gesellschaft zu Berlin, No. 7, Jan. 17, 1879. —*Hjort, J.* Norw. med. Gesell., March, 1878. —*Hiess, J.* Beiträge zur Physiologie dere Gsichtsempfindung, 1878.

Ingleby. Shakespeare's Color-Names: Nature, vol. xix. No. 481.

Jeaffreson. Color-Blindness in Diseases of the Brain and Optic Nerve: Lancet, 1872, pp. 601, 635, 670, and Ann. d'Ocul., 1873, t. lxx. p. 196, 1873. —*Janssen.* Mémoire addressé à M. le Ministre de l'Instruction publique: Cosmos, Jan. 4, 1868. —*Jackson, Hughlings.* Colored Vision: Roy. Lond. Ophth. Hosp. Rep., 1875, p. 331. —*Jones, Wharton.* Failure of Sight from Railway and other Accidents: London., 1869. —*Jordan, W.* Die Farben bei Homeros: Jahrb. f. classische Philologie, Fleckeisen, tome cxiii., 1876. —*Jüngken.* Lehre d. Augenkrank: Berlin, 1832. —*Javal.* Daltonisme: Revue des Sciences méd., Oct. 15, 1878, p. 644. La France médicale, June 1, 1878; Sur la Vue humaine dans les Temps préhistoriques, Bull. Soc. d'Anthropol., 1877, p. 481. —*Jeffries, Dr. B. Joy.* Dangers from Color-Blindness in Railroad Employés and Pilots, 9th Ann. Rep. Mass. State Board Health, 1878; Incurability of Congenital Color-Blindness: Bost. Med. and Surg. Jour., March 28, 1878; Relative Frequency of Color-Blindness in Males and Females, ditto, July 25, 1878; Color-Blindness, Institute Technology lecture, Advertiser, Boston, April 13, 1878; Color-Blindness, its Dangers and its Detection, 1879, Boston, Houghton, Osgood, & Co.

Klob. Farbenblindheit bei Mangel des Corpus callosum und Hydrocephalie: Jahrb. f. Kinderheil, Bd. iii. 3, p. 201, 1860. — *Krieger.* Ueber Licht- und Farbenscheu: Deutsche Klinik, Nos. 50–52, 1850. — *Krieger.* Dyschromatopsie; Ann. d'Ocul., t. xxxiv. p. 284, 1856. — *Klug.* Farbenempfindung bei indirectem Sehen: Græfe's Archiv., xxi. 1, p. 251. — *Krukow.* Objective Color-Perception on Periphery of Retina: Moscow, 1873. — *Kunkel.* Ueber die Abhängigkeit der Farbenempfindung von der Zeit: Pflugers Archiv. f. ges. Physiol., ix. p. 197. — *Knoblauch.* Santonin: Deutsche Klinik, 1854, No. 35. — *Knapp.* Color-Blindness in Atrophy of Optic Nerve: Archives of Ophth. and Otol., vol. vi., Nos. 1, 2, p. 198; Die geschichtliche Entwickelung der Lehre von Sehen: New York, 1863. — *Krause, E.* Kosmos, June, 1877, p. 264–275, et 428–433, August, 1877, Sept., 1877; Nature, Dec. 12, 1878, p. 120. — *Kalischer.* Zur Ausbildung der menschlichen Sinne: Die Gegenwart, No. 38, p. 185; Die Farbenblindheit: Die Natur., Nos. 7, 8, 9, 11, 12, 1879. — *Kunstle.* Recension von Holmgren's Farbenblindheit: Deutsch Archiv. f. klin. Med., Bd. xxiii. p. 217. — *Kries, Dr. J.* Beiträge zur Physiologie der Gesichtsempfindung: Phys. Institute zu Leipzig, 1878. — *Kitao, Diro.* Farbenlehre: Inaug. Diss. Göttingen, 1879. *Koller.* Die Farbenblindheit, Med.-Chirurg. Centralbl.: Wien, 1879, xiv. 98, 109.

Laurence. Sensibility of the Eye to Color: Phil. Mag., 1861, p. 220. — *Leber.* Anomalies de la Sensation des Couleurs dans les Affections oculaires: Klin. Monatsbl., 1869; Græfe's Archiv., xv. 3, pp. 26–107, 1870, xvii. 2, 241. — *Leber.* Klin. Monatsbl., 1873, pp. 467–473. — *Lembert.* Cas de Pseudochromie; Gaz. hebd., No. 16, 1855. — *Longet.* Traité de Physiologie: Paris, 1850, t. ii. p. 97. — *Lembert.* Pseudochromie: Ann. d'Ocul., 1857, t. xxxviii. p. 275. — *Lefevre.* Action de la Santonine: Compt. rend. de l'Acad. des Sci., 1859, xlviii. p. 448. — *Landolt.* Percezione dei Colori alla Periferia della Retina: Annali di Ottalmologia, 1874; Anno. iii. Fasc. 2–3; Klin. Monatsblatt f. Augenheil, 1873, p. 376. — *Lamansky.* Ueber die Grenzer der Empfindlichkeit des Auges für Spectralfarben: Græfe's Archiv., xvii. 1, p. 123; Poggendorff's Ann., Bd. cxliii. p. 633. — *Leibreich.* On Defects of Vision in Painters: Macmillan's Mag., April, 1872; Nature, vol. v. pp. 404, 506; Brit. Med. Jour., i. pp.

271, 296, 318. Die Fehler des Auges bei Malern: Der Naturforscher, 1872, No. 47. — *Liegey*. Cas de Daltonisme congénital: Jour. de Méd. de Bruxelles, April, 1874, p. 327. — *Lacon, Sir Stilling*. Revue maritime, 1853. — *Landolt, E*. Procédé pour déterminer la Perception des Couleurs, Ann. d'Oculistique, 1875, p. 74; De l'Amblyopie hystérique, Arch. de Phys. norm. et path., 1875, p. 628; Klin. Monatsblatt f. Augen., 1873, p. 376; Chromatometer; Correspondenzbl. f. schweiz Aerzte., 1878, Nov. 22, Nov. 15. — *Lederer, A*. Farbenblindheit und mangelhafter Farbensinn mit Rücksicht auf den Signaldienst und der Marine, Wiener med. Wochenschrift, Jan. 12, 1878; Mitth. aus dem Gebiete des Seewesens, vol. vii. No. 1. Pola. 1879. — *Landolt*. Annal. d'Ocul., 1877, 2, p. 154. — *Le Conte*. Binocular Vision; Phil. Mag., vol. xxvii., 1877. — *Landolt et Charpentier*. Compt. rendu. t. lxxxviii. p. 495, Acad. des Sciences, Feb. 18, 1878; Notice in Archives générales, p. 505, April, 1878, p. 118, July, 1878; Congres. per. Sci. méd. 5 Session, Genève, 9–15, Aug., 1877. — *Leipzig*. Ethnographisches Museum: Fragebogen zur Untersuchung des Farbensinnes der uncultivirten Völker, 1878. — *Ledger*. Philadelphia, July 26, 1878. — *Löw*. Ueber die Farbenbezeichnungen in den Indianasprachen: Sitzungsb. d. Münchener anthropolog. Ges., June 22, 1877. — *Lort, Rev. M*. Phil. Trans., vol. lxviii. p. 611, 1779.

Mandelstamm. Beitrag zur Physiologie der Farben: Græfe's Archiv., xiii. 2, p. 399; Gaz. hebd., 1867, p. 399. — *Maxwell*. Experiments on Color and Color-Blindness, &c.: Edinb. Trans., 1855, xxi. pp. 275–297; Edinb. Jour., (2) i. pp. 359–360; Proceed. Edinb. Soc., iii. 299–301; Phil. Mag., (4) xiv. 40; Edinb. Jour., (2) i. 361, 362; Athen., 1856, p. 1093; Edinb. Jour., (2) iv. 335–337; Inst., 1856, p. 444; Rep. of Brit. Asso., 1856, 2, pp. 12–13; Nature, vol. iv. p. 13. — *Muncke und Gehler*. Phys. Wort., 1828: Leipzig, Bd. iv. p. 1428. — *Melloni*. Bibl. Univ. de Genève, Aug. 1847. — *Moigno*. Répertoire d'Optique, 1851, t. ii. et iii., translated in Smithsonian Reports, 1866, p. 211. — *Marché*. Des Alterations de la Sensibilité: Paris, 1860. — *Magnus*. Geschichtliche Entwickelung des Farbensinnes: Leipzig, 1877. — *Meckel*. Archiv. f. Physiol., i. 188; Ann. Phil., 1822, Feb. — *Müller, J. J*. Theorie der Farben: Græfe's Archiv., xv. 2, p. 208; Poggendorff's Annal. der

Physik, Bd. 139, pp. 411–593. — *Mungo, Ponton.* Colors and their Relations: Quart. Jour. of Sci., x. p. 74. — *Moxon.* Xanthopsia in Jaundice; Lancet, i., 1873, p. 130. — *Mayer.* History of Young's Discovery of his Theory of Colors; Am. Jour. Sci. and Art, vol. cix. (3d ser. vol. ix. p. 251). — *Mol.* Onderzoek op Kleurblindheid; Nederl. Tijds. v. Geneeskunde, 1875, No. 7, p. 89. — *Morton.* Ein neus Chromatrop; Poggen. Ann., B. clvii. p. 150. — *Michel, J.* Die Prüfung des Sehvermögens und der Farbenblindheit beim Eisenbahnpersonal und bei den Truppen; München, 1878. — *Magnus und Cohn.* Farbenblindheit in hiesigen Schulen; Deutsch. med. Wochenschr., iv. ii. — *Magnus.* Die Entwickelung des Farbensinnes: Jena, 1877. Neueres zur Theorie und Praxis der Farbenblindheit; Deuts. med. Wochens., No. 20, 1878; Zur spectroscopischen Untersuchung Farbenblinder; Centralblatt f. Aug., April u. Oct. u. Dec., 1878; Histoire de l'Évolution du Sens des Couleurs, 1878, Paris; Die Farbenblindheit, ihr Wesen und ihre Bedeutung, Breslau, 1878; Zur Entwickelung des Farbensinnes, Klin. Monatsblatt f. Aug., Nov., 1878; Die Farbenblindheit, Nord und Sud, 1878, Heft 21, p. 325; Beiträge zur Kenntniss der physiologischen Farbenblindheit; Græfe's Archiv., xxiv. 4, 1878. — *Medico.-Chir. Trans.* 1816, vol. vii. p. 477. — *Minder, F.* Beiträge zur Lehre von der Farbenblindheit: Berne, 1878. — *Muncke.* Gehler's physikal. Wörterbuch: Leipzig, 1828, t. iv. p. 1428. — *Müller.* Handbuch der Archäologie der Kunst: Breslau, 1848, p. 51. — *Mackenzie, W.* Diseases of the Eye: London, 1835, p. 860, 2d ed.; Am. ed. 1855, p. 881. — *Mayer.* De affinitate Colorum (Opera inedita, 1775). — *Magnus.* Höhe des Procentsatzes der Farbenblindheit: Schles. Gesellsch. f. vaterland. Cultur., Sitzung am 25 Oct., 1878; Breslauer Zeitung, No. 537, 1878; Die physiologische Farbenblindheit, Das Ausland, Stuttgart, Jan. 20, 1879, No. 3; Untersuchung von 5489 breslauer Schülern und Schülerinnen auf Farbenblindheit, Breslauer aertzl. Zeitschrift, No. 2, Jan. 25, 1879.

Noel. De la Chromatopseudopsie, Paris, 1857; Courier des Sciences, July 31, 1864. — *Newton.* Optics, lib. i. pars 2, prop. 3. — *Noel.* Thèse de Paris, 1839. — *Nagel.* Der Farbensinn: Berlin, 1869. — *Nicholl.* Med.-Chi. Trans.,

1818, vol. iv. p. 359, vii. 477, ix. 359; Ann. of Phil., N. S. iii. 128. — *Niemetschek.* Ueber Farbenblindheit: Prag. Vierteljahrsschr., 25 Jahrg. Bd. 4, pp. 224–238. — *Nuel.* (Louvain). L'Amblyopie Alcoolique et le Daltonisme: Acad. méd. de Belgique; Bull., Août, 1878; Ann. d'Oculist., Sept., Oct., 1878, p. 105. — *Nelson.* Color-Blindness: Chicago Railway Review, Mar. 30 and June 1, 1878.

Opel, J. J. Einige Beobachtungen ueber part. Farbenblindheit: Jahresberich. d. phys. Ver. zu Frankfort a. M., 1859–60, pp. 70–144; ibid., 1860–61, pp. 42–47; ibid., 1861–62, pp. 48. — *Oesterlin.* Handbuch d. Heilmittel, 1861, 7 Aufl.

Phipson, T. L. Action de la Santonine sur la Vision: Gaz. hebd., No. 13, 1859; Compt. rendus de l'Acad. des Sci., xlviii. p. 593. — *Pole.* Color-Blindness: Proceed. Roy. Soc., viii. 172–177, 1856; Phil. Magaz., (4) xiii. 282–286; Phil. Trans. Roy. Soc. Lond., 1859, vol. 149, p. 323; Nature, Oct. 24, 1878, p. 676, and Oct. 31, Dec. 12, 1878, Dec. 19, 1878. — *Potton.* Recherches sur le Daltonisme: Gaz. de Lyon, March, 1854; Archives d'Ophthalmologie, t. i. p. 158, et t. ii. p. 137, 1854; Archiv. gén. de Méd., Nov., 1854, p. 617, et l'Union méd., Apr. 8, 1854, p. 174. — *Purkinje.* Achromatopsie: Berl. Encycl. Wört. d. med. Wissensch., Bd. i. s. 259. — *Parry.* Med. Trans. Coll. Phys., London, vol. iv. p. 56, 1813. — *Prevost.* Mém. de la Soc. de Phys. et d'Hist. nat. de Genève, t. xii. p. 196. — *Preyer.* Die Verwandschaft der Töne und Farben: Jenaische Zeitschr. f. Med. u. Naturwiss., pp. 376–388; Pflugger's Archiv., i. pp. 229–329, 1868; Med. Centralbl., 1872, No. 8. — *Purkinje.* Berl. Encycl. Wört. d. med. Wiss., Bd. i. p. 259, 1828; Physiologie der Sinne, Bd. ii. p. 15. — *Picha.* Ueber Farbenblindheit und ihre Beziehungen zur Beurtheilung der Dienstesuntauglichkeit: Der Feldarzt, Nov. 4, 1878. — *Plateau, J.* Mém. Acad. des Sci. de Brux. t. viii. 1834; Philos. Mag., 1839, 3d ser., No. 14, p. 330; Mém. de l'Acad. belg., 42, 1878. — *Peclet, E.* Traité élém. de Physique, t. 2, p. 362, 3d edit., 1838. — *Plutarch.* Lehrmeinungen der Philosophen, lib. iii. cap. 5. — *Porta Baptista.* De Refractioni: Neapoli, 1593, lib. ix. trop. 10, p. 200. — *Phillips.* Color of Steam: Lond., Edinb., and Dub. Phil. Mag., 4th series, vol. iv., 1852, p. 128. — *Podmore.* Nature, vol. xix.

p. 73, 1878—*Prior, R. C. A.* Nature, Dec. 12, 1878, p. 119.—*Page, H. W.* Prevalence of Color-Blindness: Lancet, Jan. 13, 1877, p. 46.

Raehlmann. Daltonismus und Young-Helmholz Theorie: Græfe's Archiv., xix. 3, pp. 88–106, 1873, xx. 1, p. 232, xx. 1, p. 15, xxi. 2, p. 27, 1875; Ann. d'Ocul., t. lxxii. p. 60, 1874; Græfe's Archiv., xxii. 1, p. 29.—*Rose, Ed.* Wirkung des Santoninum: Virchow's Archiv., Bd. vii. 2, p. 72, xvi., 1859, p. 223, Bd. xxviii. 15, 1860, Bd. xxxviii. p. 30, 1863; Archiv. für path. Anat., Bd. xx. p. 225, 1860, Bd. vii. p. 72, Bd. xxx. p. 442; Græfe's Archiv., vii. 2, pp. 72–108.—*Rose, Ed.* Unters. Methode Farbenkranker: Berl. klin. Wochenschr., No. 31, 1865; Pogg. Annal., Bd. cxxvi., 1865.—*Rosier.* Observations sur le Physique et l'Hist. nat., vol. viii., 1779, p. 87, vol. xiii.—*Ruete.* Lehrb. d. Ophth., 1855, B. i. pp. 179–191.—*Reade.* Experimental Outlines for a New Theory of Color: London, 1816.—*Robin et Littre.* Dict. de Médicine, Paris, 1865, p. 1394.—*Ricco.* Un Caso di Daltonismo; Annali di Ottalmologia, Anno. v. Fasc. i. p. 59, 1876. Ueber die Farbenwahrnehmung; Græfe's Archiv., xxii. 1, p. 282; also more extended in Atti della R. Academia di Scienze di Modena, 1875. *Vide* also Annali d'Ottalmologia, Anno. iv. p. 315.—*Rahmer.* Zur Casuistik spinaler Augenleiden; Inaug. Dissert.: Breslau, 1873.—*Reich.* Subjective Erscheinungen bei intraoculärem Druck.; Klin. Monatsb. f. Augenheil, 1874, p. 238.—*Romberg.* Das Stakenrecht auf See: Bremen, 1870.—*Reynand.* Mémoire sur l'Eclairage et le Balisages des Côtes de France, 1864.—*Rood, Ogden.* Observations on a Property of the Retina first noticed by *Tait* in Edinb. Proceed., 1869–70, vii. pp. 605–607; Am. Jour. Med. Sci., Jan., 1877.—*Ragona-Scina.* Su taluni Fenomeni che presentano i Cristalli colorati: Racc. fis. chim., ii. 207, 1847.—*Rosenstiehl.* De l'Emploi des Disques rotatifs pour l'Étude des Sensations Colorées: Compt. rend., t. lxxxvi. p. 343.—*Robertson, A.* Ann. d'Oculist., t. lxiii., p. 114 —*Roustan.* Traitement par la Lumière: Montpellier, 1874, p. 42.—*Rüte.* Lehrbuch d. Ophthal: Braunschweig, 1845, p. 86.—*Rayleigh, Lord.* Lectures Royal Institute, 1878.—*Reuss, Dr. A. von.* Ueber Farbenblindheit. Wiener Klinik, Mar., 1879; Wiener med. Presse, 1879, No. 9.

Schelske. Farbenblindheit: Græfe's Archiv., vii. 2, p. 104, ix. 3, p. 39, 1863; ibid., ix. 3, p. 49; ibid., xi. 1, p. 175, 1865. — *Schirmer.* Erworbene und angeborene Anomalien des Farbensinnes: Græfe's Archiv., xix. 2, p. 194; Berl. Klin. Wochenschrift, p. 55, 1873; Verhandl. der Wurzburg phys.-med. Gesellschaft, 1873; Sitzungsberichte der Bernischer Naturforsch. Gesellschaft, 1872. — *Schultze, Max.* Gelben Flech: Bonn, 1866. Uber Staebchen und Zapfen der Retina: Arch. für mikr. Anat., Bd. iii. p. 215, 1867. — *Seebeck.* Mangel an Farbensinn: Poggendorff's Annal., Bd. xlii., 1837, No. 10, p. 177. — *Sommer.* Chromatopseudopsie: Græfe u. Walthe., Jour. Berlin, 1823, Bd. v. s. 19–44, Bd. v. 4, 1824. — *Sous.* Du Daltonisme: Bordeaux, 1865, p. 19. — *Szokalski.* Essai sur les Sensations des Couleurs: Ann. d'Ocul., t. ii. p. 11, et. t. iii. p. 1, 1839–1840. Essai: Paris, 1841, Bruxelles, 1840; J. Müller's Archiv., 1842, lvii. — *Scott.* Phil. Trans., London, 1778, vol. lxviii. pp. 611–615; Empfindungen der Farben, Giessen, 1842; Ann. d'Ocul., vol iii. 1841. — *Smith.* Cause of Color and Theory of Light: 1859, Rep. Brit. Asso., vol. ii. p. 22. — *Stellwag von Carion.* Ophthalmologie: Erlangen, Bd. ii. 1, s. 634, 1856. — *Schopenhauer.* Ueber das Sehen und die Farben, 3 Auflage: Leipzig, 1871. — *Stein.* Zur Theorie der Körperfarben: Pogg. Annal., Bd. cxliv. p. 260. — *Sekulic.* Ultraviolet Strahlen sind unmittelbar sichtbar: Pogg. Annal, Bd. cxlvi. p. 157. — *Schœn.* Ueber die Grenzen der Farbenempfindungen in path. Zustand.: Klin. Monatsb. f. Augenheil, 1873, p. 171; Berl. Klin. Wochen., 29, 1874; *vide* also Græfe's Archiv., xx. 2, p. 273. — *Sauer.* Sichtbarkeit ultravioletter Strahlen: Pogg. Annal., 1873, Bd. clv. p. 602. — *Stilling, J.* Lehre von der Farbenempfindungen, Klin. Monatsb., 1873; Prüfung des Farbensinn, Cassel, 1877; Ueber den Stand der Farbenfrage, Archiv. f. Augenheilkunde, vii. 1. pp. 10–37. — *Schrœder.* Farbige Schatten: Klin. Monatsb. f. Augenheil, 1873, p. 354. — *Schöler.* Bestimmung einer der drei Grundfarben: Græfe's Archiv., xx. 2, p. 87. — *Stilling.* Methoden zur Prüfung des Farbensinnes: Bericht. Ophth. Gessel., Heidelberg, 1877. Ueber Farbensinn und Farbenblindheit, Rede, 51: Versammlung der Naturforscher und Aertze in Cassel, 1878. Lehre von der Farbenempfindungen: Klin. Monatsblatt, f. Aug., 1873; Prüfung des Farbensinnes, Cassel, 1877; Farbige Schatten bei Tageslicht, Centralblatt, f. Aug., Juni, 1878; Blau- Gelbblindheit mit unverkurztem Spectrum, ditto, Mai, 1878, p. 99. — *Seely, W., jun.* Yellow Vision in Santonine Poisoning: The Clinic, xiv. 6, Cincinnati, Feb. 9, 1878. — *Schreffer.* Accidental Colors: Jour. de Phys., t. xxvi. 1785. — *Smith.* Phil. Mag., series 3, vol. i. p. 249, et vol. ii. p. 168. — *Spurzheim.* Phrenology, 3d ed. p. 276. — *Stewart, Dugald.* Philosophy of the Human Mind, 1792–1802; His Case in Chambers' Edinb. Journ., vol. iv. No. 171; Brewster's Optics, p. 311. — *Schuster.* Zeitschrift. f. Gymnasialwesen, xv. Bd. ii. p. 721. — *Scöhn.* Die Lehre vom Gesichtsfeld: Berlin, 1874. — *Scott.* Phil. Trans., lxviii. p. 611, 1779. — *Statistiche Correspondenz.* 1878, No. 42, Ueber die Haufigkeit des Vorkommens der Farbenblindheit. — *Smith, Prof. Robertson.* Nature, Dec. 6, 1877. — *Sartisson.* Farbenblindheit und Eisenbahndienst: St. Petersburg med. Wochenschrift, No. 38. — *Sous, G.* Couleurs dans l'Atrophie progressive de la Papille: Bordeaux Médicale, No. 14, p. 106. — *Sehenkl.* Lehre vom Farbensinn und seinen Störungen: Prager. Vierteljahrschrift, i. 1879. — *Schassler.* Harmonische Farbenverbindungen: Westermannische Monatshefte, 1879, Heft i. — *Sattler.* Kritik. Jenaer Litteratur. Zeitung, 1879, No. 11.

Trichinetti. Chromatopseudopsie: Ann. Univer. de Méd. No. 1, Milano, 1844. — *Tyndall, J.* Phil. Mag., (4) xi. No. 139, pp. 329–333; Silliman's Jour., (2) xxii. pp. 143–146; Arch. d. sc. Phys., xxxii. 221–225; Athenæum, Jan. 29, 1853; Ann. d'Ocul., t. xxx. p. 143, 1853; Dub. Phil. Mag., May, 1856. — *Tourtal.* Chromasie des Auges: Meckels Archiv., 1830, p. 129. — *Taylor.* Scientific Memoirs: London, 1846, vol. iv. p. 185. — *Treitel, Th.* Inaug. Dissert., 1875, Königsberg. — *Thomas Paul.* Revue Littéraire, July 7, 1877; Athenæum Belg., Jan. 6, 1878. — *Tourtal.* Müller's Archiv. f. anat. phy. Med., 1842. — *Tuberville, Dr. D.* Phil. Trans., No. 164, p. 736, Aug. 4, 1684. Lowthrop's Abridgment, vol. iii. part 1, p. 40. — *Tucker.* Edin. Phil. Jour., vol. vi. — *Talbot.* Phil. Mag., ser. 3, vol. x. p. 361.

Vernon. Congenital Myopia and Limited Color-Blindness: St. Barth. Hosp. Rep., vol. ii. p. 93. — *Vierordt, K.* Messung der Stärke des farbigen Lichtes: Tübingen, 1871. — *Valhon-*

nesta y Vendrell. Classification y Contrasta de los Colores segun el S. Chevreul: Barcelona, 1874. — *Vitello.* Opticæ libri decem. Ed. Risner, Basiliæ, 1572, lib. x. 67, p. 462. — *Volkmann.* Ueber die Empfindung welche ensteht wenn verschiedenfarbige Lichtstrahlen auf identische Netzhautstellen fallen: Müller's Archiv. f. Anat. und Phys., 1838, p. 373. — *Völckers.* Ueber Farbenmischung in beiden Augen., ditto, p. 60. — *Virchow.* Die Erziehung des Farbensinns: Berliner Gesellschaft f. Anthropologie, July 20, 1878.

Wartman. Daltonismus: Häser's Repertorium, 1839, Bd. iv. p. 125. — *Wartman (de Lausanne).* Daltonisme: Genève, 1844 et 1849; Archiv. gener. de Med., Févr., 1846; Archiv. d'Anat., p. 56, 1846; Bull. de Brux., 137, 1849; Institute, 1849. — *Wardrop.* Morb. Anat. Hum. Eye: London, 1818, p. 196, vol. ii. — *Weicher.* De nonnullis coloribus, &c.: Leipzig, 1857. — *Wilson.* Statistics of Color-Blind Persons: Month. Jour., 1853–1854; Year-Book of Facts, 1858, p. 138; Researches on Color-Blindness, 1855. — *Witcke.* Wirkung des Würmsamens: Med. Zeit. des V. f. Heil. in Preussen, No. 7, 1852. — *Woinow.* Farbenempfindung: Græfe's Archiv., xvi. 1, 1870, p. 212, xvi. 1, p. 251, xvii. 2, p. 241, xxi. 1, p. 223; Klin. Monatsblät., Bd. ix. p. 377; Græfe's Archiv., xvii. 2, 241, 1871, xxi. 1, p. 223; Ann. d'Ocul., t. lxvii. p. 112, et lxviii. p. 169, 1872; Revue Médicale Russe, 1874, 1–2, et 1874, 6. — *Warlomont.* Chromatopseudopsie: Ann. d'Ocul., t. lxxiv., 1875, p. 1. — *Watson, Th.* Lectures on Prin. and Prac. of Physic, 1862, vol. ii. p. 604. — *Whisson.* Phil. Trans., lxviii. ii. 611. — *Weber.* Ueber Farbenprüfung: Klin. Monatsbl., 1873, p. 486. — *Weinhold.* Ueber die Farbenwahrnehmung: Poggendorf's Annalen, Neue Folge, B. ii. p. 631. — *Wartmann, Eli.* Memoir on Color-Blindness: Taylor's Scientific Memoirs, 1846, trans., noticed in Rep. Brit. Ass., 1841, p. 40; Silliman's Jour. Sci., Jan., 1842, vol. xlii. p. 62. — *Wiegmann.* Die Malerei der Alten in ihrer Anwendung und Technik: Hannover, 1836, p. 210. — *Whewell.* Athenæum, Aug. 28, 1841, No. 722. — *Wallace, Mr. A. R.* Color in Animals and Plants: Macmillan's Mag., Oct., 1877. — *Wolfe, Dr. J. R.* Color-Sight and Color-Blindness: Med. Times and Gazette, April 5, 1879.

Young, Th. Phil. Trans., 1801, part 1, p. 33; 1802, p. 38; Lectures on Nat. Phil., 1807.

Zimmermann. Gelb- und Grünsehen nach Santoningebrauche: Deutsche Klinik, Nov. 14, 1855. — *Zehender*. Zur Entwickelung des Farbensinnes: Klin. Monatsbl., Nov., 1878, p. 478. Zeitschrift d. königl. preuss. statist. Bureau.; xviii. Jahrg., Heft iii. u. iv. Beitrage zur Statistik.

INDEX.

D.

E.

F.

G.

H.

I.

J.

K.

L.

U.

V.

W.

Y.

www.ingramcontent.com/pod-product-compliance
Lightning Source LLC
LaVergne TN
LVHW011200110826
845150LV00006B/1277

9781425572914